ISLAND IN AN EMPIRE

Education, Religion, and Social Life in Newfoundland, 1800–1855

PHILLIP McCANN

BOULDER PUBLICATIONS

McCann, Phillip, author
Island in an empire : education, religion, and social life in Newfoundland, 1800-1855 / Phillip McCann.

Includes bibliographical references.
ISBN 978-1-927099-70-4 (paperback)

1. Newfoundland and Labrador--History--1763-1855. 2. Newfoundland and Labrador--Social life and customs--19th century. 3. Newfoundland and Labrador--Social conditions--19th century. 4. Newfoundland and Labrador--Religion--19th century. 5. Education--Newfoundland and Labrador--History--19th century. I. Title.

FC2172.M4 2016 971.8'01 C2016-900415-5

Published by Boulder Publications
Portugal Cove-St. Philip's, Newfoundland and Labrador
www.boulderpublications.ca

Copy editor: Iona Bulgin
Cover and interior design: John Andrews

Printed in Canada

Newfoundland Labrador

We acknowledge the financial support of the Government of Newfoundland and Labrador through the Department of Tourism, Culture and Recreation.

We acknowledge the financial support for our publishing program by the Government of Canada and the Department of Canadian Heritage through the Canada Book Fund.

Contents

History is made in such a way that the final result always arises from conflicts between many individual wills, of which each again has been made what it is by a host of particular conditions of life ... each individual will is obstructed by everyone else, and what emerges is something that no one willed.

—Frederick Engels (1890)

PREFACE

In 1883 Joseph Hatton and Moses Harvey co-authored a book entitled *Newfoundland: Its History, Its Present Condition and Its Prospects in the Future.* In a chapter dealing with the early years of representative government in the 1830s, the authors described them as "a dark and troubled period" in which Protestants and Catholics were arrayed against each other in the political arena, disrupting the peace of social and commercial life. "Over this period of political and religious rancor," they asserted, "it is best to draw a veil, and consign the memory of it to oblivion."

Today it is possible to lift the veil and to rescue these years from oblivion. The essays in this volume reveal a different picture of life in the island and in St. John's and trace in detail transformations in educational, political, and religious spheres. Religio-political strife was evident, but largely in the period following 1830, after three decades of relative social peace. During these early years the citizens of St. John's in particular enjoyed a vibrant social life. The theatre, the circus, vaudeville, concerts, exhibitions, museums, and literary societies flourished, and sporting events such as the Regatta and horse racing became fixtures of the social scene. A middle class arose, interested in the consumption of fashionable commodities and in exclusive schooling.

These essays examine these and other issues; they were written at different times, and for different audiences, over the last 25 years. They happen to be subjects in which little or no research has been done, and for which adequate, if not voluminous, material is available. My aim was to attempt to answer the traditional scholars' questions about the past: "what happened in history, when, and why?" In several instances research revealed unexpected outcomes which threw new light on aspects of the subjects under review, or added further evidence to existing narratives. Though placed in broad chronological order, the essays are not intended to form a connected narrative history of the first half of 19th-century Newfoundland; rather they are studies of discrete topics. Nevertheless, certain themes common to the whole period emerge, as is shown in the Afterword. The somewhat arbitrary dates of the beginning of the 19th century and the achievement of responsible government in 1855 have on occasion been exceeded for the sake of clarity. The footnotes refer to sources and I have avoided making them extensions of the text. As I do not subscribe to any religious or political body, I believe I can claim a degree of impartiality in relation to the religion and politics of the period. All historians, however, have a particular world view based on their background and experiences, and the reader will notice that I am opposed to racism and imperialism whenever and wherever they appear; it is not good enough, in my opinion, to excuse expressions of these prejudices on the ground that they were typical of their time. On another issue, scholars still dispute the importance of the role of social classes in society, but no one who studies the Newfoundland scene in the 19th century can avoid encountering blatant examples of class division, nor class struggles in the broadest sense.

On the British background I have consulted some secondary sources of the pre-postmodern era, which I have found to be well researched and clearly written. If readers consider there are a large number of British references, it must be remembered that the majority of the inhabitants of Newfoundland in the first four decades of the 19th century were British by birth, and turned to the mother country for ideas and practices, which they integrated into the Newfoundland fishing society and economy. Accordingly, rather than a narrow concentration on indigenous Newfoundland issues, I have placed the island's development in the wider context of the British Empire and its many influences on economic, religious, and social life. This is a scholarly work, based largely on manuscript sources and contemporary newspapers. I have, however, attempted to write as simply and clearly as possible, in hope of appealing to the general reader as well as to the academic community. If the essays collected here stimulate further research and interest in early 19th-century Newfoundland history, particularly unexplored aspects of education, religion, and social life, and the role of women in society, they will have served their purpose.

The contribution of women to the history of the period has not been given separate treatment in this volume, mainly because the activities in almost all the chapters were largely the province of men. Women are given their due where they did play a role, for example in the theatre. As for Labrador, a separate monograph would be necessary to cover its contribution.

This book is a product of the pre-digital age. It has not been put together by pressing keys and printing texts, but by taking notes in longhand in libraries, archives, and museums in Newfoundland, mainland Canada, England, Ireland, and Italy (the Vatican archives), and written up with the aid of my trusty word processor, a pencil. Nevertheless, I am grateful to the numerous individuals who have assisted in many ways. I am indebted to Memorial University's scheme of allotting student assistants to researchers on a termly basis (MUCEP). Too many to mention individually, I thank them all for their assiduity in fact-checking and hunting up obscure references in Memorial's excellent Queen Elizabeth II Library and its adjunct, the Centre for Newfoundland Studies. I am grateful to the members of the General Office of the Department of Financial and Administrative Services in the Education Building who typed my often bizarre manuscripts with unfailing skill and courtesy.

Finally, I must record the death of Rebecca Young, a research assistance beyond compare who aided the revision of the text. Rebecca died at the age of 27 in 2015.

Phillip McCann, PhD, FRHS

INTRODUCTION

Phillip McCann is the pre-eminent historian of education as it has developed in Newfoundland and Labrador, and other historians necessarily rely on his publications to inform their own thoughts about our history. At the same time, though, he has looked into many other aspects of the Newfoundland past.

For example, it was Dr. McCann who started the necessary scholarly reinterpretation of the Confederation period of the 1940s, with a paper to the Newfoundland Historical Society in 1983,* and, as this volume shows, he has always been interested in where the province (as it now is) and its society came from. Much of his work has been devoted to the evolution of the school system during the first half of the 19th century, and this interest is reflected in the essays in this collection. It was a formative period in many ways, during which a relatively new colonial society began to sort itself out and find its place within the British Empire.

Newfoundland was, in the imperial context, a complicated and ambiguous place. In 1800 it was still regarded in London as a transatlantic migratory fishery subject to naval administration. It took some time, after the end of 125 years of Anglo-French warfare in 1815, for the appropriate departments of the British government to understand that Newfoundland had changed. Fishing and sealing remained its only major industries, but it had become a settler society composed for the most part of English and Irish immigrants and their descendants, with associated demands and problems. The island, and to some extent Labrador as well, were also encumbered by British fisheries agreements with France and the United States which were to cause problems for many years.

It was not until the mid-1820s that Newfoundland was at last formally recognized as a colony, and it was given representative government in 1832. These long-delayed changes reflected its new

---

* Phillip McCann, "British Policy and Confederation," 1983, published in *Newfoundland Studies* 14:2 (1998), 154–168.

status. However, the migratory fishery had disappeared, Britain no longer needed a "nursery for seamen" (insofar as it ever had needed one), and Newfoundland did not appear to be a place for large numbers of British emigrants. But it was strategically important, and there was never any discussion about casting it off. Newfoundland was a British colony (if a minor one) and would remain so: its internal problems needed to be addressed, and this was best done by devolving much of the responsibility to its inhabitants.

The provision of public schooling was central, and that is the subject of much of what follows in this volume. In Britain, Newfoundland, and elsewhere in British North America, education was a vexed question in this period and long afterwards. The fundamental issue was the relationship that should exist between schools (at all levels) and the various Christian churches, sometimes complicated, as in New Brunswick, by the presence of francophone populations. In Newfoundland, in spite of some support for non-denominational education, the result was separate but parallel church-affiliated school systems—Roman Catholic, Anglican, and Methodist, with other denominations being added later. This outcome was practical and politic, though by no means ideal, and should be seen as part of the mid-century understanding that each denomination was entitled to its fair and proportionate share of influence, place, and pay.

At the same time, Dr. McCann demonstrates the existence of a class consciousness that cut across denominational allegiances. His essays on mumming, the varied forms of entertainment that were available (at least in St. John's), and the annual Regatta show that there existed genuinely communal events and practices that had nothing to do with the churches, but which were usually respectful of the accepted social hierarchy, the existence of class and economic inequality being taken for granted. In education though, denomination trumped class as a final determinant.

Another divisive element was the growing gap between St. John's and the rest of the colony. There were some relatively important centres elsewhere—Harbour Grace, Carbonear, Trinity, and Bonavista, for example—but St. John's was where most of the elite clustered, the merchants, lawyers, politicians, and senior clergy. During the first half of the 19th century, the town emerged as the administrative, economic, and educational centre of the colony with no real challengers. The colony's leaders, who were based there, faced the difficult task of providing basic services, including schools, to a small and scattered coastal population—approximately 125,000 in 1860, largely native-born, of whom perhaps 2 per cent were professionals or otherwise worked outside the fishery.

Newfoundland society was divided by geography, social class, and religious affiliation. But at the same time, by mid-century there had developed a local nationalism, similar in nature to the nationalisms that developed in other colonies of settlement. It combined pride in being a Newfoundlander with pride in being part of the British Empire. This did not prevent criticism of the Mother Country and its government, far from it. Indeed, one of the unifying national myths was that if Newfoundland was backward, in spite of its rich resources on land and in the sea, it was because the Mother Country had deliberately retarded its progress in order to promote the migratory fishery. Dr. McCann addresses the roots of this nationalism in Chapter 13.

Thus there developed assumptions, beliefs, and understandings that were shared by most if not all Newfoundlanders, and which overlay the society's divisions and tensions. Among them was the acceptance that in education, the central concern of the essays that follow, the churches would control the public school system. They did so until 1998. One wonders whether Bishops Fleming and Feild ever imagined that the educational division which they had largely brought about would last so long.

Phillip McCann has made a major and significant contribution to Newfoundland historiography. His judgments and interpretations, like those of all historians, will be debated and challenged. He has, though, provided a solid basis from which to proceed. This is a substantial achievement, to which the essays in this volume bear witness.

James Hiller, Professor Emeritus, Department of History, Memorial University of Newfoundland

Abbreviations

AAD	Archives of the Archdiocese of Dublin
AASJ	Archives of the Archdiocese of St. John's
AAQ	Archives of the Archdiocese of Quebec
AFK	Archives of the Franciscan Order, Killiney
APF	Archives of Propaganda Fide, Rome
ASCD	Archives and Special Collections Division, Memorial University of Newfoundland
BFBS	British and Foreign Bible Society
CCHA	Canadian Catholic Historical Association
CO	Colonial Office, England
Courier	*Morning Courier and General Advertiser*
DCB	*Dictionary of Canadian Biography*
ENL	*Encyclopedia of Newfoundland and Labrador*
Express	*Newfoundland Express*
Gazette	*Royal Gazette and Newfoundland Advertiser*
Herald	*Weekly Herald and Conception Bay Advertiser*
Indicator	*Newfoundland Indicator*
JGA	Journal of the General Assembly
JHA	Journal of the House of Assembly
JLC	Journal of the Legislative Council
Ledger	*Public Ledger*
LMS	London Missionary Society
Mercantile Journal	*Newfoundland Mercantile Journal*
Mercury	*Conception Bay Mercury*
MGA	Member of the General Assembly
MHA	Member of the House of Assembly
MMS	Methodist Missionary Society
NBNASEP	Newfoundland and British North American Society for Educating the Poor
NSOED	*New Shorter Oxford English Dictionary*

NSS	Newfoundland School Society
Parl. Deb.	Parliamentary Debates
PP	Parliamentary Papers
Patriot	*Patriot and Terra Nova Herald*
Post	*Morning Post and Shipping Gazette*
Sentinel	*Sentinel and Conception Bay Advertiser*
SPCK	Society for the Promotion of Christian Knowledge
SPG	Society for the Propagation of the Gospel
Star	*Star and Conception Bay Journal*
Telegraph	*Telegraph and Political Review*
UCA	United Church Archive
Vindicator	*Newfoundland Vindicator*

CHAPTER 1

Empire, Missionaries, and Schools, 1800–1836

> [E]very Englishman is born with a certain miraculous power that makes him master of the world. When he wants a thing, he never tells himself that he wants it. He waits patiently until there comes into his mind, no one knows how, a burning conviction that it is his moral and religious duty to conquer those who possess the thing he wants. Then he becomes irresistible. Like the aristocrat, he does what he pleases and grabs what he covets: like the shopkeeper, he pursues his purpose with the industry and steadfastness that come from strong religious conviction and [a] deep sense of moral responsibility. He is never at a loss for an effective moral attitude. As the great champion of freedom and national independence, he conquers and annexes half the world, and calls it Colonization. When he wants a new market for his adulterated Manchester goods, he sends a missionary to teach the natives the Gospel of Peace.
>
> —G.B. Shaw, *The Man of Destiny* (1895)

EMPIRE

In the early years of the 19th century, while Britain was at war with Napoleon, thousands of young Irishmen, fishers and farm workers for the most part, would annually throng the small hamlet of Passage East, then as now a cluster of grey stone houses on the banks of the River Suir, 7 miles downriver from Waterford. For nearly all of them the green hills of Waterford and Wexford would be the last glimpse of their native land. At the same time the wide sweep of Poole harbour would be the last of England for many of their English contemporaries from the coasts and rural hinterlands of Devon, Dorset, and Somerset. The destination of both was the island of

Newfoundland, 1,500 miles westward across the Atlantic where, it was believed, a good living, if not a fortune, was to be made fishing for the abundant cod along the island's rocky coastline.

The fishers were heirs to a tradition dating back over 300 years, precisely from 5 August 1583 when Sir Humphrey Gilbert claimed the island for the British crown. Almost a century earlier John Cabot's voyage had revealed that the cod was so plentiful that it could be taken "not only with the net but in baskets let down with a stone,"[1] and English and European fishing fleets subsequently harvested the stocks. Over the years English West Country expeditions began to dominate the fishery; every spring ships from Poole, Torbay, Dartmouth, and other harbours sailed to Newfoundland, racing to be the first arrivals in the east coast harbours and fishing rooms where the captains became self-styled fishing admirals.

Although the British government had historically discouraged settlement, which might have formed the basis of a rival indigenous fishery, the convenience of leaving men to prepare fishing rooms for the following season and sporadic immigration resulted in the growth of a permanent population during the later 18th century. Then in the first decades of the 19th century came an influx of settlers from southeast Ireland and southwest England. By 1836 the population had reached 75,000.[2] Partly as a result of this, for the first decade and a half of the 19th century, Newfoundland prospered. The value of exports to Britain, the West Indies, and the Catholic countries of southern Europe was estimated by a member of the British House of Commons at £1 million per annum during these years, from a possession which cost a mere £4,000 annually to maintain. MPs of all parties at Westminster declared that Newfoundland was of vital importance to the commercial and maritime strength of the British Empire.[3]

The British ruling elite had recovered in a remarkable way from

---

1 St. J. Chadwick, *Newfoundland: Island into Province* (Cambridge, 1967), 4, 5.

2 J.J. Mannion, introduction to *The Peopling of Newfoundland*, ed. Mannion (St. John's, 1977), 5–8.

3 Parl. Deb. 1813–14 11, "Estimate of the Charge of Defraying the Civil Establishment of the Island of Newfoundland," 5; 1815 21, 15 June 1815, 823–26; 1817 36, 18 June 1817, 1023, 1025.

the catastrophic loss of the American colonies in 1783 to fight a successful war against France and to extend the bounds of the colonial Empire. In broad perspective, the Empire in the 18th century was essentially an Atlantic one; in the 19th century it became largely an Eastern one, in which free trade replaced commercial regulation. The Industrial Revolution transformed Asia and much of the rest of the world from suppliers of raw materials and luxury goods to consumers of the products of the machine age. By the second decade of the 19th century, Britain had conquered or subordinated 43 colonies containing 200 million people.[4] Newfoundland was an island in an Empire which stretched from Africa to India, from the Mediterranean to Asia.

The ideology of the project has been explored by Catherine Hall in *Macaulay and Son: Architects of Imperial Britain* (2012). Hall focuses on the importance of the Evangelical strain which pervaded much of the outlook of supporters of the Empire, and by extension the missionary movement. Christianity, the Evangelicals believed, fitted Britain to be an imperial power; they envisaged a Christian empire of British subjects under the providential rule of God. The notion of providence was central to the Evangelical creed; it assumed the presence of a God who governed and sanctioned all human activity, from personal life to imperial outreach. This was consonant with Zachary Macaulay's conviction, when secretary of the Africa Society, that one of the advantages of Empire was that "our customs, manners and opinions would spread rapidly, from the power of example."[5]

The imposition of British values, ways of thought, customs, and manners on "backward" peoples was the counterpart of military subjugation. Richard Gott, in *Britain's Empire: Resistance, Repression and Revolt* (2011), charts the conquest of countries across the globe, from Africa to India, from Ireland to Ceylon. In contrast to most histories of Empire, Gott brings to the forefront the resistance and rebellion of many peoples caught in the imperial net, some suc-

---

4 P. Brendon, *The Decline and Fall of the British Empire, 1781–1997* (London, 2007), 28.

5 C. Hall, *Macaulay and Son: Architects of Imperial Britain* (Yale, 2012), 9, 11, 62, 87ff.

cessful, some not. Far from the romantic views of Empire, his narrative shows in some detail that Britain's Empire was captured and maintained by maximum force.[6] During the 19th century, Britain engaged in over 30 wars across the globe, wars to extend her imperial interests or consolidate the Empire. Ian Hernon, in *Britain's Forgotten Wars*, sums up the deployment of the Empire's armies:

> [which] subjugated, conquered, exploited, evicted and even wiped out entire races. By the standards of the time motives were often "pure"—the propagation of Christianity, trade, remorseless imperial conquest, glory, riches, social advancement—but the results were still fire-blackened villages, scorched hunting grounds empty of game, the destruction of civilisations older than our own, mass slaughter, epidemics, social inferiority and poverty.[7]

Viewing the Empire as a whole, it is difficult to counter Michael Paris's contention that Britain was "an aggressive warfare state committed to the use of violence to maintain commercial predominance and territorial expansion."[8] It is important to emphasize this point because it reveals the type of Empire of which Newfoundland was a dependent part. The degree of force employed varied, but was always present in one form or another. Not all of Britain's overseas possessions suffered invasion or massacre, but the ubiquitous presence of the navy and various units of the army kept a hold on all colonies and dependencies.

• • •

What was the precise position of Newfoundland in the imperial scheme? The island, geographically situated in the wider Atlantic Empire, was for most of its history governed, directly or indirectly,

---

6 R. Gott, *Britain's Empire: Resistance, Repression and Revolt* (London, 2011).
7 I. Hernon, *Britain's Forgotten Wars: Colonial Campaigns of the 19th Century* (Stroud, 2003), 215–16; B. Farwell, *Queen Victoria's Little Wars* (New York, 1972).
8 M. Paris, *Warrior Nation: Images of War in British Popular Culture 1850–2000* (London, 2000), 13.

by the Royal Navy.[9] Imperial policy was codified in King William's Act of 1699, which established the rule of the fishing admirals as the legal authority over property, law, and operations of the fishery, and gave appellate powers to the admiral of the protecting naval squadron. There were in fact two different types of admiral: the fishing admirals; civilians (some wealthy, mostly not) who were masters (i.e., captains) of the first English fishing ship to enter a harbour on the island, and who took on the title of the admiral of that port for the fishing season. Masters of the second and third ships became vice- and rear-admirals respectively. The other type of admiral was the admiral of the squadron of the Royal Navy, who was commissioned to act as governor.

During the 1730s, following the establishment of naval governors and a civil magistracy in 1729, the fishing admirals and the justices of the peace contended for legal authority, but the Royal Navy increasingly began to exercise political and legal control over the Newfoundland station, strengthened by the emergence of a surrogate system of justice in the outports largely administered by junior naval officers. In consequence, the role of the local fishing admirals declined, and by mid-1750s the navy had firmly staked its claim as the "unquestioned arbiter of power and authority." This was consistent with British imperial policy, which regularly employed the navy as the standard-bearer of English law and royal sovereignty throughout the Empire. In Newfoundland the navy imposed an authoritarian regime, using the criminal law to exact retribution for real or perceived threats to order, often against the Irish. Apart from hanging, punishments included banishment, burnings on the hand with a hot iron, whippings (up to 100) with a lash, imprisonment in irons, and a range of fines. Naval hegemony declined in the early 19th century, but as late as 1838 a visitor noted that an armed sloop carrying naval officers and magistrates was sent on a mission of inquiry to the outports every year, adding that "the mother country, here as elsewhere in all her possessions, maintains her power."[10]

---

9 The following is based on J. Bannister, *The Rule of the Admirals: Law, Custom and Naval Government in Newfoundland, 1699–1832* (Toronto, 2003).
10 E.W. Tucker, *Five Months in Labrador and Newfoundland during the Summer of 1838* (Concord, 1839), 67, 68.

In addition to naval forces, military garrisons had been stationed in Newfoundland since the middle of the 17th century, usually in St. John's and Placentia. Until the end of the Napoleonic wars in 1815 their primary purpose had been to protect the fishery. Afterward the forces of Empire became subject to the authority of the civil government. The soldiers of the garrison were called upon to quell civil unrest, actual or threatened, often at election times, notably at St. John's in 1831, 1836, and 1840, and at Harbour Grace in 1840. The garrison was withdrawn in 1870 as part of the Empire-wide reduction of military establishments. Soldiers of the garrison had become an established part of civil life, taking part in local sport and entertainment. However, their presence and their pageantry—military reviews, salutes, and various ceremonies (not to mention displays of force) contributed to an awareness among the populace of the Empire to which they belonged.[11]

The British government had direct control over Newfoundland's affairs through the office of governor. Captain Richard Henry Bonnycastle, stationed with the Royal Engineers in the island, noted that a governor was subordinate to no other authority than the queen and her ministers, "which gave him a weight not possessed by the lieutenant in other provinces." All departments of state were under the governor's guidance and supervision; he was Vice-Admiral, Commander of the Troops, Chancellor, and Commissioner. It was no accident that the judiciary, in the early 19th century, was the most developed aspect of the colonial government. A Chief Justice and Justices of the Supreme Court, plus circuit courts, were in place by 1826, and judges were members of the Council, with the Chief Justice as president. The latter was also in charge of the colony during the governor's absence.[12]

The power exerted by the state, whether civil, naval, or military, was complemented by the influence of ideas. Members of church and state were convinced that religion, in the shape of Protestant Christianity and the further shape of the Church of England, was an

---

11 G.E. Gunn, *The Political History of Newfoundland* (Toronto, 1966), 20, 33, 67, 71; *ENL*, s.v. "Military Governors."

12 R.H. Bonnycastle, *Newfoundland in 1842*, 2 vols. (London, 1842), 2:87; S. Cadigan, *Newfoundland and Labrador: A History* (Toronto, 2009), 98.

essential element in the preservation of social order. In 1786, William Knox of the Society for the Propagation of the Gospel, and Undersecretary of State for the Colonies, had declared: "the Prevalence of the Church of England in those Colonies is the best Security that Great Britain can have for their Fidelity and attachment to her Constitution and Interests." Believing with Edmund Burke that the English considered the church establishment "the foundation of their whole constitution," the imperial ruling class sought to establish a viable colonial church. In 1787 the High Anglican Charles Inglis was appointed bishop of Nova Scotia, with jurisdiction over Newfoundland. Other colonial bishoprics followed in other parts of the Empire—Quebec (1793), Calcutta and New South Wales (1814), and the Caribbean in the 1820s. Colonial churches, under the leadership of colonial bishops, were considered "indispensable adjuncts to the civil authorities," providing "moral leadership, social cohesion, and education."[13]

As far as Newfoundland was concerned, governors held similar views. Both James Gambier and Erasmus Gower, in the first decade of the 19th century, maintained that the Church of England (which was not established in Newfoundland) was essential to peace and good order. Governors and the British government gave financial and material support to the Anglican church in Newfoundland.[14] The instructions of Governor Sir Thomas Cochrane in 1826 enjoined him to maintain the church as the dominant religious and educational institution on the island. Cochrane believed that religion, though not exactly an opiate, encouraged habits of industry and economy, and that "an efficient Church establishment" was a means to social and political order. The church's position was underlined by Anthony Hamilton of the London-based Ecclesiastical

---

13 A. Porter, "Religion, Missionary Enthusiasm and Empire," in *The Oxford History of the British Empire Vol. III: The Nineteenth Century*, ed. R.W. Louis (Oxford, 1999), 3:223–25.

14 CO 194/43, Gambier to Hobart, 12 Dec. 1803; CO 194/44, Gower to Camden, 9 Feb. 1805, Gower to Windham, 18 Mar. 1806; CO 194/46, Gower to Castlereagh, 11 Apr. 1807; P. O'Flaherty, *Old Newfoundland: A History to 1843* (St. John's, 1999), 123–24; CO 194/57, Pickmore to Bathurst, 11 Dec. 1816.

Commission: in the proportion that the population connect themselves with the Established Church "they will be found Loyal and Faithful Subjects of the Crown."[15] The degree to which Britain was determined to make Newfoundland a Protestant colony was revealed in 1838, when the Reform movement submitted a table to Governor Henry Prescott containing a list of all persons receiving a salary or fees from the government. The document showed that 94 per cent of civil servants were Protestant; Roman Catholics received only 2.3 per cent of civil salaries.[16]

• • •

The white settler colonies and dependencies—the Americas, Australia, New Zealand, South Africa, Canada, Rhodesia, Kenya, and Newfoundland—differed from other colonial possessions in having populations largely made up of immigrants, many of them (adventurers apart) the poor and oppressed of the mother country. In the years following the end of the Napoleonic wars in 1815, thousands of new settlers, many of them ex-soldiers, convicts, or dispossessed peasants, flooded into the largest of these colonies, sometimes assisted by government or by private entrepreneurs. In many cases these immigrants, particularly ex-officers, took a renewed interest in the Empire and began to extend its dominion by aggression against the indigenous inhabitants. As Gott states, "tragically, and almost overnight, many of the formerly oppressed became themselves … the imperial oppressors."[17]

Newfoundland can be taken as an example, though on a much smaller scale, of a site of the destruction of indigenous peoples—in this case the Beothuks—at the hands of white settlers. The narrative, traced by Frederick W. Rowe in *Extinction: The Beothuks of Newfoundland*, reveals that by the 1780s the fishers-furriers of the northeast coast of the island were trespassing on Beothuk lands and often shooting the inhabitants on sight. Despite official attempts at

---

15 CO 194/72, Cochrane to Bathurst, 10 Nov. 1826; CO 194/80, Cochrane to Murray, 11 Mar. 1830; CO 194/75, A. Hamilton to Horton, 12 Mar. 1827.
16 J. Greene, *Between Damnation and Starvation: Priests and Merchants in Newfoundland Politics 1745–1855* (Montreal and Kingston, 1999), 172.
17 Gott, *Britain's Empire*, 2, 205–206.

conciliation, Rowe estimates that by the early 19th century, white aggression and disease had reduced Beothuk numbers to a critical point. In Ralph Pastore's words, they had become "a beleaguered and dwindling population eking out a living on the run from a dominant culture." The tribe was few in number—possibly less than 2,000 in all—scattered and poorly armed, and their only attempted resistance appears to have been theft of settlers' goods and some isolated killings. Rowe concludes:

> there is no defence or apology possible for the actions of some of the settlers. They did murder Beothuks and they committed other indefensible outrages against them, and the sum total of their actions must be regarded as a factor contributing to the decline and eventual extinction of that people.[18]

MISSIONARIES

If the extinction of the Beothuks was an action peculiar to Newfoundland, the island came within the orbit of an international movement with the arrival, in 1799, of an emissary of the London Missionary Society (LMS). It was one of the half-dozen such societies founded in the late 18th and early 19th centuries by Protestants interested in proselytizing the inhabitants of territories opened up by British trade to the East. Although missionaries believed they were bringing Christianity and civilization to benighted peoples under God's providence, modern critics have taken the view that missionary work was a species of "moral conquest" and missionaries part of the "advance column of imperalism's cultural assault on indigenous subjectivities."[19]

Missionary enterprise was worldwide, and Newfoundland was

---

18 F.W. Rowe, *Extinction: The Beothuks of Newfoundland* (Scarborough, 1977), 8, 22; J. Howley, *The Beothuks or Red Indians* (Cambridge, 1915; facsimile edn., Toronto, 1974); R. Pastore, "The Collapse of the Beothuk World," *Acadiensis* 19, no. 1 (1990): 52–71.

19 S. Thorne, *Congregational Missions and the Making of an Imperial Culture in Nineteenth Century England* (Standford, 1999), 9; S. Neill, *A History of Christian Missions* (Harmondsworth, 1966), 249–50.

drawn into the net. In 1799 a missionary from the LMS arrived on the island. Some local persons must have known of its existence, for the emissary journeyed in response to an appeal. "We have lately complied with a request from Twillingate" reads an entry in the LMS Report for 1799, "and Mr. Hillyard … is now on his passage there." John Hillyard, a student of the Society's academy at Newport Pagnell, arrived in Newfoundland in June 1799, and proceeded to Twillingate, taking the place of a fisher who practised family worship. He gave scriptural lessons to children and adults, converted 30 of the inhabitants, and preached in neighbouring communities.[20]

In July 1800 Hillyard reported that a church and school had been operated during the winter—about 40 children could say the Assembly's catechism—and an evening school from 7 p.m. to 10 p.m. for young men who were working during the day. The schools, he believed, "will be very useful informing the minds of those formerly absorbed in ignorance and darkness." He did not find his duties easy; on Mondays he was "too much fatigued by the duties of the Sabbath" to teach school, and generally found that "the hurry of the fishing season" interfered with his missionary activities.[21] Hillyard left for a sojourn in England in 1802. During his absence the people petitioned for a school teacher. A letter to this effect, preserved in the LMS archives, throws a poignant light on the literacy level of the people and their desire for education:

> we are A Poor Elitrate Pople … we cannot ingage any Perticler Sum, as to maintain A Minister, … Some I belive would—Deprive themselves of Nesserys for their own and Children's—Instruction, if any one should be willing to come Amongest us. by keeping scool and all would [?]. Eightey Pounds yearly … and as to the scoole to reade and wright and figuer as far as division will be sufficient/this I mention hoping you may provid one for us that might not be sutable elsewhere …

20 C.S. Thorne, *The Story of the L.M.S.* (London, 1894), 22; R. Lovett, *The History of the London Missionary Society 1795–1895* (London, 1899), 2:528–29, 629.

21 LMS Newfoundland 1, Hillyard to Hardcastle, St. John's, 18 July 1800; Hillyard to Hardcastle, Twillingate, 4 Nov. 1800.

In 1803 Hillyard returned for a second term of four years. Twillingate continued to be the centre of his work, but he found time to visit "many settlements where multitudes of souls no less ignorant than the heathen, are totally destitute of religious instruction," including Harbour Grace, Bonavista, and Trinity.[22]

Hillyard continued to make Twillingate his base until 1805, when he was invited to be pastor of the church at St. John's. In 1807 he left Newfoundland to become pastor of a church at Yarmouth, Nova Scotia, and his connection with the island ceased. The Rev. W.J. Hyde served as the LMS missionary from 1813 to 1816, and was active in founding and maintaining a Sunday School in Portugal Cove. The Society's connection with Newfoundland ended with the departure of Hyde. The mission, according to R. Lovett's history of the LMS, "never took vigorous root." Lovett, true to the imperial mindset, described the inhabitants of Newfoundland as "heathens," and the indigenous peoples as "savages," living in an "extremely barbarous and hostile state."[23]

Nearly a century before Hillyard began his ministry, John Jackson of the Society for the Propagation of the Gospel in Foreign Parts (SPG) was appointed chaplain to the garrison in St. John's, a post he held from 1701 to 1705. Jackson was followed by Jacob Rice, who officiated from 1705 to 1712. Thereafter, as R.J. Lahey's monograph on the SPG shows, there was one or more SPG representatives in the island every year throughout the 18th century. By the 1780s the SPG was sending four missionaries to Newfoundland, and at the turn of the century they numbered five, plus four teachers.[24]

Although SPG missionaries on the whole fulfilled their duties adequately, and in some cases selflessly, their calibre varied. In the

---

22 LMS Newfoundland, Moors to Kingsbery, Twillingate, 29 Oct. 1802; Lovett, *History*, 629; Hillyard to Secretary, Harbour Grace, 14 Sept. 1804, in *Transactions of the Missionary Society* (London, 1804), 2:200–201.

23 LMS Newfoundland 1, Hyde to Burder, St. John's, 24 Dec. 1813; Hyde to Burder, St. John's, 25 May 1814; Hyde to Burder, St. John's, 9 June 1815; Lovett, *History*, 627, 629.

24 R.M. Christensen, "The Establishment of SPG Missions in Newfoundland, 1703–1783," *Historical Magazine of the Protestant Episcopal Church* 20 (1951): 207–29; R.J. Lahey, "Newfoundland Material Contained in the Annual Reports of the SPG 1704–1800," unpublished typescript, ACSD.

first decades of the 19th century, they endured severe criticism from Dissenters and Methodists. One of the latter, George Cubitt, alleged that they were lukewarm about conversion, and that some frequented "balls and card parties[;] no one will suspect them of evangelism." "It is much to be lamented that these missionary clergymen," wrote the Congregationalist minister Rev. James Sabine, "have not been men of a missionary character." Both denominational and personal rivalries were possibly at work here; in 1816 the SPG clergyman David Rowland had complained that Cubitt and Sabine were illegally performing marriages, which led to their arraignment before Governor Pickmore.[25] In fact, several of the clergy were university men, who fulfilled their mission ably.

The calibre of missionaries in the field varied. Some found the winter weather upsetting; others, like the Methodist John Walsh, were prepared to shoulder the burden: "The salvation of souls is of unspeakable importance," he declared, "and whether this great work is carried on under the torrid or the frigid zone, it is equally precious in the sight of God and his saints."[26] The focus of the "great work," for both Anglican and Methodist missionaries in Newfoundland, was the eradication of "vice," which they interpreted in terms of both intemperance and Sabbath-breaking. The missionaries who were sent to Newfoundland in the early 19th century were members of a generation of Britons who had been exposed to the full force of the Evangelical-inspired crusade against vice, with popular amusements, "licentious" books and plays, drunkenness, and Sabbath-breaking the main targets.[27]

Intemperance shocked the missionaries profoundly and they attempted, not always successfully, to combat the almost universal consumption of liquor. According to the Methodist William Wilson, at this period strong liquor was considered almost a necessity of life. Rum was imported in large quantities, and the favourite drink, calibogus (rum and spruce beer), was consumed on every possible oc-

---

25 MMS N. Am. 1, Cubitt to Marsden, St. John's, 17 Jan. 1817; Rev. J. Sabine, *A View of the Moral State of Newfoundland* (Boston, 1818), 5; *ENL*, s.v. "Sabine, James."

26 MMS CNA 3, Walsh to Society, St. John's, 3 Jan. 1822.

27 I. Bradley, *The Call to Seriousness* (London, 1976), 94–118.

casion by the working classes. Thomas Angwin, another Methodist, was pained to observe that "[d]rinking is indulged in to an amazing extent," and Edward Wix of the SPG declared that drinking alcohol led to depravity "such as would have roused execration in the most licentious days of heathen Rome."[28]

The other great sin to be combatted by the missionaries was Sabbath-breaking. The work of catching and curing fish occupied families for the entire week, including Sunday. This trespassed on the spiritual territory of the missionaries, and what fishing families regarded as a necessary part of their livelihood the missionaries castigated as transgression. John Lewis in Burin, whose spelling was not equal to his convictions, fervently depicted the clash between sin and survival:

> The violation of the Sabbath apears to me to be one of the most Flagrant Sins that a man can comit and since I have been here I have been compeled to witness the Lords day abused and violated in the most glaring and profligate manner. But as people here with one voice say that they are compeled from necessity to be employed about the Fish on the Sabbath and I have decidedly set my face against it and have endeavoured to show the evil of it.... should they observe it [the Sabbath] they could make but one [catch a week] and to tell ungodly that one hundred quarters of Fish got in a lawful manner with the blessing of God is better than two hundred got by Sabbath breaking is to them quite unreasonable ...[29]

The missionaries, in their efforts to convert and civilize the inhabitants, found that they were working against the customs and practices that contributed to the very existence of the fishing community. The seasonal rhythm of the fishery, with the seven-day working week in summer, followed in winter by preparation for the

---

28 W. Wilson, *Newfoundland and Its Missionaries* (Cambridge, MA, 1866), 347–52; MMS N. Am. 98, T. Angwin to Society, Grand Bank, 23 Apr. 1833; E. Wix, *Six Months of a Newfoundland Missionary's Journal, from Feb. to Aug., 1835* (London, 1836), 245–46.
29 MMS N. Am. 1, Lewis to Society, Burin, 7 July 1817.

next season and spring sealing voyages, were to the fishers the basis of life. To the missionaries, activities of the fishery were a breeding ground of vice. They had been brought up in a developing industrial-capitalist society based on competition, the division of labour, strict utilization of time, and year-round regularity. They found themselves in a community which operated on seasonal work, mutual aid, and a certain independence of outlook. Newfoundlanders, observed the Anglican missionary the Rev. Julian Moreton, generally thought that the missionary was in Newfoundland for the sake of his salary; furthermore, there was a prevalent belief that the SPG was a branch of the national government, whose funds were derived from taxes, and thus indirectly maintained by the fishing families. But "a chief obstacle" to missionary work, he concluded, was their "studied independent bearing" and the habit of doing things "in their own time."[30]

• • •

The missionaries of the SPG had been active in Newfoundland since the beginning of the 19th century. Their fellow labourers in the field, the Methodists, were later arrivals. They were the heirs of John Wesley, the Anglican clergyman, whose conversion to a holy life in 1738 was the starting point of a nation-wide and eventually worldwide religious movement. Wesley preached that an initial sense of sin could be vanquished by the belief that Christ had died to justify (i.e., pardon) the sins of the individual. Methodism was an experiential type of religion which inspired zealous and enthusiastic preachers to take the message to the masses. "Revivals"—outpourings of religious hysteria, marked by screaming, singing, praying, and clapping—became the hallmark of popular Methodism.[31]

Following a threat by the British government in 1811 to curb Methodist enthusiasm, the movement gradually became respectable. Its members, in the words of novelist George Eliot, were of "the modern type which reads quarterly reviews and attends in chapel

---

30 Rev. J. Moreton, *Life and Work in Newfoundland* (London, 1863), 24–27.
31 D. Hempton, *Methodism and Politics in British Society 1750–1850* (London, 1987).

with pillared porticoes."[32] When the Methodist Missionary Society was formed in 1813, it turned part of its energies to work abroad.

Methodism eventually reached Newfoundland not, however, by the agency of the Society but by the efforts of an individual, Laurence Coughlan.[33] Born in Ireland, converted to Methodism there by lay preachers, ordained by a bishop of the Russian Orthodox Church, and discountenanced by Wesley, he was ordained as a priest by the bishop of Chester in 1766; Coughlan then set sail for Newfoundland as an SPG missionary at the invitation of Dissenters in Carbonear. His work at Harbour Grace was increasingly opposed by his subscribers, the principal merchants and planters of Conception Bay, mainly because he reverted to old-style Methodism—organizing small groups and classes and shocking the respectable by preaching against sinners in language which, according to William Wilson, "Newfoundland had not heard before." His preaching apparently made the fishers less deferential to the merchants. His adversaries petitioned for his removal, and he was forced to leave for England in 1773. For 40 years after his departure Methodism in Newfoundland, in J.W. Grant's words, consisted "of barely glowing embers." Eventually, however, it took hold, and its ethos became rooted in the populace; "it retained a tradition of periodic and highly emotional revival," with informal and unstructured worship and a negative moralism.[34]

Calvin Hollett elaborates on this aspect in *Shouting, Embracing and Dancing: The Growth of Methodism in Newfoundland, 1774–1874* (2010), elevating the popular, revivalistic side of the movement, and playing down the importance of its organizational and missionary structure. He argues that the attainment of the status of a District of the Wesleyan Methodist Conference of Brit-

---

32 George Eliot, *Adam Bede* (Oxford World's Classics edn., 2008), 35.

33 The following paragraphs rely on H. Rollmann, "Laurence Coughlan and the Origins of Methodism in Newfoundland," in *The Contribution of Methodism to Atlantic Canada*, ed. J.W. Grant and C.H.H. Scobie (Montreal and Kingston, 1992), 53–76.

34 J.W. Grant, "Methodist Origins in Atlantic Canada," in *Contribution of Methodism*, ed. J.W. Grant and C.H.H. Scobie, 37ff.; Wilson, *Newfoundland and Its Missionaries*, 139.

ain by Newfoundland Methodism in 1815 was "in many respects a hindrance to its expansion," and that the District meeting was a "professional body" made up entirely of self-serving and poorly educated missionaries, forming "an impediment to the growth of Methodism."[35] This is less than fair to the preaching and teaching of the more dedicated missionaries—John Lewis at Port de Grave, James Hickson at Bonavista, William Wilson, when in Island Cove, Perlican, and Hants Harbour, John Walsh at Blackhead, and Ninian Barr at Bonavista—who took services or taught school on virtually every day of the week. James Hickson, for instance, began Sunday at 6 a.m. with a prayer meeting, preached at 11 a.m. and 6 p.m., taught school in between, and devoted every evening of the week to preaching or a prayer meeting.[36]

By "the growth of Methodism" Hollett appears to mean the increase in the number of revivalist meetings—the outcome of the enthusiastic work of grassroots activists, which he maps in some detail in all the regions where Methodism was growing. He characterizes early Newfoundland Methodism as a demotic spiritual movement, "a vernacular religion, in which quenching a thirst for the experiential was the essential trait." Revivalism was widespread over time and space. In the small settlement of Haystack, Placentia Bay, in the 1820s people "melted into tears"; on the northeast coast in 1834 people's faces were "beaming with joy"; "[w]e have got him by heart, too," they cried in Grand Bank and Fortune in 1848; seven years later at Bonavista "transport(s) of joy" were experienced.[37] An Anglican clergyman, observing a revival in Twillingate, was disturbed by what he called "these outrageous and absurd proceedings," with their "wild cries … maniac actions … dancing and jumping … praying, raving and cavorting," which went on for most of the night.[38]

Methodist's emotional bond with the people, however much

35 C. Hollett, *Shouting, Embracing and Dancing with Ecstasy: The Growth of Methodism in Newfoundland, 1774–1874* (Montreal and Kingston, 2010), 56, 57, 252.

36 MMS N. Am. 1, Hickson to Society, Bonavista, 6 Dec. 1816.

37 Hollett, *Shouting, Embracing and Dancing*, 253.

38 Ibid., 173–74, citing letter of Thomas Boone, 31 Dec. 1860.

it might dismay members of the more hierarchical and decorous Church of England, was a source of its strength. The Methodist missionaries were good singers, wrote William Wilson, and hymns and music took "a high stand" in their activities; hundreds who cared nothing about preaching were "charmed to Methodist assemblies by the music." Mass participation, and the devoted work of the more active missionaries, gave an impetus to the development of Methodism, which flowered in the mid-19th century into an organization with considerable political and educational influence. In Hollett's words:

> Methodism expanded by the passion and ardour of fishermen and their families, especially in revivals. It was this experience of the heart that fuelled a lay army of class leaders, lay readers, local preachers, exhorters, and Sunday school teachers who in just over a century built Methodism to such a degree that it gave a third dimension to the culture of Newfoundland—one in which deference gave way to self-assurance.[39]

SCHOOLS

Among the missionaries sent to Newfoundland by the SPG and the Methodists there were, as we have seen, some who became guilty of moral failings or lack of zeal, not to mention a lack of empathy with the fishers' way of life, which would have tended to reduce the general effectiveness of their mission. But if missionaries are to be judged by the material effect of their labours, they were successful in an important sphere—the establishment of schools. In the period between 1800 and the passing of the first Education Act in 1836, all three societies—the LMS, the SPG, and the Methodists—founded or promoted day and Sunday Schools (and a few evening and adult classes) in some 60 locations, mainly on the northern Avalon Peninsula and Trinity Bay, with a number on the Burin Peninsula and the islands of Notre Dame Bay. Over 125 schools were founded, Methodists accounting for 49, of which 28 were Sunday schools.

---

39 Wilson, *Newfoundland and Its Missionaries*, 375; Hollett, *Shouting, Embracing and Dancing*, 260.

The SPG established 74 schools of all types, including 44 Sunday schools, about the same percentage as the Methodists.[40] The total was large, but it is likely that many of the schools did not last the whole period.

Missionary correspondence supplies details of the location of some of the schools that were established. John Burt, for the SPG, reported in 1826 that the Society had established schools at Harbour Grace, Carbonear, Bay Roberts, Bareneed, Ship Cove, Bay de Verde, Bread and Cheese and Island Cove, and Salmon Cove, with an average attendance of 35 boys and 32 girls. Five years later William Bullock listed SPG Sunday Schools at Trinity, Catalina, English Harbour, Salmon Cove, Bonavista, New Harbour, Heart's Delight, Heart's Content, New Perlican, Silly [Scilly] Cove, and Grates Cove; the average number of boys and girls in attendance (excluding Grates Cove) was 16 and 14 respectively.[41] Some of these were Sunday schools. The rationale for the institution was provided by the SPG missionary at Harbour Grace, Lewis Amadeus Anspach:

> 1: … it affords those many children whose parents are really poor, an opportunity to learn their Catechism and reading, who without it would have continued in that state of ignorance in which they had hitherto been brought up. 2: It affords the same opportunity to the children of those who are able but not willing to bear the expense of schooling, and whose children consequently stand in the same unhappy state as the last. 3: During the fishing season, from May till October, children as soon as they can handle a line are sent to the Bay Fishery, and are at home only on Sundays, when it is a great advantage to them to find a school opened for their reception. Add to this that they thus acquire a habit of distinguishing the Lord's day from the rest of the week, of spend-

---

40 LMS NFLD. Corr. 1802–1817; SPG NFLD. Corr. 1801–1836; MMS NFLD. Corr. 1815–1836; *An Account of the State of the Schools in the Island of Newfoundland Established or Assisted by the SPG* (London, 1827), Appendix, Bishop of Nova Scotia to the Society (4 Jan. 1828), 83.

41 SPG C/CAN/NFL 3, J. Burt to Society, Harbour Grace, 21 Dec. 1826; SPG C/CAN/NFL 4, W. Bullock to Society, Trinity, 29 June 1831.

ing that day in a manner very different from that to which they were used before, of attending divine service &c.[42]

Many of the SPG schools were day schools. Several were modelled, as far as circumstances allowed, on the principles of Dr. Andrew Bell's monitorial system, in which a single teacher, assisted by several monitors, instructed large numbers of pupils in one classroom. How these schools operated in practice in Newfoundland outports in the early 19th century is shown by accounts of three schools conducted respectively by William Lampen, William Tulk, and John Thomas. Lampen was appointed to Harbour Grace in 1796 at a salary of £10 per annum, increased to £15 in 1798. He immediately set about teaching children to read and say their prayers and catechism; he attracted 41 day scholars, and eight in an evening class, plus eight admitted free "on the Society's bounty."[43] By 1805 his parishioners had contributed £65 toward the building of a new schoolhouse; later they requested him to take over missionary duties, including reading prayers and delivering the sermon on Sunday.

Lampen always had plenty of pupils. At the turn of the century he informed the Society that he had 14 in his day school and was teaching 32 "young men" to read and cipher in a night school (the only one, he claimed, in the whole island) and giving tuition to 28 others. He also organized a Sunday school. He was unusual for including writing in the curriculum and using Dixon's *Spelling Book* to teach reading. The Society supplied him with children's books which helped his pupils to make "greater progress in learning than [he had] known them some years past." His pupils included children of Roman Catholic parents, but he instructed them in the principles of the Established Church.[44]

By 1812 Lampen was teaching 80 children and 10 young men in his day and night schools. He found the Sunday School "of great utility"; the children were taught "to read, spell, say their catechism and constantly to attend the church." In 1813 his daughter assisted

42 SPG C/CAN/NFL 2, Anspach to Dr. Morris, Harbour Grace, 15 Jan. 1807.

43 Lahey, "Annual Reports," entries for 1896, 1897, 1898.

44 SPG Proceedings, 1804–1805, 32; 1812–1813, 34; SPG C/CAN/NFL 1, Lampen to Society, Harbour Grace, 18 Nov. 1801, 30 Oct. 1802.

him by teaching the very young children.[45] Lampen had his reward. In 1810 Admiral Duckworth, on a visit to Harbour Grace, reported that he "saw Mr. Lampen with 70 of his scholars round him, as well girls as boys, of truly creditable appearance. His labours must indeed be of extreme benefit to a numerous but little wealthy society." Duckworth felt he was "so worthy an object of consideration" that he recommended to Lord Liverpool, the Colonial Secretary, that Lampen receive a government allowance of £20 per annum. Lampen died in 1820, having taught for 36 years. "Great, indeed, was the number of those who received their sole education from him," wrote the SPG, "and his memory will long be retained with respect and gratitude."[46]

The story of William Tulk also reveals something of the life and tribulations of early 19th-century missionary teachers.[47] A Dorset man, he first went to Newfoundland in 1807 to work as a SPG teacher in Burin, at a salary of £15 per year. The house in which he lived, with a schoolroom attached, was built by the local people. In a letter to his brother in 1815 Tulk expressed a wish to visit England, but consoled himself with the thought that "[he was] making many poor parents happy in this rockey wild, and unchristian country." He was able to leave for England in 1821, but before his departure a misfortune occurred. He had initially understood that his residence was rent-free, but on entering it he was informed that a rent of £14 per annum would be charged, virtually the whole of his salary. Shortly after taking up his abode a group of Methodists arrived in Burin who wished to preach in his schoolroom. Tulk refused, which led some of the Methodists to withdraw their children, thereby reducing his income from fees. He then removed to Great Burin with his wife and three children, where he had to pay a rent

---

45 SPG C/CAN/NFL 1, Lampen to Society, Harbour Grace, 19 Nov. 1812, 19 Nov. 1813, 15 Dec. 1813.

46 CO 194/49, Duckworth to Liverpool, 25 Nov. 1810; SPG Proceedings, 1821, 60.

47 I am grateful to Mr. and Mrs. H. Baker of Dorset, England, for supplying me with a letter of William Tulk of Burine to his brother, dated 10 June 1815, on which the following is partly based. Cf. also SPG C/CAN/NFL 2, J. Parsons to Society, Dorset, 20 Jan. 1821; Parsons to Society, 23 Apr. 1822; SPG C/CAN/NFL 3, Tulk to Hamilton, Great St. Lawrence, 17 Nov. 1827.

of £6 per annum.

Tulk arrived in England in January 1821 after a voyage of six weeks. He was befriended by the Rev. J. Parsons, vicar of Sherborne, Dorset, who wrote to the SPG on his behalf. The Society had treated Tulk in a somewhat cavalier fashion, delaying payment of his salary, neglecting to reply to his letters, and failing to send him any school books; such books as he had were supplied by Parsons. One of the reasons for Tulk's visit to England was to obtain the assurance of a proper supply of books for his scholars. But more importantly he wished to persuade the Society to consider his reduction of income and allow him the rent of his new house in addition to his salary. Alternatively, he suggested, the Society might buy the premises for £60. A further £20 would enable him to have a chimney, which would enable him to live there in winter as well as summer. He also wished to improve his qualifications by undertaking instruction in Dr. Bell's monitorial system and offered to go to London for that purpose if the Society would pay the expense, or, if not, would learn the system at the local National School, at no cost to the Society.

By 1827 Tulk was in charge of a school at Great St. Lawrence, with about 30 children in attendance. The Revs. Blackman and Burt supplied him with books, including spelling books and cards, and religious literature ranging from the Bible and *The Book of Common Prayer* to introductory texts on various aspects of Christianity. In the winter of 1827, an "alarming malady" struck the community, which resulted in the closing of the school for a long period, with a consequent loss of fees. No medical assistance was available, but Tulk, an aged and infirm man, did his share of visiting the sick; his plight was severe enough for him to petition the bishop of Nova Scotia for assistance. Tulk was described by the Rev. Parsons as "much attached to the Church of England," and the latter believed that Tulk had imbibed "a considerable portion of the humility and piety" of his wife's spirit. Though obviously a dedicated teacher, the letter he wrote to his brother showed him to have a somewhat insecure grasp of grammar, punctuation, and spelling, not uncommon in men of his class and calling at the time.

Another stalwart of the SPG was John Thomas of Scilly Cove. In 1799, in a letter to the Society, written in an elegant script, he stated that he read the service of the Established Church and gave a sermon every Sunday, catechizing the children afterwards. His greatest duty, however, was "to instruct the children under [his] care their duty to God and man in the best manner [he] possibly c[ould]." His pupils numbered 26, whom he taught gratis. Twenty-two years later he informed the SPG that he was 81 years of age, had been resident in Newfoundland for 44 years, had read the prayers in church for 30 years, and "kept school for most of that term." He did not charge fees because of the poverty of the parents, and when his son married and left home, he had nothing to depend upon but his salary from the SPG.[48] By the year 1827, when Thomas was 87 years of age and very infirm, John Inglis, bishop of Nova Scotia, recommended that Governor Hamilton continue his salary as a pension.[49]

Teachers employed by the SPG were paid a low salary. Schoolmasters and catechists existed on £10, £15, or £20 per annum. Missionaries were, however, paid handsomely, receiving a salary of £200 per annum, increased to £250 in 1821; by 1828 Archdeacon George Coster and the Rev. Charles Blackman were drawing £300.[50]

In the mid-1830s, the comfortable salaries of SPG missionaries were heavily cut. Radicals and liberals in the British House of Commons, who had long opposed the mission, succeeded in persuading the government to reduce the grant to the SPG prior to its abolition; the subsidy, it was alleged, was excessive, it supported a monopoly of one religion, and the funds were often mismanaged. The grant was reduced to £12,000 in 1832, to £8,000 the following year, and to a final grant of £4,000 in 1834. In 1834 the SPG had granted its 12 missionaries in Newfoundland £2,636; the following year it was halved to £1,315.[51] This retrenchment weakened the work of the SPG vis-à-vis the Methodists.

---

48 SPG C/CAN/NFL 2, Thomas to Society, Silly [Scilly] Cove, 28 Oct. 1799; SPG C/CAN/NFL 3, Thomas to Society, Silly [Scilly] Cove, 10 Nov. 1821.
49 SPG C/CAN/NFL 9, Inglis to Hamilton, 11 July 1827.
50 *Colonial Journal* 1, no. 3 (1816); SPG Proceedings 1821, 57; 1828, 238.
51 Parl. Deb. 2nd ser. 10, 12 Mar. 1824, 963–70; Parl. Deb. 2nd ser. 21, 6 Apr. 1829, 455–62; Parl. Deb. 3rd ser. 5, 25 July 1831, 283–302; *Gazette*, 8 Oct. 1833, A.M. Campbell (Sec. SPG) to Bishops of Quebec and Nova Scotia, London, 21 July 1833; SPG Proceedings, 1834, 187; 1835, 271.

• • •

Methodist missionaries were industrious promoters of both day and Sunday schools. They recognized that the latter, in particular, were an expeditious means of introducing young children to the basics of literacy; they were cheap, needed only one day's supervision, and usually required no separate building. Sunday schools were "absolutely necessary" in this country, maintained the Methodist John Pickavant in 1815, and answered far better than day schools in a situation where children worked in the fishery during the summer weeks, but were free on Sundays. By 1833 the Methodists claimed 25 Sunday schools in operation, with 1,592 pupils.[52]

William Wilson, who taught a Methodist Sunday school at Bonavista, described its routine:

> At half past eight o'clock the flag is haul[ed] up as a signal for school. At nine it commences with singing and prayer when the greatest order is observed among the children. After the second mention of the Hymn the children are told to rise. After singing they are ordered to kneel after prayer the names are called over and the children then retire to their respective classes. Those in the spelling classes devote the whole of their time in reading and spelling. Those in the Bible and Testament first repeat a portion of scripture given them the preceding—then say a column of spelling, afterward read a chapter. At half an hour before the commencement of public service I generaly arrange the children in the front of the reading desk and question them either respecting the Scripture they have been commiting to memory or the lesson they have been reading, I then explain to them whatever I conceive they have not understood ...[53]

Since the main subject in these schools was scriptural knowledge—of the Bible, the catechism, perhaps a few tracts or religious

---

52 MMS N. Am. 1, J. Pickavant to Society, St. John's, 2 Dec. 1815; MMS N. Am. 98, Haigh to Society, Brigus, 26 June 1833.

53 MMS N. Am. 3, Wilson to Society, Bonavista, 14 Nov. 1822.

books—it was assumed that the ability to repeat passages by heart would provide children with the means of salvation. William Wilson, and William Faulkner, missionary at Hants Harbour, felt that reading was a step on the road to embracing Methodism, and that children's aptitude for learning should be regarded, in his words, as "presaging future good to our interests."[54]

These utilitarian assumptions found at least one critic in the ranks. George Ellidge, missionary at Port de Grave, was convinced that youthful exuberance could not be contained by the rigidities of schooling, nor by early labour:

> love of reading is scarcely ever acquired by a young man in Newfoundland. If he came to the age of nine or ten years, he generally delights much more in playing about … than he does in the routeen of a school, not to remark that at this age he is commonly needed as an Auxiliary to his father, and after this period so many are his interruptions to a regular attendance on either Night or Sunday School and so much is he taken up with the companions of his own age … that his little stock of learning is rather diminished than increased hence we can hardly ever get any that are able and disposed to read our work and consequently their attachment to us as a denomination of Christians is not so much as it ought to be.[55]

Few of the missionary schools were of high quality. Apart from limitations imposed by geography, demography, and lack of infrastructure, they were primarily a means of indoctrination rather than institutions of secular learning. Most of the SPG schools, wrote Bishop John Inglis of Nova Scotia in 1827, after a widespread investigation, "hardly deserve the name." Outport schools, declared the Methodist John Pickavant six years later, were "of the lowest de-

54 MMS N. Am. 3, Wilson to Society, Bonavista, 14 Nov. 1822; MMS N. Am. 97, Faulkner to Society, Hants Harbour, 1 Dec. 1830.
55 MMS N. Am. 98, Ellidge to Bunting, Port de Grave, 23 Dec.1834.

scription," and in St. John's but of "an ordinary kind."[56] Nevertheless, a number of children must have imbibed the elements of literacy.

Although missionaries in Newfoundland were few in number—in 1817 the Methodists had 11 missionaries in the island, the SPG only six, for a population in the mid-1820s of 55,000[57]—they had some claim to have laid the foundation of popular education in the island. They not only pioneered the provision of schoolrooms but also furthered the concept of education—that children should have access to institutions devoted specifically to learning. This, however, was achieved at the cost of separating schools and children on denominational lines—an inevitable outcome of missionary influence. Missionaries, as we have seen, were the spearhead of the British Empire's mission to Christianize and educate countries beyond its borders. Seen in this light, the religio-educational landscape in Newfoundland in the first decades of the 19th century was less an indigenous growth and more a consequence of Newfoundland's status as an integral part of the British Empire.

---

56 SPG C/CAN/NS 9, John Inglis, Nova Scotia, to Hamilton, 11 July 1827; MMS N. Am. 98, Pickavant to Watson, Port de Grave, 9 Feb. 1833.

57 Hollett, *Shouting, Embracing and Dancing*, 37; SPG Report 1825, 166; J.J. Mannion, ed., *The Peopling of Newfoundland* (St. John's, 1977), 13.

CHAPTER 2

Merchants and Evangelicals: The Origin and Early Years of the Newfoundland School Society, 1823–1855

> Merchants and master manufacturers are ... the two classes of people who commonly employ the largest capitals. The interest of the dealers ... in any particular branch of trade or manufactures, is always in some respect different from, and even opposite to, that of the public. To widen the market and to narrow the competition, is always the interest of the dealers ... who have generally an interest to deceive and even oppress the public.
>
> —Adam Smith, *The Wealth of Nations*, Books I-II

> I never feel as if I was pleading for schools, when pleading for this Society, because its schoolmaster in a majority of instances is all that the people have; he is their priest and he is their preacher, he reads to them the liturgy of the church and he reads them a sermon; he cannot administer to them the sacraments of the church, but he prepares them for these, in case any wandering missionary should visit them; I feel that this Society is a Missionary Society—I might say a Missionary Society to the heathen, but they are your own countrymen.
>
> —Rev. Francis Close, in a sermon to the Newfoundland School Society (1839)

Fish merchants, Evangelical Christians, schools for the poor: at first sight they appear to have nothing in common. In the peculiar economic and social conditions of early 19th-century Newfoundland, however, merchants and Evangelicals joined forces to found the Newfoundland School Society,[58] which in 1823 set out to bring Christian education to the children of the island's fishing families. Religious fervour and mercantile enterprise united to establish an organization which lasted exactly 100 years, inscribing a unique, if minor, chapter in the annals of missionary history. The founder of the Society, and its leading spirit, was Samuel Codner, a Devon merchant and committed Evangelical, who realized that the rock on which the Society had to be built was the powerful and influential merchant class which had long dominated the Newfoundland economy.

Historians, notably Keith Matthews in his thesis "A History of the West of England Fishery" (1968), W. Gordon Handcock in *Soe longe as there comes noe women: Origins of English Settlement in Newfoundland* (1989), and Sean Cadigan in *Newfoundland and Labrador: A History* (2009), have traced the domination of the Newfoundland fishery by West of England merchants from the 17th century onward. The Dorset town of Poole became the focus of the enterprise, with the Newfoundland settlement of Trinity the most important entrepôt on the island. The turmoil in the North Atlantic following the American Revolution paved the way for the decline of the migratory West Country fishery and for a more stable settlement, with migrant labourers marrying and setting up household production. With the supply of provisions from the New England states cut off, many merchants turned to supplying residents with goods from Europe on credit. By the early 19th century the fishery had become, in Governor Duckworth's words, "decidedly sedentary," declining from 330 fishing ships in 1788 to 130 in 1804.[59]

Fishing operations were largely in the hands of planters, resident small-boat owners who sometimes hired "servants," that is, individual fishers. Merchants were finding that they could procure cured fish in return for provisions and fishing gear on easier

58 The Society went through several changes of name throughout its history, ending up as the Colonial and Continental School Society. For convenience, it will be referred to by its popular name, the Newfoundland School Society, throughout this chapter.

59 CO 194/53, Duckworth to Bathurst, 2 Nov. 1812; CO 194/44, Gower to Camden, 24 Dec. 1804.

terms from planters who operated a household fishery (with the women doing the shore work) than from the employment of their own shoremen at high wages. In this period some of the oldest and wealthiest trading families retired or left for other fields of activity. The trade became dominated by some 40 or more "new adventurers," most of whom had originated as agents or captains, but many of the less-powerful fishing merchants owned their own ships, owners of bye-boats who came out from England annually and employed several thousand men; there were also local middlemen and some Scottish and a few Irish traders. From the ranks of this group emerged the leading men of the early decades of the 19th century.[60] Codner was one of them, having entered the family business in the island in 1788.

Samuel Codner's Evangelical vision was shared by many in England, some of whom he recruited to form the Newfoundland School Society. The Evangelicals were a small but influential group, centred in Clapham, London; they founded nearly 200 religious, moral, educational, and philosophical societies, and won over Members of Parliament and government, High Church clergy, bankers and industrialists, members of the professions and services, and important merchants.[61] As described in Chapter 1, their interests also extended to the Empire.

Samuel Codner was born in Teignmouth, Devon, in 1776 and came from a family which had long connections with the Newfoundland fishery as bye-boat keepers and merchants. His introduction to Newfoundland began in 1788 when, at the age of 12, he joined the family firm in St. John's, and by 1794 he was acting as agent for the firm of Daniel Codner and Co. In 1819 he began to trade on his own account from Teignmouth, and later Dartmouth; in the 1820s he was importing provisions—foodstuffs, wine and

---

60 PP, 1817, VI, Report from the Select Committee on Newfoundland Trade, evidence of G. Garland, 4; K. Matthews, "The West Country Merchants in Newfoundland," Lecture to the Newfoundland Historical Society, 10 Dec. 1968; W.G. Handcock, *Soe longe as there comes noe women: Origins of English Settlement in Newfoundland* (St. John's, 1989), 215–16, 241–42.
61 F.K. Brown, *Fathers of the Victorians* (Cambridge, 1961), 9.

beer, clothing, and fishing gear.[62]

As joint secretary of the Teignmouth Bible Society since 1820 Codner had been instrumental in sending Bibles to Newfoundland, and he utilized the voyages of his ships to deliver Bibles to Portugal and Italy. Codner was heir to a long tradition of Bible Society activity in Newfoundland. The first recorded shipment of Bibles reached Newfoundland in 1807, and supplies to the island of the Authorized Version continued on an almost annual basis throughout the 18th and early 19th centuries.[63]

• • •

The birth of the Newfoundland School Society took place in the depth of the depression that followed the catastrophic crisis in the fishery in the winter of 1816–1817. The calamity was devastating, all the more so because it followed a period of prosperity. With the coming of peace in Europe and between Britain and the United States in 1815, exports of fish (mainly to Spain, Portugal, and the Mediterranean) rose to nearly a million quintals, fetching good prices. Wages were high—up to £70 per season for fishers and between £90 and £140 for splitters. As Shannon Ryan observes, there was full employment, high wages, a large catch, and almost insatiable markets—in fact, "the most prosperous and pleasant year of the whole period." Then, with the conclusion of peace, came "a very great fall" in the price of fish in foreign markets, increased duties on fish in Spain, competition from French fishers under treaty regulations, and the general increase in the expenses of the trade.[64] These sudden events had a destructive effect on the fishery; the human cost to the citizens was also considerable. For many, the world seemed to have been turned upside down: respectable citizens formed armed night

62 *Devon and Cornwall Notes and Queries* 13 (1925–26), 196; *Mercantile Journal*, 6 July 1826, 17 May 1827.

63 BFBS Home Correspondence, Codner to Society, 1820–1821; J. Fingard, "'Grapes in the Wilderness': The Bible Society in British North America in the Early Nineteenth Century," *Histoire Sociale—Social History* 5, no. 9 (1972): 5–31.

64 S. Ryan, *A History of Newfoundland in the North Atlantic to 1818* (St. John's, 2012), 191; PP, 1817, VI, Report from the Select Committee on Newfoundland Trade, evidence of G. Garland, 4–6.

patrols to protect property; in St. John's, thousands of "hardy industrious men" were daily walking the streets, "without money, without provisions, without lodgings, without employment," dependent on casual charity for subsistence and sleeping in makeshift shelters and old hulks on the beach; indigent members of the middle class, ashamed to be seen as mendicants, crept about the streets after dark, looking for food; bankrupt merchants reinvented themselves as attorneys for victims of the crash.[65]

Many starving workers took the situation into their own hands. In the words of George Garland to the Select Committee on Trade:

> a lawless, because starving population, has been seen in various parts, breaking open the merchants stores, and carrying off their property, or seizing the vessels that arrived with provisions; and in both cases, setting the police (such as it is) altogether at defiance. In one instance, going with arms in their hands, demanding and enforcing a supply of provisions from the sitting magistrates.

Graphic accounts of attacks on stores and ships at Brigus, Carbonear, and St. John's, by others giving evidence, added to the picture of merchants menaced by gangs of starving men. Edward Kemp expressed the general fear that "stores once forced, no sort of property will be safe"; and John Elson, agent for G.J. Kemp's business, warned that "neither the persons nor property of those engaged in trade here will be safe in future."[66] There is no narrative account of the economic decline of these years, but the incidental record is strong. According to the statistics of D.W. Prowse, total exports sank from £1,183,000 in 1815 to £637,000 in 1823; exports of cod fell from over 1 million quintals in 1815 to 825,000 in 1819; customs duties, which yielded £17,000 in 1815, brought in only £7,000 in

---

65 PP, 1817, VI, Report from the Select Committee on Trade, 13, 23; CO 194/63, Hamilton to Bathurst, 17 Jan. 1820.

66 PP, 1817, VI, Report from the Select Committee on Trade, 3, 8–12; CO 194/61, Butterworth to Bathurst, 5 Jan. 1818.

1822.[67] These deficiencies in the cod fishery led to starvation across the island, graphically chronicled by Governor Charles Hamilton, a committee of merchants, and the Grand Jury.[68]

The evidence favours the view that the depth of the post-war depression was reached in 1821. Was it a coincidence that this was the year that Codner experienced a revelation that led him to become the founder of the Newfoundland School Society? Aubrey Spencer, when bishop of Jamaica, reminded the Society that at this juncture Newfoundland was experiencing "hopelessness ... despair ... and absolute destitution." But against this dark horizon, he continued:

> the star of your Society arose. It was then that a pious and benevolent individual devoted himself to the work of bringing this huge amount of wrong and suffering to the notice of a Christian public ... The Society's schools ... were diffusing the renovating elements of piety, order, and consequent happiness among a thousand homes.[69]

The "pious and benevolent individual" was, of course, Samuel Codner. He had been activated to spread the Christian message by a near-death experience in 1820. In that year he was returning to England in the brig *Mercury* after the summer fishing season. Three hundred miles west of Ireland a storm arose which threw the vessel on her beam ends, broadside to the waves. Disaster seemed imminent and Codner vowed that, if by some miracle his life were saved, he would devote the rest of his days to "spreading the message of the Kingdom of God." The storm abated before the ship foundered, and Codner reached England in safety. Within a year chance provided a spur that led him to put his vow into practice. In October 1821, advised to visit Margate for his health, he attended the inau-

---

67 D.W. Prowse, *A History of Newfoundland* (London, 1895), Table I, 692; Table VIII, 697; Table XXXII, 713.

68 CO 194/61-62-64, Hamilton to Bathurst, 1818, 1821, encl. Petition to His Majesty from the Merchants of St. John's Trading to the West Indies; Grand Jury to Forbes, 13 Oct. 1821.

69 SPG Proceedings, 1845–46, Spencer to Society, 28 May 1846, in Occasional Paper No. XX, July 1846.

gural meeting of the Isle of Thanet Auxiliary Bible Society. The chief speaker was no less a personage than the Prime Minister Lord Liverpool, President of the Bible Society, who stated that the British had an "important duty" to circulate the Scriptures throughout "their extensive colonies and foreign possessions."[70] "As I listened to his Lordship," Codner related later, "I considered how negligent I had been, for I knew that the one of our colonies to which I was more immediately attached, much needed Christian instruction; and from that day I commenced my efforts for a School Society ..."[71]

Codner acted on his intention quickly. In February 1822 he wrote to the Methodist MP Joseph Butterworth, enclosing a leaflet "Schools in Newfoundland" (cost: £700 per school, plus teacher's salary); over £200 had already been subscribed by individuals, the Methodist Missionary Society, and merchant houses. In November of that year he approached the government for support, emboldened by the presence in the administration of Evangelicals—Lord Bexley and James Stephen—and Bathurst, the Colonial Secretary, a sympathizer. After securing an interview with Bexley, Codner sent a memorial on Newfoundland schools to the government, and a further leaflet to Bexley proposing the institution of a Society to provide schools for the people of the island under Anglican teachers.[72] He followed this with an interview with the prime minister, Lord Liverpool, who concurred in the design to found the Society, appointed himself Vice-Patron, donated £30, and empowered Codner to secure the support of Lord Bathurst, the Colonial Secretary.[73]

The way was now open for the founding of the organization. The meeting to establish "The Society for the Education of the Poor in Newfoundland" took place at the London Coffee House,

70 J.D. Mullins, *Our Beginnings: Being a Short Sketch of the History of the Colonial and Continental Church Society* (London, n.d. [1823]), 4; G.H. Bolt, *The Codner Centenary* (St. John's, 1923), 1; Monthly Extracts from the Correspondence of the BFBS, no. 52, 30 Nov. 1821, 55–56.

71 *The First Annual Report of the Committee of the Society for the Education of the Poor in Newfoundland* (London, 1824), 13.

72 MMS N. Am. 3/30, Codner to Butterworth, 16 Feb. 1822; D.M. Young, *The Colonial Office in the Early Nineteenth Century* (London, 1961), 18, 58; CO 194/66, Codner to Bexley, 14 Apr. 1823.

73 *The First Annual Report*, speech of the Rev. H. Budd, 34.

Ludgate Hill, London, on 30 June 1823. It was hurriedly organized and sparsely advertised, and sympathetic ladies were not informed, so the attendance was thin, and Lord Bexley, Lord Calthorpe, and William Wilberforce sent letters of apology for their absence. The meeting was dominated by Evangelical clergy and laymen with support from sympathizers connected with Newfoundland—notably Francis Forbes (a former Chief Justice), Joseph Butterworth, and John Wells, MP for Poole, an Evangelical. Unsurprisingly, the general theme of the meeting was the superiority of educational reform over practical measures as a solution to the ongoing fishery crisis. Wilberforce, in a letter to Bexley read at the meeting, set the tone: "The Establishment of Schools will lead the way to every other improvement."[74] Forbes, elaborating on this, declared that if a solution to the present crisis in the fishery were to be found, it would lie not in practical relief but in the provision of "wholesome moral institutions, and especially schools"; he continued:

> In proportion as the poor were intelligent they would become industrious—as they were industrious, they would be moral—as they were rendered moral they would be religious—and as they were religious, they would be useful and happy. Any other relief than schools for the poorer classes must fall short of the object.

Wells added that the Society's influence would maintain the populace "in contentment and good order towards the government," and render them more ready for obedience to the laws. Shortly after the meeting the Committee issued a statement expressive of the merchants' view of the Society as a bulwark for the protection of property and commercial interests:

> The moral evils must increase in proportion to the increase of population, unless some more efficient means of instruction are adopted; and when we consider the dangers and depredations to which the property of the resident inhabit-

74 *The First Annual Report*, 5, 10, Wilberforce to Bexley, 27 June 1823.

ants, of the absent merchants, and of the masters and sailors of the fishing and trading vessels, is necessarily exposed on a long line of coast, presenting various opportunities for fraudulent and improper practices, it is obviously of the utmost importance, on commercial as well as moral grounds, to adopt immediate measures for inculcating sound principles among the rising generation.[75]

At the end of July 1823, Wilmot Horton, Secretary at the Colonial Office, informed Codner that Lord Bathurst had agreed to three requests "the Newfoundland merchants were anxious to receive":

1. That the Society should receive a grant of land on which to build schools, houses and playgrounds in any part of the Island.
2. That all teachers be allowed a free passage in HM ships or transports from England to Newfoundland.
3. That the local government be instructed by HMG to give "all the aid and support within their power" to every school of the Society.[76]

After due consideration Codner and his merchant allies decided that land grants were insufficient and that an assurance of regular monetary funding was crucial to the future of the Society. A memorial for Bathurst to this effect was prepared and forwarded at the beginning of 1824. It contained 140 signatures, with 18 merchant houses—including Newman, Brooking and Garland, & Co., Bully Job and Co., Newman and Co., Slade Elson and Co., Rennie Stewart and Co., and Baine Johnstone and Co.—appending their names, together with those of numerous Newfoundland notables and Devon worthies connected with the trade. The petition requested a grant to the Society of £2,000 "or such other sum as His Majesty's Government shall be pleased to bestow." Faced with this extensive display

75 *The First Annual Report*, speech of Forbes, 16–17, speech of John Wells, M.P., 11–12; *Christian Observer*, Aug. 1823, 521.
76 CO 43/63, Horton to Codner, 28 July 1823.

of support, the government relented—up to a point. In June 1824, Horton wrote to Governor Hamilton:

> Lord Bathurst having had under his consideration the Memorial of the Merchants and others connected with the Island of Newfoundland, requesting some assistance from His Majesty's Government in aid of the expense to be incurred by the Newfoundland School Society, I am directed by Lord Bathurst to desire that you will pay from the Balance of Crown Rents in your hands the sum of Five Hundred Pounds towards the expense of the Buildings and One Hundred Pounds per annum for the Salary of a Schoolmaster.[77]

Thus the British government refused to give direct financial support to the Society; instead, it ordered that the smaller and less stable administration of Newfoundland should be the paymaster. The Colonial Office had been quite prepared to help found a quasi-missionary society and to offer it some practical support; it was not, however, disposed to finance its activities. The Society had no choice but to accept the situation. The arrangement, however, did ensure that the Society gained a measure of financial stability which enabled it to begin operating successfully. The Annual Report for 1827 showed that schools were in operation in seven locations, with 165 day scholars, 460 Sunday School children, and 274 adults under tuition. Twenty Associations were active in England.[78]

The Society was from the beginning an Evangelical body: the president was Lord Bathurst, the treasurer was John Wells, MP, and Codner the honorary secretary, with Evangelicals a majority among the vice-presidents and committee members. The dynamism of Evangelicalism, with its emphasis on outreach and conversion, was essential to its operation. The Evangelical ethic, nevertheless, had its dark side, not only in its attitude to children (as will be shown later) but also evident in contempt for the lower orders of society.

---

77 CO 194/68, "To the Right Honourable Earl Bathurst, Secretary of State for the Colonial Department" (n.d. [Feb. 1824]); CO 195/17, Horton to Hamilton, 30 June 1824.
78 *World*, 19 May 1827.

This was openly revealed at the third annual meeting of the Society. Speakers at the meeting were scathing in their condemnation of the condition and character of the Newfoundland people. Lord Bexley had declared, in his opening remarks, that "considerable ignorance" was rife and that the poorer classes were "entirely uneducated," and the Rev. Edward Bicketsteth believed that "ignorance in the highest degree" prevailed. But worse was to follow. The Rev. Henry Budd went further in asserting that "there was a degree of vice and depravity existing which could not be contemplated without shuddering," and that the female part of the population was in a "gross state"; steadiness and cleanliness was a rare occurrence among them. He added that the lower order of females were "remarkably vicious and depraved."[79] Patrick Morris, who was present at the meeting, was incensed by these slanders and on his return to Newfoundland dashed off a letter to Bexley to repudiate "[t]he strange and most unnatural stories" related at the meeting, stories which were "utterly groundless and without foundation." Although Morris claimed that Newfoundlanders "are very much like the people of other countries—not much worse nor much better," he proceeded, perhaps understandably in the circumstances, to paint a somewhat rosy picture of Newfoundland society, education, and religion. The women, he stated, were characterized by "a steady attention to their domestic duties, and correctness of conduct in every point of view"; crime was absent and "bitter sectarian hostility" was unknown. Possibly the object of the traducers of the Newfoundland people, Morris concluded, "is to represent us as great sinners, that they may have the merit of converting us into great saints."[80]

• • •

The Society began its operations in Newfoundland in 1824, shortly after the question of financial aid was settled. In the spring of that year the first group of teachers—Mr. and Mrs. Jeynes, Mr. William Fleet, and "a female monitor"—were ready to commence

79 Ibid.
80 P. Morris, *Remarks on the State of Society, Religion, Morals, and Education at Newfoundland … in a Letter, Addressed to the Right Honourable Lord Bexley* (London, 1827), 5.

their voyage to Newfoundland. Their journey was, however, delayed by a dispute over transport in one of His Majesty's ships—a small social comedy in itself. The only available vessel was the *John and Isaac* of 142 tons, which was bound by charter not to take more than two passengers; the teachers attempted to make arrangements with the master to occupy his berth and to eat with him. The captain, accustomed to taking only officers and their wives and unused to this inversion of social rank and precedent, not unnaturally refused, and it took the intervention of the Colonial Office with the Commissioners of the Navy to get him to share his accommodation with teachers rather than with officers.[81]

The teachers arrived at the end of August. One was surprised and captivated by the appearance of St. John's:

> Instead of craggy rocks, and barren houseless land, the neighbourhood of St. John's is, at this season (September), very fertile—the crops of hay gathering, potatoes, oats, and a great variety of vegetables growing; cottages, with their gardens, scattered about, the new roads, &c., make it appear to us, indeed, a new-found-land ...[82]

The teachers had been met by Messrs. Cock and Brooking, agents of the Society, who then introduced them to clergymen and ministers and also to the Chief Justice, who received them with "great kindness and condescension," exceptional treatment for teachers who, had they remained in England, would never have received such lionization. They immediately set to work visiting houses in St. John's in order to assess the probable number of children requiring education. A storeroom next to a bakery was taken as a temporary schoolroom. A notice of this, together with an appeal for funds and for information on the state of education in the outports, was inserted in the local press; parents wishing to send their children to the school had to obtain written recommendations from a clergy-

81 The situation can be traced in the correspondence of Codner, Horton, and Tipping, at CO 194/68 and CO 43/64, 1824.

82 SPG Proceedings, 1824–25, 66.

man or "two respectable inhabitants." The advertisement pointed out that the schools were interdenominational, that the Authorized Version of the Bible would be read without note or comment, that instruction in the catechism and formularies of the Established Church would be given after the usual school hours, and that the object of the Society was "the moral and religious instruction of the poor children of Newfoundland."[83]

The first school was opened in St. John's on 20 September 1824, and 75 children, almost equally divided between boys and girls, were soon enrolled. Within two years the school had been transferred to a commodious stone building on Duckworth Street, rented for £35 per year and able to accommodate about 450 children. Outside St. John's the strategy of the Society was to set up a school in the larger outports, under the supervision of teachers from England, then gradually to open branch schools in the smaller surrounding communities, staffing them with monitors—"well taught and pious individuals"—trained in the larger schools.[84]

Much of the guidance on religious and educational policy was provided by Evangelical ministers in sermons to the Society's annual meetings in London, and this advice was followed by teachers in the island. Their overriding aim was the conversion of children and adults to "vital Christianity." The Rev. Henry Melvill drew attention to this aspect of the teachers' work in a sermon to the Society: "There is no more necessary result of conversion, than the wish to convert others." The Rev. Baptist Noel, in an earlier sermon, had frankly declared that the operations of the Society "tend to convert the unconverted among those to whom they extend."[85]

It was not only the children that the teachers were seeking to evangelize. To the populace at large their activities took the form of a mission. In fact, the Society's Proceedings for 1837–1838 defined the teachers' duties as three: first, that of schoolmasters; second, that of friendly visitors; third, that of catechists or lay readers.[86] The

83 Ibid., 63–65; *Mercantile Journal*, 16 Sept. 1824.

84 SPG Proceedings, 1824–1825, 65; 1825–1826, 36; 1838–1839, 14.

85 SPG Proceedings, 1837–1838, 8; 1830–1831, 2.

86 SPG Proceedings, 1837–1838, 3; CO 194/84, Marshall to Hay, 28 Feb. 1832.

schools, the Society explained, operated as centres of conversion for the whole population around them, forming a site for interviews, libraries, visiting the sick, and tract distribution. Consistent with conversion were two other strands of policy—an insistence on treating Newfoundland as an outpost of Britain and a desire to ensure that teachers were purveyors of British Evangelical attitudes to the education of children. The Society, and ministers in sermons, insisted that settlers in Newfoundland were "fellow subjects and fellow men" and "still altogether British," allied to the mother country by "bonds of language and blood"[87]—sentiments which made some impression on the teachers.

But the main influence of ministerial sermons was on the sphere of education of young children. Advice stopped just short of insisting that scriptural knowledge should take precedence over secular learning. The former should be given as early as the nursery years, and the aim of instruction was to make children "wise unto salvation" rather than "wise unto head knowledge." The saving of souls exceeded in importance the teaching of reading and writing, for the lower orders were unable to be lifted out of their "proper stations" by learning even the 3Rs, though the Rev. C.T. Noel was constrained to admit that secular learning "has its advantages."[88]

"It is our desire and endeavour," explained one teacher, "to give the dear children committed to our charge a Biblical education," and his colleagues, while paying due attention to the teaching of literacy, loaded the curriculum with scriptural knowledge, which had to be learned by heart. Quotations from the Bible were also used to disciplinary effect. If children were caught out in childish misdemeanours, they were chastised with all the force of Biblical invective. Examples of "frightening little children into being Evangelical little children" (Ford K. Brown's words) were not uncommon. At Harbour Grace a boy expelled for blasphemy returned to school within four weeks, confessing he had been a very wicked boy and had prayed to God to forgive him. Another teacher reassured his charges that al-

87 *The First Annual Report*, 5; SPG Proceedings, 1829–1830, 28–29; 1830–1831, 12.

88 SPG Proceedings, 1824–1825, 49, 56; 1827–1828, 26, 30–33; 1828–1829, 25; 1830–1831, 5.

though now lying was not punished with instant death as in the case of Ananias and Sapphira, yet the day was approaching "when every liar would be sentenced to everlasting woe." Two scholars who had lied took this to heart and recalling the line in the hymn "every liar must have his portion in the lake that burns with brimstone and fire" resolved henceforward to memorize the fifth chapter of Acts to keep themselves on the path of truth. The effect on the children of fishing families of this division of youthful innocents into sinners and saints, with dire warnings of the wrath to come for the former and of happy release for the latter, is difficult to estimate. But Brown contends that these practices could be construed as a form of religious terror, with unforeseen consequences for the children's psychological health.[89]

• • •

The growth of the Society, from the 1820s to the 1840s, was materially aided by the efforts of the first resident governor, Thomas Cochrane, and the first Church of England bishop, Aubrey Spencer. Cochrane, a career naval officer who eventually became Admiral of the Fleet, took office in 1825. He followed the policy of the Colonial Office in giving extensive aid to the Society's activities. In June 1826, at Bathurst's request, he extended to Mark Willoughby, the assistant secretary of the Newfoundland School Society, all the assistance in his power in increasing the number of the Society's schools, and in 1828, on Willoughby's second visit, urged him to stay for over a year in order to further the work of the Society. Between 1828 and 1830 Cochrane had made to the Society 18 separate grants of land for schools and playgrounds in 13 different outports and also at St. John's. In 1829, on Cochrane's orders, all arrears of rent on land held by the Society were cancelled and future rent waived. In 1835 Cochrane addressed the annual meeting in London and "strongly recommended the Society to the continuance of public favour."[90]

---

89 SPG Proceedings, 1825–1826, 45–46; 1827–1828, 45–46; 1835–1836, 5; 1836–1837, 5; Brown, *Fathers of the Victorians*, 463.

90 CO 195/17, Bathurst to Cochrane, 8 June 1826; CO 194/72, Cochrane to Bathurst, 30 Oct. 1826; CO 194/82, Codner to Goderich, 28 Feb. 1832; *Gazette*, 27 Apr. 1830; The Rooms Provincial Archives Division, GN 2/1, Proclamation of Cochrane, 10 Nov. 1829; SPG Proceedings, 1834–1835, 15–16.

Cochrane's assistance in increasing the number of schools led to expenditure outrunning receipts; by the end of 1826 arrears of £1,000 were posted. Codner thereupon arranged an interview with Lord Liverpool, the prime minister, and tried to secure an increase in the grant to £2,000 per year and an increase in the annual payment to £500. This request was refused, as were further appeals for aid in the next five years. In 1834 the Newfoundland legislature discontinued its grant to the Society. Willoughby immediately sent in a petition, to no avail.[91] Shortly afterwards Cochrane stepped up the pressure by supporting a memorial to the Colonial Secretary signed by over 200 "merchants, planters and inhabitants" requesting funding for the provision of schools. Lord Glenelg (son of the Evangelical Charles Grant) was sympathetic but maintained Colonial Office policy by urging the petitioners to seek funding from the local legislature. Fortunately for the Society, the Newfoundland Assembly passed the colony's first Education Act which, desiring to support educational efforts beyond the establishment of public elementary schools, included a clause allocating an annual grant of £300 to the Society.[92]

If Governor Cochrane had materially aided the Society in the 1820s and early 1830s, Bishop Spencer assisted it largely as a spiritual counsellor during (and after) his tenure as bishop of the diocese from 1839 to 1844. Aubrey George Spencer was born in London in 1795 of minor aristocratic lineage,[93] and studied for the priesthood at Magdalen Hall, Oxford, a college Evangelical in both orientation and theology. He was ordained a priest in 1819 and sent to Newfoundland under the auspices of the Society for the Propagation of

---

91 CO 194/73, Robinson et al. to Horton, 5 Sept. 1826; CO 194/75, Codner to Horton, 13 Jan. 1827; CO 194/82, Codner to Goderich, 26 May 1831; JHA 1834, 9 May 1834, 134–35.

92 CO 194/88, Cochrane to Spring Rice, 1 Nov. 1834, encl. The Memorial of the Undersigned Merchants, Planters, and Other Inhabitants; CO 195/18, Glenelg to Prescott, 4 June 1835; 6 Geo. 4, cap. 13, An Act for the Encouragement of Education in This Colony (6 May 1836), Ch. I.

93 The following paragraphs, unless otherwise stated, are based on H.R. Russell, "Evangelicalism in the Anglican Church in Nineteenth-Century Newfoundland" (MA thesis, Memorial University, 2005), 54ff.; *DCB*, s.v. "Spencer, Aubrey George"; *ENL*, s.v. "Spencer, Aubrey George."

the Gospel, serving as a missionary in Ferryland (1819–1820) and Trinity (1820–1822) before leaving for a 17-year sojourn in Jamaica.

Spencer arrived in Newfoundland as the first Church of England bishop in July 1839. Shortly after his arrival he became vice-president of the Society. He then began strengthening the position of the church in an Evangelical direction, dividing the diocese into deaneries, increasing the number of clergy, founding a theological training school, and travelling around the island opening numerous churches and schools. He also established a number of chapelry schoolhouses and ordained several of the Society's teachers as deacon schoolmasters. Spencer was wholly committed to Evangelicalism. The tone of his sermons, in comparison with those of the more fervid Evangelicals, was reasonable and restrained, focusing on repentance and holiness rather than on threats of everlasting damnation. He also supported the teaching of secular knowledge—the arts and sciences—"which dignify and embellish life," and believed that the schools of the Newfoundland School Society—"seminaries of pure and evangelical knowledge"—had given to Newfoundlanders for more than 20 years "the elements of secular learning in direct connexion with Scriptural truth."[94] Spencer had left Newfoundland—"that dreary and difficult land"[95]—in 1843 in order to restore his health in the warmer clime of Jamaica. But during his stay in Newfoundland his undeviating support of the Society was fundamental to its success. It reached the peak of its progress during his episcopate, although the Society to some extent filled a gap in school provision left by the decline of the public elementary system during the late 1830s and early 1840s.

In 1840 the Society had in operation 52 schools, with 3,234 pupils; five years later the numbers were 44 and 3,907 respectively. It could still call on merchant and popular support; a petition to the Newfoundland Legislative Council in 1850 from merchants, tradesmen, and householders of St. John's collected 251 signatures, calling

94 SPCK Annual Reports 1839–1842; SPG C/CAN/NFL 4, Spencer to Campbell, 30 Dec. 1840, 26 Apr. 1841; SPG Proceedings, 1842–1843, 9–10, and 1845–1846, A Sermon ... by the Bishop of Jamaica, 3–14; Russell, "Evangelicalism," 83–103.

95 SPG Proceedings, 1843–1844, Spencer to Bexley, 4 Feb. 1844, 12–13.

for the renewal and continuance of the administration's grant to the Society. It also acted as a distributor of religious literature; by 1844 it had put in circulation through its teachers 20,000 copies of the Bible and 500,000 religious tracts and books "breathing the doctrinal and unctual spirit of the blessed Reformation." The Society's teachers, despite a lack of alignment with community values, and their desire to make children "wise until salvation," had enabled many pupils to obtain a secular education (the Central School in St. John's leading the way) and some to attain a degree of social mobility.[96]

Spencer was succeeded as bishop by Edward Feild in 1844. Despite the fact that as a High Churchman he was at the other extreme of the Protestant spectrum from the Evangelical Spencer, initially he attempted, with some reservations, to carry on relations with the Newfoundland School Society where Spencer had left off. Before leaving England he had attended the annual meeting of the Society at Exeter Hall. Although he could have been under no illusions as to the Society's Evangelical orientation, he was willing to give it the benefit of the doubt as an ostensible Church of England body. He intended, however, to inspect their schools "very narrowly," stating that if he found them confined to the purposes of education, he would assist them; but should he discover "proceedings and endeavours" of a non-educational nature, he would report it to the Committee. Within a month he found something of a non-educational nature in the Society's schools and teachers. Of his arrival he wrote in his diary:

> The Newfoundland School Society's teachers are generally respectable and amiable men and doing good by their example and influence with the people—but as teachers they are very inefficient and unsatisfactory. Their schools are wretchedly found in books and of a very dubious, heretical character … They are certainly taught nothing in these

96 SPG Proceedings, 1839–1840, 1845; JLC 1850, App., [Petition]; "From Merchants and Others of St. John's …" SPG Proceedings, 1844, 24; 1837–1838, 5; 1838–1839, 6; *Record*, 15 May 1845.

schools to make them understand or love the Church ...[97]

A year later he wrote to the Rev. E. Hawkins of the SPG that he was "at sixes and sevens with the Newfoundland School Society," feeling that it needed an application of church education, as it "calls itself Church and acts dissenter." The following year he wrote to Hawkins again, asking why the bishops and the church could not "take up" the Society and "make it a Church Society ..." If this were not done, he suspected that the Society would get into the hands of the Colonial Church Society—"and what help or comfort could [he] then expect from or through it?" He granted that the Newfoundland School Society had been of "immense value," though upon "conditions and principles to which [he could] not subscribe."[98] Feild then urged the English bishops to use their influence with the Society to alter its rules in favour of greater Church of England influence. The Committee, at a meeting in July 1846, accordingly changed the name to the Church of England Society for Educating the Poor of Newfoundland and the Colonies, and drew up a new set of rules. Under the new regulations Feild, as bishop of the diocese, was given the right to approve the superintendent and to license the teachers, and his clergy were granted access to the schools to report on their progress. Religious instruction would be in the Holy Scriptures (i.e., the Authorized Version of the Bible) and, except where the parents objected, in the formularies of the Church of England. There was no change in the distinctive principles of the Society the Committee emphasized, but the new rules would enable it to become "in all the Colonies the handmaid of the Church in the cause of Scriptural education."

Feild became vice-president of the Society and effectively exercised control over its operations. As a result of these changes the Society lost the support of the *Record*, England's leading Evangelical newspaper, and a staunch supporter of the Society for many years;

---

97 *Record*, 29 Apr. 1844; R. Rompkey, ed., *The Diary of Bishop Feild in 1844* (St. John's, 2011), entry for 2 Aug. 1844.
98 SPG C/CAN/NFL, Feild to Hawkins, 19 June 1845, 19 Mar. 1846.

it could not condone Feild's "Tractarian leaven."[99] In letters to the *Record* and at the Annual Meeting of 1847, the Society asserted that the conduct and principles of the teachers remained unchanged, and that their selection, appointment, and dismissal rested with the Committee. Nevertheless the Society lost support in England. In November 1848 Feild resigned the vice-presidency and membership of the Society, feeling that his name and "supposed co-operation" were a hindrance to its work. The way was now clear for the Society to regain its lost support by returning to its former constitution. This was accomplished at a Special General Meeting on 12 June 1849, following advice from Samuel Codner, other leading members, and ex-Governor Cochrane. The "Church of England" was retained in the name, but the Committee secured the right to appoint and remove teachers without the bishop's veto, and to ensure that superintendents were laymen. The latter provision conveniently got rid of the Rev. T.F.H. Bridge, formerly an Evangelical stalwart, but now a henchman of Feild.[100] Leaving Feild "to his conscience and his God,"[101] the Society, on 1 January 1851, took the next logical step—amalgamation with the ultra-Evangelical Colonial Church Society, founded in 1835 to send out missionaries to the colonies. The new Society was henceforward to be known as the Colonial Church and School Society, and the move was seen as a means to its rejuvenation.[102]

• • •

There could hardly be a greater contrast between the leisured

---

99 F. Jones, Bishop Feild (PhD diss., Cambridge, 1972), 140; SPG Proceedings, 1845–1846, "Statement Respecting the Extension of the Operations of the Newfoundland and British North America Society to All the Colonies of Great Britain" (30 July 1846).

100 *Record*, 19, 26, 30 Nov., 7 Dec. 1846, 19 Apr. 1847; Leaflet entitled "Reply of the Committee to Certain Charges ..." (30 Mar. 1847), *Record*, 19 Apr. 1847; *Christian Remembrancer* 29, no. 70 (1850), 499–500; Feild to Society, 7 Nov. 1848, *Record*, 14 June 1849.

101 *Record*, 14 June 1849. The words were those of the Rev. E. Hollond at the Special General Meeting, 12 June 1849.

102 Guildhall Library, NS 15674, Colonial Church and School Society General Committee Minute Book 1850–1855; SPG Proceedings, 1850–1851, 19.

existence of Bishop Feild, not to mention that of the lords, bishops, politicians, and clerics who formed the leadership of the Society, and the life of the fishing families. To fully understand the structure and workings of the Society, distinct from the world of the policy-makers, account must be taken of the environment in which fishing families worked, the ramifications of the merchant-fisher relationship, and the variance between the aims of the Society and their resolution on the ground. Sean Cadigan, in *Hope and Deception in Conception Bay*, argues that fishing families were locked into a situation that offered very little scope for improvement. Whereas Upper and Lower Canada had a flourishing agricultural economy, often state-aided, which led to industrial capitalism, Newfoundland did not undergo a similar development because the climate and soil could not produce it. Thus planter families were bereft of the productive means which would open up alternatives to merchant credit, on which perforce they had to rely. The merchants, on their part, transported provisions and immigrants to the island and exported fish and cod oil. They supplied fishing families with food and equipment on credit and took fish and oil in return.[103]

In 1817 James Stewart, a Scottish merchant, describing himself as an impartial bystander of nine years residence, supplied the Colonial Office with an account of merchant commercial practices. The merchants had a dominant position, he wrote, by virtue of their monopoly of the import of provisions necessary for the subsistence of the planter-fishers. The merchants were "greatly protected," he continued, by possessing the "double advantage" of selling goods at their own prices and receiving payments in fish which they bought at prices they also fixed. If the value of fish caught was less than that of the provisions advanced, the merchant would advance winter supply on credit, thus putting the family into debt. "[T]he advantages which the (merchants) are permitted to assume over such a useful and valuable description of their fellow subjects," wrote Stewart, "is most unreasonable, and unjust, and must operate powerfully

103 S.T. Cadigan, *Hope and Deception in Conception Bay: Merchant-Settler Relations in Newfoundland, 1785–1855* (Toronto, 1995), 3–15.

against the improvement, and extension of the fishery."[104]

The planter-fisher families, however, cannot be considered simply as slaves of the merchant. The truck-credit system, which arose on the northeast coast of the island in the late 18th and early 19th centuries, had in fact evolved as a species of compromise between merchants and fishers, as historians Ellen Antler and Cadigan both have suggested. The merchants gave up control of the process of production of the fish but maintained the supply of provisions (largely on credit), the setting of prices and the control of marketing. The fishers secured a much prized, albeit limited, independence within the system, based on open access to the sea, the production of part of their subsistence, and control over the catching and curing of fish. The typical fishing family owned and reproduced its own means of production—houses, boats, flakes, sheds, gear, tools, etc., and cultivated root crops, kept livestock, and collected wood for fuel. They sold the product of their labour, not their labour power. In this sense they were semi-independent commodity producers; the unit of labour was the family, not the individual, and the domination of the merchants was at the point of exchange, not at the point of production.[105]

• • •

There was a clear divergence between the lives of the fishing families and those of the merchants. The former were concerned in individual struggles for existence; the latter, though they differed in nationality, politics, and religion, were united as a class by the pursuit of profit, an objective, as Cadigan observes, in which they were primarily interested. In fact, they acted as merchants in the dictionary definition of the term: "A person whose occupation is the pur-

---

104 CO 194/60, Stewart to Bathurst, 4 Mar. 1817, encl. "Observations on the Affairs and Present State of the Island of Newfoundland."

105 E.P. Antler, "Fisherman, Fisherwoman, Rural Proletariat: Capitalist Commodity Production in the Newfoundland Fishery" (PhD diss., University of Connecticut, 1981); S.D. Antler, "Colonial Exploitation and Economic Stagnation in Nineteenth Century Newfoundland" (PhD diss., University of Connecticut, 1975); G.M. Sider, *Culture and Class in Anthropology and History: A Newfoundland Illustration* (Cambridge, 1986), 21–29; Cadigan, *Hope and Deception*, viii–xi.

chase and sale of goods or commodities for profit." But rather than investing in the Newfoundland economy the largesse they acquired by the exploitation of the fishers, they mostly left the island, taking their wealth with them, as Stewart pointed out.[106]

As a class the merchants generally prospered, to the extent of acquiring a fortune or at least a solid remuneration. Their riches were considerable. According to Handcock, by the 1780s the main establishments of Poole merchants were valued at £60,000; Benjamin Lester (1724–1802) shortly before his death was assessed in Poole at £3,000 in export and import rates, by far the largest for any local merchant. He also owned a substantial part of Poole and two country estates. Late 18th-century merchants bequeathed substantial fortunes: Joseph White left £130,000, John Green £40,000, and John Slade £70,000. In the Dorsetshire port of Poole alone eight families—the Whites, Jolliffes, Spurriers, Lesters, Garlands, Kemps, Jefferys, and Slades—amassed great wealth from the labours of the fishers, built magnificent mansions, some of which can be seen to this day, and played a major social role as Members of Parliament and civic worthies.[107]

Steven Antler calculated that the average income for the wealthiest half of the 900 or so merchants in the mid-Victorian period was $600 per annum, compared to the per capita Canadian income (in 1880) of $135 per annum, and the average per capita Newfoundland income (1845–1880) of $56. Antler has also been one of the few historians to attempt to calculate the amount that merchants in general exported from Newfoundland. Using a "simple model," he estimated that net capital export between 1845 and 1855 averaged $421,000 per annum, with a high of $710,000 in 1855 and a low of $237,000 in 1847. Over the period 1845–1884 he estimated that capital exports averaged roughly 4.5 per cent of the national product. Antler further argued that if exported wealth had been invested in the Newfoundland economy (in 1884, for instance), it would

---

106 Cadigan, *Hope and Deception*, viii; *NSOED*; CO 194/60, Stewart to Bathurst, 4 Mar. 1817.

107 Handcock, *Origins of English Settlement*, 217, 220; *ENL*, s.v. "Lester, Benjamin"; C.N. Cullingford, *A History of Poole and Neighbourhood* (Chichester, 1988), 118–39.

have realized, assuming 10 per cent depreciation, no less than $4.7 million of capital equipment. Had such monies been applied to improving education, the need for the Newfoundland School Society would hardly have been necessary.[108]

The merchants who supported the School Society were in a paradoxical position. On the one hand they were supporting an organization committed to educating, Christianizing, and ameliorating the lot of the children of fishing families; on the other, the truck-credit system they operated was restricting the family's life chances and by extension any large-scale transformation of their children's existence. Despite the jolt to their position in 1816–1817 and after, merchants collectively possessed sufficient wealth to subsidize the Society to a far greater extent than the Newfoundland government. Their aid to the Society was, however, on the whole limited to the signing of petitions, some services to schools and teachers, and relatively modest monetary support; in 1855–1856 only a dozen merchant firms paid their small annual subscription.[109]

• • •

Although the Society lasted exactly a hundred years until 1924, after the mid-19th century decline set in, and in 1856 the Society was forced to issue an "Appeal to British Merchants and Manufacturers" for "Liberal contributions." By 1865 the number of schools had dwindled to 19, and fluctuated around this figure to the beginning of the 20th century. The waning of the Society can partly be attributed to a transformation in the religious atmosphere brought about by Bishop Feild. In his hands the Church of England was transformed from an essentially Evangelical body into a Tractarian one, with predictable effects on the Society. In the latter part of the century the Society drew closer to the Church of England. Their schools began to be inspected by Canon William Pilot, the church's Superintendent of Education, and Chief Justice Sir Hugh Hoyles,

---

108 S. Antler, "The Capitalist Underdevelopment of Nineteenth Century Newfoundland," in *Underdevelopment and Social Movements in Atlantic Canada*, ed. R.J. Brym and R.J. Sacuman (Toronto, 1979), 195–97; Antler, "Colonial Exploitation and Economic Stagnation," Table 6.5.1, 132.
109 SPG Proceedings, 1855–1856, 201–202.

a staunch Anglican, was for many years president of the Society. It continued as a ghost of its former self until its demise in 1923.[110]

At its peak between the early 1820s and the early 1850s the Society made signal contributions to education and religion in Newfoundland. It provided a parallel educational service to the government's public elementary schools, and its teachers significantly contributed to the religiosity of the population and its attachment to Britain. Beckles Willson, a Canadian author who visited the island in the mid-1890s, found Newfoundlanders to be "wonderously religious"; at the same time the eminent author Rudyard Kipling was impressed by Newfoundland's loyalty to the Empire, and Premier Whiteway declared that, when England might be in difficulties, "Newfoundland will not be backward in shedding its blood for her,"[111] a prophecy that tragically became true in the slaughter of 1914–1918.

110 SPG Proceedings, 1856, "Appeal to British Merchants and Manufacturers"; SPG Proceedings, 1865–1900.

111 B. Willson, *The Tenth Island* (London, 1897), 42; Kipling's remark is quoted in the preface and Whiteway's in the foreword.

CHAPTER 3

Religion, Ethnicity, Education, and the Social Order: The First 30 Years of the Benevolent Irish Society, 1806–1836

> May the Rose, Thistle, and Shamrock be ever entwined for the happiness, prosperity, and independence of the United Kingdom.
>
> —Aaron Hogsett, Chairman of St. Patrick's Day festival, 1828 (*Royal Gazette*, 25 March 1828)

When we speak of the Benevolent Irish Society (BIS) and the Orphan Asylum School (OAS) we engage with the Irish in early 19th-century Newfoundland, and when we turn to these immigrants we connect with the Irish diaspora that scattered the sons and daughters of Erin across the globe. Beginning in Tudor times, and with a massive upsurge following the famine of 1848, Irish emigration left its mark chiefly in the United Kingdom and North America, with sizeable elements in Australia and New Zealand. As Tim Pat Coogan observes in his magisterial survey of the subject, "the Irish diaspora is the outworking of two forms of colonialism, those of mother England and Mother Church."[112] This is true of Newfoundland where, in the early 19th-century the British, while denying self-government to a fractious dependency, struggled to establish a viable Protestant state in a society in which Irish Catholics were rapidly increasing in numbers.

The Irish, as the historical geographer John Mannion has shown, had come to Newfoundland long before the great exodus following

112 T.P. Coogan, *Wherever Green Is Worn: The Story of the Irish Diaspora* (New York, 2000), ix, xi–xii, 233ff.

the famine of 1848.[113] In the mid-18th century the Irish wintering population in the fishery began to outnumber the British. In 1754, 46 per cent of the winter population was Irish, and during the next 20 years some 60 per cent of male migrants were Irish—by far the most substantial exodus across the Atlantic from Ireland in the 18th century. It was a seasonal migration rather than a settlement, but in the second half of the century, Irish female emigration increased, leading to the growth of permanent communities, coincident with the decline of the migratory fishery in the decades around 1800. In the years 1810–1815 14,000 Irish passengers arrived in Newfoundland, and a similar number in 1825–1831. In fact, 75 per cent of all passengers arriving in the first third of the 19th century were Irish. In 1827 Catholics numbered 52 per cent of the population of Newfoundland; in 1836 the figure was 51 per cent.[114] More than 70 per cent settled in St. John's and its hinterlands, and by 1836 St. John's was essentially an Irish town, with three-quarters of its residents claiming Hibernian ancestry.

The Irish settlement in Newfoundland was unique in the small spatial extent of both its origin and destination. The vast majority of Irish immigrants came from the four counties of Kilkenny, Wexford, Waterford, and Tipperary within a 30-mile radius of the port of Waterford, but most embarked at Passage East, then as now a bleak village of stone houses downriver from the city. No other region in America drew such an overwhelming proportion of immigrants from so geographically compact an area in Ireland for so long a time. The concentration of the Irish in large and increasing numbers in and around St. John's at the turn of the century was the soil out of which grew the BIS. It was founded on 5 February 1806 by "a group of Irish gentlemen" who gathered for the occasion in the London Tavern, "the great social meeting house of the city." Their aim was to relieve "the wants and distresses of their Countrymen and fellow creatures at large." All the prominent Irishmen of the city were present, including representatives of the military, merchants,

113 Unless otherwise stated, the following paragraphs are based on J. Mannion, "Tracing the Irish: A Geographical Guide," *The Newfoundland Ancestor* 9, no. 1 (1993): 4–18.

114 Gunn, *Political History*, Table II, 206.

and the administration, and from among them a committee was formed to draw up a constitution.[115]

Under the rules, membership was open to "Natives of Ireland, Sons of Irishmen, or Women descendants of any present or future Member of this Society"; they were encouraged to wear a sprig of shamrock on St. Patrick's Day, and officers to don a green sash decorated with a harp and crown on public days. Committees of Charity, and of Review and Correspondence, were also established.

The first officers of the BIS were:

Captain Winckworth Tonge, President
Lieutenant Col. John Murray, Vice-President
Mr. Joseph Church, 1st Assistant
Lieutenant John McKillop, 2d. Do.
Mr. Henry Shea, Secretary
James Macbraire, Esq., Treasurer[116]

Tonge and Murray were officers attached to the garrison, McKillop was in command of HMS *Rattler*, and McBraire and Shea, both merchants, were officers of the Volunteers. Shea, father of the politician and reformer Ambrose Shea, was the only Catholic on the Committee. Paradoxically, what was to become a Catholic preserve was founded by Irish Protestants—a reflection of the absence of local Irish Catholics of any prominence at this period.[117]

What motivated this group of Irishmen to found the BIS? There appears to have been several reasons: a desire to stress their own distinctive ethnicity and at the same time to prove their loyalty to the Protestant political establishment; a need to distance themselves from their potentially subversive Catholic compatriots then pour-

115 *Rules and Constitution of the Benevolent Irish Society* (St. John's, 1807), 3; *Centenary Volume Benevolent Irish Society of St. John's, Newfoundland 1806–1906* (St. John's, 1906), 10.

116 *Rules and Constitution*, 4, 8–11, 14.

117 *Centenary Volume*, 19–20; Prowse, *History of Newfoundland*, 382; N.A. Veitch, "The Contribution of the Benevolent Irish Society to Education in Newfoundland, from 1823 to 1875" (M.Ed. thesis, Saint Francis Xavier University, 1965), 26.

ing into the fishery; and to encourage the indigent, both Irish and others, to learn the value of self-help through labour.

As service officers and merchants, the leaders of the BIS would be aware of the tumultuous international upheavals that ushered in the new century. The American and French revolutions, war, economic instability, and human migration were transforming the established social and political order in Europe, the North American continent, and the island of Newfoundland itself. In 1797 mutiny broke out among the crew of HMS *Latona*. An uprising of the followers of the United Irishmen, with the apparent aim of taking over St. John's, followed three years later; James Louis O'Donel, the first Catholic bishop, sided with the British in helping to nip the revolt in the bud.[118]

These explosive events at the turn of the century shocked the supporters of order into believing that revolution and infidelity were in the air. Before leaving Newfoundland in 1800, Governor William Waldegrave feared that Newfoundland was "of all places in His Majesty's Dominions the one most prone to adopt the doctrines of Liberty & Equality." Brigadier-General John Skerrett told the Colonial Office in 1801 that the "constant topics of United Irish supporters were 'Papers and Songs on Revolutionary Subjects.'" Equally alarming to the authorities was the circulation in St. John's of Thomas Paine's *The Age of Reason* and *The Rights of Man*. According to the Protestant missionary L.A. Anspach, these works had more weight among the public mind "than either the Bible or the acts of Parliament." This highly volatile social situation convinced the leadership of the BIS that the rules of the new society should contain injunctions to the members to support the government and obey the laws: "in all cases to behave as good and Loyal Subjects, zealously to exert themselves in support of the Laws of our Country, to avoid all controversy on Religious or Political subjects ..."[119]

These admonitions found most resonance among a specific section of the Irish Catholic population—members of a growing

---

118 *DCB*, s.v. "O'Donel, James Louis."

119 *DCB*, s.v. "Waldegrave, William"; CO 194/43, Skerret to Pelham, 22 Sept. 1801; L.A. Anspach, *A History of the Island of Newfoundland* (London, 1819), 228; *Rules and Constitution*, 11.

middle class in St. John's. Noel Veitch, in his thesis on the BIS, puts the membership of the Society at between 100 and 120;[120] nearly all would have belonged to this middle-class group, able to afford the relatively high subscription, not to mention the donations—usually 4 shillings and sixpence—expected of BIS members. Every person, on joining the Society, paid $4, plus 2 shillings and sixpence to the secretary, and an annual membership fee of 18 shillings. A further shilling was extracted to pay the expense of the meeting. A fine of 1 shilling was payable by those absent from a meeting without cause. Between February 1806 and September 1807, £470 was collected from these sources. The Society, however, had not established itself in the popular mind as an institution worthy of support. In 1811 and again in 1813, the president lamented the "indifference" and lack of "patriotic zeal" on the part of those of his countrymen toward the BIS, "for whose benefit and advantage it was principally established."[121] Although the poorest Irish accepted the Society's charity, the mass of working Irish were not in harmony with the Society's ideology, nor were they able to afford the high fees and donations.

Although the BIS was exclusively Irish in leadership and its members overwhelmingly Roman Catholic, for the first 15 years or so of its existence the Committee was largely staffed by Protestants. "The Catholic and Protestant wear the same undying foliage, and it would be impossible to say which of them [was] proudest of his country," observed a commentator in the local press. In 1811, for instance, the Committee consisted of six Protestants and one Catholic, but by the early 1820s Catholics—Patrick Morris, Aaron Hogsett, Patrick Doyle, and others—were elected to the Committee; Patrick Morris became the first Catholic president in 1823, and his fellow Catholic Timothy Hogan chairman of the OAS Committee in 1827.[122]

---

120 Veitch, "Contribution of the Benevolent Irish Society," 28.

121 *Rules and Constitution*, 9; *A Report of the Members Names Belonging to the Benevolent Irish Society* (St. John's, 1807), 10; *Gazette*, 21 Feb. 1811, 25 Feb. 1813.

122 Rock, "St. Patrick's Day," *Mercantile Journal*, 28 Feb. 1822, 16 Mar. 1826, 22 Feb. 1827; *Gazette*, 21 Feb. 1811; *Centenary Volume*, 35.

One of the most important activities of the Society in its early years was its charitable work. Faced with social problems arising from the pressure of population on an inadequate infrastructure, not to mention the increasing number of widows and orphans thrown onto destitution by the hazards of the burgeoning fishing industry, the Society's Committee of Charity interpreted its remit widely. It set out to distribute relief to those "as they shall think deserving"; to place children whose parents could not support them with good masters so that they would become useful members of the community; to relieve the aged, the infirm and the disabled; and to encourage industry and check vice and immorality.[123]

These aims were largely in accord with the prevailing attitude to the relief of the poor in Britain, where charity was guided by two principles—that it should be limited to the "deserving poor" and that relief should not allow the lower orders to rise out of their "station in life."[124] As the BIS was largely an organization for the relief of the poor, the Committee of Charity was the Society's most important body, donating relief in both money and kind and providing various services. Financial assistance to individuals in its first year varied from £6 or £7 for large families to a few shillings for individuals; bread, butter, molasses, tea, and fish were staples of the food distribution, as shown in a table of recipients from 3 March to 17 May 1806, included in *Report of the Members Names*:

---

123 *Rules and Constitution*, 8.

124 J.R. Poynter, *Society and Pauperism: English Poor Relief, 1795–1834* (London, 1969).

	No. in Family	Lbs. Bread	Lbs. Butter	Lbs. Tea	Gals. Molasses	Lbs. Fish
Casey and Family	2	84	12	3	3	84
Mary Ryan	1	14	2	½	½	14
Thomas Keefe	1	42	6	1½	1½	42
Catharine Eustace	3	84	12	3	3	84
David Condon, in part	1		9	1½	1½	14
Edmond White	1	28	4	1	1	28
John Glody and Family	6	168	24	6	6	168
John Murphy and Family	6	168	24	6	6	168
Mary Glinn and Child	2	35	5	1½	1½	35
Marks Cody and Family	4	70	10	2½	2½	70
Ann Slattery	1	14	2	½	½	14
Stephen Cleary	1	14	2	½	½	14
Pierse Cummins	1	28	4	1	1	28
		749	116	28¼	28¼	768

Amounting to £34 : 17 : 1

The Society's relief activities were various, but tended to fluctuate with the state of the economy. In 1823 a special meeting of the BIS issued an address to the public which declared that the prime object of the Society was to encourage people not only to look to the sea but also to cultivate the land as a secondary resource against beggary and want. The following year a committee was appointed to oversee the production of potatoes. Seed potatoes were distributed to 62 families, a practice that continued for many years. In 1828 the Society was able to state that, since its inception, it had distributed £8,000 to "distressed objects" without reference to country or creed. Two years later, however, the Society was forced to issue an "APPEAL to the charitable inhabitants of St. John's." The situation was serious enough for the St. Patrick's Day

Festival for that year to be cancelled.[125]

• • •

In order to strengthen the finances of the Society and secure a stable income, the Society decided to hold an annual Charity Ball, the profits of which would go to the newly opened OAS. The first Charity Ball organized by the BIS took place on 5 April 1831.[126] Held at the schoolhouse, it was given a certain cachet by the patronage of the governor, Sir Thomas Cochrane (prevented from attending by indisposition), and of the wives of leading citizens: Mrs. Tucker, Mrs. Buchan, Mrs. Lawler, Mrs. Brenton, Mrs. Brooking, and Mrs. Kielly. Stewards, with Chief Justice Tucker at their head, were recruited from prominent members of both religious communities. "Pleasure beamed on every countenance ... a more brilliant and splendid scene was never before witnessed in this town," enthused the *Newfoundlander*. The lower room, in which the dance took place, was brilliantly lit with lamps, and was decorated (under the supervision of Captain Bonifant, RN) with ornamental pillars covered with evergreens and flowers to form sylvan bowers, between which were hung transparencies representing Britannia, St. Patrick, St. George, and Charity. The Patronesses, seated on a raised platform at the head of the room, began to receive guests, eventually numbering over 200, at 8 p.m. Dancing began an hour later to an orchestra seated behind mock fortifications at the other end of the room. Quadrilles and reels were the most popular, and continued "with great animation and undiminished spirit until the early hours of the morning." The company was refreshed with tea, lemonade, wines, sandwiches, cakes, and fruit "in great abundance," served in adjoining rooms. An upstairs room was given over to card playing.

This type of ball closely resembled, in its organization, those which were common in England at the time. In fact, the account of the *Newfoundlander* was almost identical with the description of the Charity Ball at Rochester in Charles Dickens's *Pickwick Papers*,

---

125 *Centenary Volume*, 35, 36; *Gazette*, 4 Mar. 1828.

126 The following paragraphs, unless otherwise stated, follow accounts in *Newfoundlander*, 31 Mar. and 7 Apr. 1831.

down to the decorated ballroom, the musicians in their niche, local notables as guests, quadrille as the main dance, the variety of refreshments, and the adjacent room set aside for cards. The St. John's Ball, with tickets at 15 shillings for gentlemen and 10 shillings for ladies, raised £82 for the OAS.[127] From then on, the "Irish Ball" became a social event of the first order, and continued throughout the following decades.

The other event of the year, and politically the most important, was the celebration of St. Patrick's Day every 17 March, when "Erin's sons, and their descendants, who are even *more Irish than the Irish themselves*, will ... commemorate the glorious advent of the TRUE FAITH to the Old Land of Heremon ..."[128] The St. Patrick's Day dinner was not merely a justification for wining and dining; it was an occasion for the Irish elite not only to commemorate their tutelary saint but also to make loyal declarations to England, its crown, and constitution.[129] The day was celebrated with a dinner at one of the hotels in St. John's or at the OAS after it opened. The room was usually decorated with evergreen branches and transparencies of various English and Irish iconic figures. The evening began at 6 p.m., with a dinner, typically described as consisting of "the choicest viands and wines that could be procured," served to a large number of guests—160 in 1831, and over 200 in 1836. The proceedings usually lasted all night, until 6 or 7 a.m. In 1832 a local reporter stayed to the end:

> the evening was passed in an uninterrupted flow of wit, song, cordiality and good feeling. Some of the <u>prime ones</u> remained, as usual, "till morning grey began to peep"; when they had light sufficient to sign a protest against their de-

---

127 Charles Dickens, *The Posthumous Papers of the Pickwick Club* (Penguin Classics edn., London, 2003), 32ff.; *Newfoundlander*, 31 Mar. 1831, 1 Mar. 1832.

128 "St. Patrick's Day," unidentified newspaper cutting, ASCD.

129 Unless otherwise stated, the following account is based on *Gazette*, 25 Mar. 1813–26 Mar. 1833; *Mercantile Journal*, 4 Mar. 1819–15 Mar. 1827; *Newfoundlander*, 14 Mar. 1828–11 Mar. 1832; *Patriot*, 25 Mar. 1834, 8, 29 Mar. 1836.

> generate brethren, who had quit the field, or were unable to take part in the pious and patriotic ceremony of drowning the Shamrock.[130]

The main item of the festival was the toasts, which offered an opportunity for florid oratory, no doubt inspired by the wine (which was laid out at the rate of six bottles per man). There were usually 30 or more toasts, each accompanied by an excerpt from a traditional air (including "Rule Britannia"), played by a military band, or on occasion by an Irish piper. Each person, in giving a toast, vied with his predecessor in a display of flowery language and unctuous praise of local guests and of England and the English, the latter category including members of the Royal Family, the British Constitution, British ministers of state, the army and navy, and the Lord Lieutenant of Ireland. Over a period the guest list comprised the governor, the Chief Justice and government ministers, officers of the army and navy, magistrates, prominent merchants, and several Protestant respectables. The toast lists, apart from the obligatory tribute to St. Patrick, "breathe an intense loyalty to England and everything English," declared the compilers of the BIS *Centenary Volume*, pointing out that it appeared that the rule forbidding members to avoid political controversy was interpreted as meaning only those opinions which flattered the pride of England could be expressed. These sentiments, the *Centenary Volume* concluded,

> were not only un-Irish, but were actually anti-Irish. They toasted the extinction of the Irish Parliament under the head "The Union—may St. George, St. Andrew, and St. Patrick be never disunited." They toasted the Government of Ireland by English ministers under the head "His Majesty's Ministers." They toasted the administration of Ireland and its affairs by English officials under the head "The Lord Lieutenant and the Government of Ireland."[131]

---

130 *Newfoundlander*, 22 Mar. 1832.
131 *Newfoundlander*, 24 Mar. 1831; *Centenary Volume*, 22.

The most blatant sycophancy came from Patrick Morris; leaving behind his reputation of a critic of English policy, he praised "the sacred person ... of George the Fourth ... the most illustrious sovereign in the universe" (satirized by the English novelist William Thackeray as "nothing but a coat and a wig and a mask smiling below it"). When the king visited Ireland, said Morris, "one shout of joy and gratitude to a beloved sovereign [burst] from every Irish heart." At a later dinner he eulogized King William IV as a "gracious and good king ... deserving the love and attachment bestowed upon him by his people," etc. Fine words for a monarch who, as a young naval officer at the Newfoundland station, has recently been described by a Newfoundland historian as having "a besmirched reputation as a dissolute womaniser and brawler."[132]

The Irish elite in the capital certainly left no doubt as to their pro-English orientation. But, the *Centenary Volume* lamented, it was achieved at a cost: "the dependency of Ireland—the absorption of Irish nationality by that of England."[133] The position of subordinating Irish national interests to England was reinforced during the tenure of the first three Catholic bishops, who gave their support to the BIS and collaborated with the governors and the local administration.

• • •

"Who is there amongst you who does not revere the memory of an O'Donel? Have not his beneficent successors followed his great example; and are they not, to this day, PILLARS of your venerable society?"[134] This was Aaron Hogsett, in his chairman's address to the 1828 Anniversary Meeting of the Benevolent Irish Society. Hogsett was not exaggerating. The participation of bishops James Louis O'Donel (1796–1807), Patrick Lambert (1807–1816), and Thomas Scallan (1816–1830) in the affairs of the BIS played an important

132 W.M. Thackeray, "George the Fourth," in *The English Humourists and the Four Georges* (Everyman's Library edn., London, 1912), 388; CO 194/71, *Mercantile Journal*, 24(?) Mar. 1825; *Patriot*, 29 Mar. 1836; Hollett, *Shouting, Embracing and Dancing*, 46.
133 *Centenary Volume*, 22.
134 *Newfoundlander*, 27 Feb. 1828.

part in reinforcing its reputation as a respected public institution.

O'Donel had arrived in Newfoundland in 1784 as prefect apostolic at the invitation of a group of Catholic merchants who had petitioned the British authorities for a bishop in order to control itinerant Catholic priests who were active in the island; soon after his arrival O'Donel had complained to Dublin that he was "pestered with strolling clergymen." He was particularly troubled by Frs. Lonergan and Power, both of whom had the support of fishing families against the merchants, whose side O'Donel had taken from the beginning. O'Donel became a bishop in 1796, and was quickly recruited to the BIS, becoming a consultant to the committee which drew up the Society's rules and regulations, and a permanent honorary member of the Committee of Charity.[135] Both Lambert and Scallan also took an active part in the work of the Society.

The first bishops had three characteristics in common. First, an aversion to conditions in Newfoundland. In 1797 O'Donel found Newfoundland "drearier than ever" and the climate "unbearable." Lambert disliked Newfoundland so much that a year after his arrival he petitioned Rome for an assignment to "a less laborious see." He lamented a lack of "all ... sublunary consolations" on the island, but solaced himself with a cellar of "wine of the best sort—Madeira, Sherry ... Port." Scallan complained that he was "almost fishified already and frozen to a mummy," soon after his arrival in Newfoundland in 1812 as assistant to Lambert, although he later declared that he found no place equal to St. John's, where he met with both comfort and respect.[136]

O'Donel and Lambert shared an antipathy amounting to con-

---

135 Cadigan, *Newfoundland and Labrador*, 78; O'Donel to Troy, 10 Nov. 1787, in *Gentlemen Bishops and Faction Fighters*, ed. C.J. Byrne (St. John's, 1984), 63; V.J. McNally, "A Question of Class? Relations between Bishops and Lay Leaders in Ireland and Newfoundland 1783–1807," CCHA, *Historical Studies* 64 (1998): 71–90; *DCB*, s.v. "O'Donel, James Louis"; *Centenary Volume*, 16; *Rules and Constitution*, 13, 14.

136 AAD 116/31, O'Donel to Troy, 11 Jan. 1797; 116/17/33, O'Donel to Troy, 28 Nov. 1797; APF S.C. Am. Sett. 3, Lambert to Di Pietio, 20 Nov. 1807, in Byrne, *Gentlemen Bishops*, 246; AAD 29/12, Lambert to Troy, 15 Oct. 1810; AFK B. 170, Lambert to Walsh, 23 Aug. 1812; AFK B. 120, Scallan to Walsh, 22 Dec. 1812; AFK, Scallan to Walsh, 29 Oct. 1824.

tempt for their plebeian fellow countrymen. O'Donel felt that there was "a deep-rooted malice in the hearts of the lower class of Irishmen to each other," which arose from "their provincial quarrels," and he condemned United Irish activists as "maddened scum." "An unprincipled and ignorant set of lawless wretches" was Lambert's verdict on Irish (and also English) immigrants. Scallan found his flock faithful Catholics, "but for the most part they are given to drunkenness, lust, and cursing."[137]

These judgments of the Catholic bishops echoed the worst feelings of British Protestants toward the Irish. The prelates disregarded the possibility that the immigrant's way of life and antipathy to the ruling elite could have originated in their background at home. The historian Gertrude Gunn traced the "racial" and religious animosities of half the population of Newfoundland to their historical experience of British rule:

> [C]onditions in the new land fostered memories of wrongs in the old. In Ireland the Irish had known defeat and coercion, plantation and union, eviction and famine; they had suffered the absence of landlords and the presence of agents; they had resented the privileges of an alien church and restrictions on national industry.[138]

All the Irish immigrants would have had some experience of the repression that followed the armed resistance of the secret society of the Defenders in the 1790s, and the uprising of the United Irishmen in 1798. The insurgence had been put down with methods of terror—house burnings, floggings, executions, massacres, and deportations. Altogether an estimated 30,000 people had been killed. The bishops' silence with regard to these atrocities aligned them with the official British position. Not surprisingly, all three prelates showed the most profound respect for the Protestant authorities in

---

137 AAD 29/11, Remonstrance of Dr. J.L. O'Donel to Governor Elliott (n.d. [1788]); CO 194/44, O'Donel to Gower, 11 Oct. 1805; AAD 29/11, Lambert to Troy, 9 Jan. 1807; APF, Cong: AS. II, Scallan to Fontana, 6 Oct. 1822, in Byrne, *Gentlemen Bishops*, 330.

138 Gunn, *Political History*, 182; Gott, *Britain's Empire*, 130–37.

Newfoundland and were gratified to dine with and enjoy the good offices of the governors of their day. "Our present governor & the Judge Advocate have made very solemn profession of friendship to me," wrote O'Donel in 1792, "the former returned me public thanks at his own table for the unremitting pains I've taken those eight years in keeping the rabble of the place amenable to the laws …"[139] He sided with the British authorities against the United Irish in the revolt of 1800, and the following year enjoined his flock to pray for the king, observe the laws, and obey the civil authorities. On his retirement in 1807, he was showered with praise by both the BIS and Protestant merchants, and given a farewell dinner at the London Tavern. In addition, he was presented with an expensive silver urn and a pension of £150 per annum. O'Donel's successors Lambert and Scallan were equally au fait with the Protestant authorities. Governor Keats recommended Lambert for a pension "for faithful discharge of his duties and his support of the government." Scallan commended himself to Governor Cochrane for "his great liberality of principle and moderation of conduct."[140]

The three prelates, rightly named "gentlemen bishops" by Cyril Byrne, came from relatively prosperous Irish farming families and received their higher education in Europe.[141] Their attitudes and actions stemmed from their ideological background. All three were men of the "throne and altar" era of the European Catholic church, described as an "aristocratic organic-hierarchical paradigm of tradition and order," which subordinated important functions of the church to the writ of the monarch, including the appointment of bishops and priests. The French Revolution—with its appeal to the Rights of Man, and the slogan of Liberty, Equality, Fraternity—profoundly alarmed the old regime. The Catholic church could not

139 AAD 116/5/155, O'Donel to Troy, 27 Dec 1793; AAD 29/12, Lambert to Troy, 15 Oct. 1810; AAQ 30CN, Scallan to Plessis, 3 Sept. 1818, in Byrne, *Gentlemen Bishops*, 317; AAD 116/5/103, O'Donel to Troy, 8 Dec. 1792.
140 AASJ, O'Donel, Diocesan Statutes, 1801; Rev. M.F. Howley, *Ecclesiastical History of Newfoundland* (Boston, 1888), 216; R.J. Lahey, *James Louis O'Donel in Newfoundland 1784–1807* (St. John's, 1984), 30, 31; CO 194/54, Keats to Bathurst, 18 Dec. 1813; CO 194/70, Cochrane to Bathurst, 29 Dec. 1825.
141 Byrne, *Gentlemen Bishops*, 21.

adapt to the post-revolutionary situation, and found itself in the arms of reaction and counter-revolution. To the aristocracy and the church hierarchy, the post-revolutionary period was a time of depravity, irreligion, and disorder. Bishop O'Donel's reaction was typical; he agonized over what he termed "the savage barbarity & inhuman cruelty" reported from Paris, and he recoiled from the sight of French Republican prisoners of war in St. John's "with large emblems of infidelity and rebellion plastered on their hats."[142]

Complementary to the bishops' fear of the French sans culottes was their hostility to the mass of the Catholic Irish in Newfoundland. Apart from preaching subordination, they supported government oppression and allowed their priests to keep unruly members of their flock in order by force. In 1815 Lambert had assisted the administration in ordering the suppression of Irish labourers angry at worsening conditions in St. John's. A Methodist observer noted that priests were in the habit of "publicly beating the contumacious of their flock." One of Scallan's priests, Father Fitzgerald, intimidated disorderly Irishmen with the aid of a well-polished blackthorn, which he had brought with him from Ireland.[143]

The bishops' support of the Protestant administration, their hostility to new ideas, and their attempts to maintain social peace harmonized with the general outlook of the BIS. From the founding of the Society in 1806 to the death of Scallan in 1830 they had assisted in forming its socio-political guidelines, but their important service was to lend the sanctity and prestige of their office to the public face of the Society, giving it a cachet it otherwise would have lacked. Equally, they assured governors and the administration that the BIS supported their rule and that they had nothing to fear from this most Irish of societies. Scallan publicly declared that he believed

142 A.R. Vidler, *The Church in an Age of Revolution* (Harmondsworth, 1971); J. Holland, *Modern Catholic Social Teaching* (New York, 2003), 32; AAD 116/5/103, O'Donel to Troy, 8 Dec. 1792; AAD 116/5/155, O'Donel to Troy, 27 Dec. 1793.

143 P. O'Flaherty, *Old St. John's: A History to 1843* (St. John's, 1999), 127; MMS Corr. N. Am. 2 [George Cubitt], "Observations on the Island of Newfoundland" (March 1819); P.K. Devine, *In the Good Old Days!* (St. John's, 1990), 72.

the object of the BIS should be "to promote the good of religion and social order, to inculcate strict obedience to the laws, and to promote the cause of virtue and morality of the flock ..."[144] None of the bishops had any ideological affinity with Protestantism, but the structure of governance in the island offered them a sense of security and identification. In an environment which they felt was uncongenial, and isolated by a social barrier from their working-class countrymen, the bishops found in the BIS a haven in which their social outlook was appreciated, and in which they could practice their own brand of Catholicism.

The main strand of the bishops' socio-religious position was, of course, their collaboration with the Protestant administration. There is little doubt that this policy, which included the regulation of the Catholic Irish workers, contributed to a period of relative sectarian harmony, from the suppression of the United Irish Revolt in 1800 to the death of Scallan in 1834. Morris may have exaggerated when he declared that "bitter sectarian hostility" was unknown at this time,[145] but compared with the religio-political struggles which characterized the later incumbencies of bishops Fleming and Mullock, the previous years were, on the whole, more peaceful. In any summary of the first three decades of the 19th century, the part played by the three Catholic bishops in their support of a Protestant regime, hitherto unnoticed, was an unconventional but significant factor in Newfoundland's historical development.

• • •

Taking advantage of the relatively peaceful religious situation, the BIS established what proved to be their most celebrated and enduring accomplishment—the unsectarian OAS. The project originated in a motion by Timothy Hogan, chairman of the BIS, who moved a resolution on 17 August 1823 proposing the establishment of an asylum for the support and education of orphans.[146] A deputation to Governor Sir Charles Hamilton secured his approbation.

---

144 Speaking at a St. Patrick's Day Festival in 1817 (*Gazette*, 25 Mar. 1817).
145 Cf. Chapter 2.
146 The Rooms Provincial Archives Division, Benevolent Irish Society Minute Book 1822–; 17 Aug. 1823 (BIS Minutes).

At a subsequent special meeting a committee was appointed to establish an asylum "without distinction of country or creed," and members contributed lavishly to a subscription fund—an annual contribution of £100 from President Morris, £50 from Bishop Scallan, £20 from Vice-President John Ryan, and £15 from Hogan, plus many smaller sums from others. The Society followed this up with a memorial to Hamilton, setting out the case for an asylum, and requesting the governor to make representation to this end to the British government. This the governor did, but with no immediate result.[147]

While the Society was still awaiting word on their request for an asylum, Morris put forward a proposal that was to prove a landmark in the Society's history: on 17 February 1825 he moved that the BIS establish a school in connection with the proposed asylum. Morris argued that a school could be attached to the asylum without heavy additional expense since the teachers could also look after the orphans. His rhetorical ability and "contagious energy" (in the words of the *Centenary Volume*) persuaded his colleagues not only to organize a school but also immediately to provide for 10 orphans and fully clothe 20 others until the asylum was ready. Shortly afterwards Morris signed a memorial to Lord Bathurst, the Colonial Secretary, requesting an annual sum from the British government for the erection and support of the proposed institution. Morris overcame the doubts of some members by arguing that many parents, desirous of education for their children, would welcome an institution conducted on "principles of fairness and liberality."[148]

When Governor Sir Thomas Cochrane arrived in Newfoundland in 1825, he was requested to become Patron of the Society, and the Committee lost little time in addressing a memorial to him, presented by Morris and Bishop Scallan, reminding him of the efforts of his predecessor in aiding the Society with donations. Cochrane replied that no money was available from the Crown Rents, but he gave them his "private support"—an annual sum of seven guineas.

---

147 *Centenary Volume*, 38, 39–40; BIS Minutes, 24 Aug. 1823; Veitch, "Contribution of the Benevolent Irish Society," 34; CO 194/66, 12 Oct. 1823.
148 BIS Minutes, 17 Feb. 1825; CO 194/71, Morris to Bathurst, 29 Mar. 1825; *Centenary Volume*, 41.

It was not until the summer of 1826 that Cochrane informed the Society that he had received authority from the British government to grant the Society "the unoccupied ground on the right side of the road leading to Fort Townshend" on which to build a school, on condition that the site was enclosed with "an ornamented fence."[149]

Earlier in the year Timothy Hogan had been elected chairman of a committee to oversee preparations for the inauguration of the proposed asylum and school. The exact date of the opening of the latter has not been determined, but Veitch, after a detailed examination of the various available sources, concluded it was fairly certain that the school opened its doors in late 1826, not in the designated building but in the house of a Mr. Gill, supervised by two teachers, Henry Simms and Mrs. Eden. One hundred and thirty-six boys and 70 girls were enrolled. These pupils, "all cleanly dressed," were paraded before the Society at the 1827 Anniversary Meeting and readily answered questions put to them, with Scallan awarding prizes to the most able. An annual subscription in support of the school was then inaugurated. After the Festival of 1831, the officers and members of the BIS gave a "sumptuous dinner" to nearly 400 children of the OAS, before a "deeply affected" audience; the event, according to the report, impressed the children "with sensations of respect and gratitude to their benefactors."[150]

Meanwhile the construction of a building to house the asylum and school had commenced. A builder from the Society's ranks, Nicholas Croke, was the contractor and, after meeting some delay, was able to complete the construction by the end of May at a cost of £999, raised by donations and aid from the Society's funds. The scholars were immediately transferred to the new premises. A contemporary drawing of the school depicts a rectangular building with 10 large windows; in 1844 a central tower and an observatory was added, making it one of the most admired buildings in the city. The curriculum of the OAS comprised the subjects common in schools

149 BIS Minutes, 14 Oct. 1825, 10 Jan. 1826, 17 Feb. 1826; *Centenary Volume*, 39; The Rooms Provincial Archives Division, GN 2/1, Brenton to Morris, 26 June 1826.

150 BIS Minutes, 17 Feb. 1826; *Centenary Volume*, 42; Veitch, "Contribution of the Benevolent Irish Society," 40–41; Gazette, 22 Mar. 1831.

for the poor: grammar, reading, writing, spelling, and arithmetic. Surprisingly, commercial subjects, navigation, and bookkeeping were also taught; Veitch suggests that the inclusion of these utilitarian subjects was due to the presence of several merchants involved in starting the school—Patrick Morris, McLean Little, Timothy Hogan, John Shea, and Patrick Doyle.[151]

The first teacher, Henry Simms, was described as "able and efficient" and a rigid disciplinarian and strict moralist. (He was later to fall foul of Bishop Fleming as one of the "dissident Catholics.") During the latter part of 1829, a Mrs. Fannon was engaged (at a salary of £25) to teach the more advanced girls plain needlework. Simms was paid £100 per annum, an excellent salary for the time. Simms also supplemented his salary with evening classes and tutoring. In 1829 he was succeeded by John Grace, who remained as teacher until his death in 1847.[152]

Given the context of the school, religion was, surprisingly, not part of the curriculum. Morris's influence was evident here. As the only member of the Committee to make his views on religious teaching publicly known—in his *Remarks on the State of Society, Religion, Morals, and Education at Newfoundland*—he emphasized that "precautions have been taken to prevent anything like undue influence in the religious instruction of the children," and condemned the "base conduct" of those (presumably the teachers of the Newfoundland School Society) who professed "liberal principles" but insidiously worked to promote "particular views." Morris supported an interdenominational regime with religious instruction by clergymen of the respective faiths outside the classroom.[153] Whether or not Morris helped to draw up the "Rules of 1826" by which the OAS was to be governed, his hand was certainly apparent in Rule 6, relating to religious instruction:

---

151 Veitch, "Contribution of the Benevolent Irish Society," 42–46; *Newfoundlander*, 29 Feb. 1828; *Centenary Volume*, 44; BIS Minutes, 17 Feb. 1827.
152 *Centenary Volume*, 42; CO 194/107, Simms to Glenelg, 3 Jan. 1838; *Newfoundlander*, 19 Dec. 1827, 27 Feb. 1828, 4 Mar. 1830; Veitch, "Contribution of the Benevolent Irish Society," 75; BIS Minutes, 17 Feb. 1847.
153 Morris, *Remarks on the State of Society*, 42, n.8.

> The Society, impressed with the importance and necessity of affording to the children under their care a strictly religious and moral education, it will be the duty of the superintending Committee to appoint certain times to be set apart for religious instruction, when the children of the different religious persuasions to which they may belong shall be instructed in such manner as their respective Clergymen shall direct. It being an object of the very first importance with the Society, to cultivate that Christian love and charity which so happily exist in the community—it will be the duty of the Committee to see that no books or catechisms should be admitted, either in the course of the literary or religious instruction, containing matter calculated to excite contempt, hatred, or any uncharitable feeling in any classes, towards persons of a different religious persuasion.[154]

The first report on the school was made by Timothy Hogan, then chairman of the Committee of the OAS, at the 1828 anniversary meeting of the BIS. Describing the school as an "edifice for the education of destitute youth," he stated that 231 male and 152 females were in attendance. He took the opportunity of making a rather flowery statement of the school's aims:

> Those inherent beauties ... which adorn the soul of man, cannot be elicited without education—and to place such a treasure within the reach of those in humble circumstances—to substitute learning for ignorance, morality for vice, and religion for infidelity—are the grand and only objects which we propose to ourselves from this institution.

Vice-President Hogsett linked learning to the elimination of poverty; he believed that "to educate the poor and promulgate learning and the only sure means to stop the current of increasing pauperism." But bread came before education; "you must feed the starving poor first, and they will be more apt to learn afterwards."

154 *Patriot*, 23 Feb. 1836.

A year later the Society declared that the OAS offered something more than learning—the institution would be of "immense advantage" to fishers and shoremen and improve the moral character of the people. During the first years of its existence, the OAS prospered as a co-educational institution open to all without distinction of country or creed. The number of children registered increased from 136 boys and girls in 1827 to a daily average of 250 boys and 215 girls in 1830.[155]

• • •

The year 1830 marked a critical change in the fortunes of the Society and the OAS. Bishop Scallan died on 28 May 1830 and his place was taken by Michael Anthony Fleming, who had arrived in Newfoundland as a priest in 1823. It was more than the replacement of one bishop by another; Fleming's accession marked a transformation in the whole atmosphere and orientation of the Catholic church, a sharpening of political life, and changes in the organization of the BIS and the OAS. If O'Donel, Lambert, and Scallan exemplified the "throne and altar" phase of Catholicism, Fleming's principles were more in harmony with ultramontanism, a current in the Catholic church which had arisen following the church's revival in 1815 following the upheavals of the French Revolution. A strong and unyielding papacy was seen as "the only salvation of the church in an age of godless, anti-Christian, and anti-clerical liberals." John FitzGerald has argued a case for Fleming as an ultramontanist.[156]

During the early years of his prelacy Fleming defined his beliefs and activities retrospectively in correspondence with Rome and particularly in a tract known as the *Relazione*, published in 1837. The latter was, in effect, a declaration to the papacy of his worthiness to remain a bishop in the face of the British government's attempts to persuade the Vatican to discipline or depose him. Fleming, stated

---

155 *Newfoundlander*, 27 Feb. 1828, 26 Feb. 1829, 4 Mar. 1830; *Gazette*, 4 Mar. 1828.

156 T. Brokenkotter, *A Concise History of the Catholic Church* (New York, 1977), 327ff.; J.E. FitzGerald, "Michael Anthony Fleming and Ultramontanism in Irish-Newfoundland Roman Catholicism, 1829–1850," CCHA, *Historical Studies* 64 (1998): 27–44.

Governor Cochrane, was "in all respects ... the reverse of his predecessors." From the beginning he declared that "a total change" was necessary; he "flung off the yoke of the Executive" and refused to flatter the rich and entertain the great. Regarding himself as a defender of the Catholic mission in opposition to the "heretical cult" of Protestantism, he reorganized and strengthened the diocese, refused to comply with disabilities imposed on Catholics, and forbade his flock to consort with Protestants or enter Protestant churches.[157]

It was a strict regime and a number of his flock rebelled against it. In 1833 Cochrane had noted that "a certain coolness had existed for some time between the bishop and the more respectable Roman Catholics" in consequence of their disapprobation of many of his proceedings.[158] The leading members of this group were Timothy Hogan, Patrick Kough, James Kent (brother of John Kent), and John Shea. They held controlling positions on the Chapel Committee of the Catholic Church, thus allowing lay persons to exercise control over ecclesiastical affairs; this was considered a normal part of congregational life under Scallan, but was abhorrent to Fleming. He was scathing in his denunciation of Hogan and his associates: "four or five and twenty petty shopkeepers and clerks at the head of whom is Hogan ... all of exceedingly low origin and perfectly uneducated."[159]

In the *Relazione* Fleming referred to them as "liberals"—a maladroit attempt to place himself in a favourable light with Pope Gregory XVI, who detested liberals. They had secured leading positions in the administration of the OAS. Timothy Hogan had been president of the OAS Committee from 1826 to 1828, succeeded by Patrick Kough for the next two years. James Kent had been secretary in 1829 and 1830, and Lawrence Barron, an associate of Kough, was

157 AASJ, M.A. Fleming, *Relazione della missione cattolica in Terranova nell America setentttrionale* (Rome, 1837) (Report of the Catholic Mission in Newfoundland in North America), 12; CO 194/87, Cochrane to Stanley, 8 Apr. 1834; APF S.M. Am. Sett. 4, Fleming to Cdl. Prefect, 21 Apr. 1838.
158 CO 194/85, Cochrane to Stanley, 20 Dec. 1833.
159 APF S.C. Am. Sett. 4, Fleming to Cdl. Fransoni, 27 Nov. 1838; CO 199/42, Fleming to Mgr. Capaccini, 13, 18 June 1835.

elected chairman in 1833.[160] This faction had friendly relations with Protestants, and interpreted the interdenominational nature of the school without strict insistence on Catholic instruction. It was these attitudes which angered Fleming:

> although the Master, the scholars, and nineteen out of twenty supporters were Catholic, although the Council of Directors which supervised that school was exclusively Catholic, it was too liberal to agree that the Master should be obliged to teach the Catechism in school, or that religious instruction be given in any form, for fear lest the Protestants take offence.[161]

Fleming had clashed with these "Liberals" before becoming bishop. The Chapel Committee had on one occasion compelled him to surrender control of a large sum of money he had collected for church purposes. On two other occasions when Fleming was a priest and later a coadjutor bishop, the group frustrated his attempts to give religious instruction to children. On the second occasion because (in Fleming's words) "500 children adorned in their festive robes would give annoyance to their Protestant friends." Fleming, unable to use the school premises, then gave the children Holy Communion "in the public church." Eventually, when he became bishop, Fleming took the unusual and perhaps legally dubious step of calling a meeting of "all the Catholic supporters" and dissolved what he termed the "Council of Liberals," the school henceforward being placed under his immediate direction. Veitch argues that this may have been an overstatement and that it was probably the after-hours religious instruction, not the school, that must have been placed under Fleming's supervision. The *Centenary Volume* stated that the bishop had not insisted on the OAS's abandoning its interdenominational character, but that he took good care that the Catholic children attending were prepared for

---

160 J.H.D. Kelly, *The Oxford Dictionary of Popes* (Oxford, 1988), s.v. "Gregory XVI"; *Mercantile Journal*, 22 Feb. 1827; *Newfoundlander*, 27 Feb. 1828, 26 Feb. 1829, 4 Mar. 1830, 28 Feb. 1833.
161 AASJ, Fleming, *Relazione*, 7.

the sacraments.[162]

The date of the expulsion of the "Liberals" is not clear, but the composition of the *Relazione* can be dated to sometime in 1835 or even earlier. Certainly none of the dissident group were elected to either the OAS leadership or the BIS Committee at the 1834 annual meeting of the Society. From then on the officials of these two bodies were drawn from Fleming's closest associates—Nugent, Kent, Morris, Patrick Doyle, John Dillon, and John O'Mara[163] and other supporters such as Lawrence O'Brien and Patrick Mullowney.

Religious instruction was not the only issue on which Fleming found fault with the structure of the OAS. He was equally concerned with the co-educational nature of the school. He deplored the system of "mixing both sexes pell mell," which, he was convinced, "produced fatal consequences to religion and morals," as the boys picked up bad habits in the fishery, and the girls, tutored by men, would lose "delicacy of feeling and refinement." Thus it was "absolutely necessary" to separate girls completely from all communication with the other sex. Suiting the action to the words, in 1833 he brought to St. John's from Galway in Ireland four sisters of the Presentation Order. On arrival they immediately set up a school for poor Catholic girls withdrawn from the OAS,[164] which thereafter functioned as a boys' school. The founding of the Presentation Sisters' school and the expulsion of the dissident group from the OAS, if not (in the *Ledger*'s words) acts of "intolerable tyranny and despotism," could fairly be described as authoritarian and regressive. The Hogan group, as we have seen, had given substantial administrative service to the OAS. Hogan, in fact, could claim to be the originator of the asylum to which the school was attached,[165] and McLean Little, another vocal

162 CO 194/42, Fleming to Mgr. Capaccini, 13 June 1835; AASJ, Fleming, *Relazione*, 7; Veitch, "Contribution of the Benevolent Irish Society," 53; *Centenary Volume*, 181.

163 CO 194/92, Aubin to Seymour, 13 Oct. 1835; *Newfoundlander*, 27 Feb. 1834; AASJ, 103, Fleming to Troy, 17 July 1836, in which he described these as "particular friends."

164 AASJ, Fleming, *Relazione*, 7–9; *Letters on the State of Religion in Newfoundland Addressed to the Very Rev. Dr. A. O'Connell, P.P. by the Right Rev. Dr. Fleming* (Dublin, 1844), Third Letter, 18.

165 *Ledger*, 8 Mar. 1836; BIS Minutes, 17 Aug. 1823.

dissident, had superintended the reconstruction of the building in 1832. Fleming's actions, in fact, had put him in an isolated position; in 1836 the first Education Act established public elementary schools on an interdenominational and co-educational basis.

The dissident Catholics had suffered a defeat. They did not take it quietly, however; they rallied their forces and on 17 March 1836 organized a rival St. Patrick's Day Festival in the Factory, which gathered together all the anti-Fleming forces in the city. "[T]hey have chosen to separate themselves," the *Ledger* stated, "and to commemorate the occasion in a manner more congenial to their own notions." From the *Patriot*'s standpoint, the "Anti-Catholic Irish" held an "Opposition Dinner." The meeting was attended by 163 people and conformed to the norms of previous festivals—decorations, transparencies, a band and an Irish piper, food and wine, toasts and speeches. The chairman, Dr. Kielly, and the vice-chairman, Bryan Robinson, were both Tories, and the guests included prominent Protestants, plus the Catholic dissidents John Shea, Timothy Hogan, and Patrick Kough. The only reference to Fleming's actions was made by Kough, who complained that he had been maligned and misrepresented by "foul slanderers and base calumniators," would-be destroyers of "the whole social fabric," who had accused him of being "apostate to the faith of my fathers" (cries of "no! no!" and "you are not").[166]

The traditional St. Patrick's Day Festival was held on the same day as that of the opposition dinner. It was a triumphalist gathering, hosted by Fleming and his supporters to demonstrate that they were now in control of the BIS and OAS. Fleming himself and several Catholic priests were present. The bishop praised the priesthood and John Kent eulogized Daniel O'Connell, both to rapturous applause. Fleming declared that priests were assailed by a few "recreant children of their own bosom" and Patrick Mullowney, chairman of the OAS, asserted that they were assembled to rally round those who had never deserted their country's cause and who practised benevolence and charity; what claim on Ireland, he asked, had those "who have on this day deserted her banners" and abandoned their

166 *Ledger*, 8 Mar. 1836; *Patriot*, 22 Mar. 1836; *Times*, 23 Mar. 1836.

benevolent society, encouraged others to do the same, and spoken out in condemnation of their bishop and his clergy.[167]

The finances of the Society, in the early 1930s, were precarious. In 1831 the Colonial Secretary had declined to give financial aid, and the Society was kept afloat by subscriptions, including monies from 15 commercial houses in 1834.[168] The position of the Society was finally strengthened by an annual grant of £100 for the OAS under the 1836 Education Act. In a meeting following the grant, Patrick Morris, the president, proposed that it was now possible for the higher branches of navigation and mathematics to be included in the OAS curriculum. A committee was then set up to explore the best way to utilize the grant. It recommended that the monies be used "to extend further the Blessings of Education," specifically to add an additional room to the school for the teaching of the "higher branches," that is, algebra, geometry, geography, astronomy, and navigation, the last subject to be open to adults. A new assistant would be engaged for the elementary class. These plans were largely put into operation during the late 1830s and early 1840s. A report for 1848 shows that the principal and primary schools enrolled 600 pupils, studying 12 subjects, including bookkeeping, mensuration, trigonometry, surveying, and navigation. In 1838 the rules of the Society were revised. A committee to superintend the OAS was established, endowed with financial control, visiting rights, and power to organize two examinations annually. It was made clear that the new rules were to supplement but not abrogate the original rules of 1826.[169] These improvements in the curriculum, the re-organization, and the salaries of the OAS were a solid foundation for the future.

In February 1837 the *Patriot* had celebrated the 31st anniversary of the Society with a rhetorical flourish:

---

167 *Patriot*, 29 Mar. 1836.

168 Crowdy to Morris, 21 June 1832, BIS Minutes, 26 June 1832; *Newfoundlander*, 27 Feb. 1834.

169 BIS Minutes, 30 May 1836, 24 Aug. 1836, 17 Feb. 1838, 1841, 1842, 1843; JHA 1848, 12 Dec. 1848, Appendix; "Rules of the Orphan Asylum School," *Vindicator*, 13 Mar. 1841.

The Benevolent Irish Society may proudly boast, that it is the only Society in the Island which, after an expenditure of nearly 400l. during the past year, and after paying up every farthing of their debts, can devote 100l. from their funds for the relief of the Indigent for the first quarter of the thirty-first year of its existence!

May it long continue to reflect a lustre on the Irish character in Newfoundland.[170]

170 *Patriot*, 18 Feb. 1837.

CHAPTER 4

*The "No Popery" Crusade and the Newfoundland School System, 1836–1843**

> Let man have an adviser, in whom he is taught to place unlimited confidence, on whom he looks as the representative of his God on earth, and he soon becomes his ready tool for good or evil ... Roman Catholics ... are told by their priests, that, as members of society, the first allegiance they owe is to the head of their church, the Pope of Rome, and the next to the government, defacto, under which they live.
>
> ... I put the question, confidently, to every honest and sensible Protestant ... whether the cause of liberty is not in danger, and likely to decline, if we any longer submit to or acquiesce in the doctrines of Popery!
>
> —W. Hogan, *Popery as It Was and as It Is* (1845)

The growth of the industrial nation-state in the last 200 years has been characterized by two interlinked phenomena: the spread of secularism—driven forward by liberalism, science, and anti-clericalism—and the introduction of systems of compulsory schooling.[171] The control over education exercised by churches and religious organizations in previous centuries has been whittled away or replaced by state schooling with legal requirements of attendance; religious instruction, particularly in the countries of the developed

---

* This chapter was first published in *Historical Studies* of the Canadian Catholic Historical Association, 58 (1991), and is reprinted with permission. The text has been edited only for style consistency.

171 Owen Chadwick, *The Secularization of the European Mind in the Nineteenth Century* (Cambridge, 1975); Pavla Miller, "Historiography of Compulsory Schooling: What Is the Problem?" *History of Education* 18, no. 2 (1989): 123–44.

world, is absent from educational institutions or present in a merely marginal role, and only in exceptional cases do we find even a segment of a national educational system run by churches. One of the most outstanding examples of church dominance of schooling in the Western world is to be found in Canada's 10th province, Newfoundland, where four main denominations—Amalgamated Protestant, Roman Catholic, Pentecostal, and Seventh Day Adventists—are responsible for the organization and control of all of the province's schools. Until recently the validity of this situation was almost beyond dispute, but during the past decade debate about the future of the denominational system has increasingly occupied the press, the electronic media, and public organizations. Should the system remain as it is, be modified, or abolished? Each position has its determined protagonists.

One feature of the controversy is the appeal to history. Supporters claim that denominational education is an expression of the response of the churches to the popular will, an inevitable and harmonious development rooted in the immemorial tradition of Newfoundland culture, and thus should remain unaltered. Critics point to the system's non-denominational origins, to the changes and conflicts that made the evolution of the system problematic rather than inevitable, and therefore open to future modification or dissolution.

Evidence can be found for both points of view, but what is beyond dispute is that public education for the children of Newfoundland began in 1836 on a non-denominational basis. Its subsequent history, however, was marked by violent disputes and divisions, culminating in the emergence, in the 1870s, of the multi-denominational system which has remained basically unchanged to the present day. The crucial period in the formation of the system was the years 1836 to 1843, when the tumultuous struggle was waged between Protestant and Catholic forces over the educational issue, culminating in an education act which instituted denominational schooling.

Disputes about the place of churches in Newfoundland education may appear today to wear a somewhat parochial aspect. In the early 19th century, however, the role of the Christian religion in the education of the masses was a hotly disputed topic in both the United Kingdom and its growing colonial empire; controversy raged over the institutional position of Protestantism as against the claims of renascent Catholicism, particularly in the so-called white-settler colonies of the Canadas, Newfoundland, Australia, and New Zealand. Newfoundland acquired full colonial status as late as 1832. Formerly merely a fishing station for West of England fleets, Newfoundland, following a wave of immigration from southwest England and southeast Ireland, in 1836 had a population of some 70,000 divided almost equally between Protestants and Catholics, nearly all of whom were engaged in the inshore fishery. The main social cleavage was between a small group of merchants and an extensive class of fishers; the latter were in thrall to the merchants through the credit or truck system, by which the product of the summer fishing season—cured fish—was bartered for winter supplies.[172]

In 1836, Newfoundland had enjoyed four years of representative government, following a long campaign for colonial status waged by political reformers. The structure and ethos of the new state, however, was essentially Protestant: a British governor, an appointed Legislative Council consisting of Protestant merchants and officials, and the Church of England established as the official religion. In the Assembly, particularly after 1837, Liberal-Catholics, with some Protestant allies, were in the majority and pursued fairly radical policies of exercising privileges, seeking control of finances, and opposing the legal system; their main success was the forcing of the resignation of the unpopular chief justice, H.J. Bolton, in 1838. Previously lacking in civic institutions, the colony was determined to introduce a range of social amenities corresponding to its status, not least a system of public education. On this issue there was, initially, general agreement among the Liberals, largely but not entirely Catholic, and the Conservatives, almost wholly Protestant.

The Education Act of 1836 was initiated by the governor, Sir Henry Prescott, who proposed "the encouragement of education" in his speech to the Assembly in January 1836, supported by a select

172 See Gunn, *Political History*, 1–33; S. Ryan, "Fishery to Colony: A Newfoundland Watershed, 1793–1815," *Acadiensis* 12, no. 2 (1983): 34–52.

committee which looked to European experience for examples of the beneficial effects of education, and given substance by the Assembly, which established nine school boards which were to include the senior or superior clergymen "of each of the several religious denominations."[173] The legislation was largely formal; no mention was made of school organization, teachers, curriculum, or religious observance, and the non-denominational nature of the "elementary schools" could be inferred only from the inclusion of ministers of all faiths on the boards.

The act was passed in the dawn of popular education; the non-denominational Irish National System had been established in 1831, providing a model for Newfoundland, and two years later England legislated financial support for the education of the poor. In the spirit of the times the select committee hoped that education would "tend to improve the morals and religious habits, encourage and direct the industry and ensure the happiness and tranquillity of the people."[174]

The act became law on 6 May 1836, and Newfoundland appeared to have established a system of non-denominational popular education which had the support of all shades of political and religious opinion. The prospect of harmonious development was, however, to be short-lived. When the governor's list of appointments to the school boards was issued in July, an astonished and furious Catholic population found that of the 117 members, only 18 were of the Catholic faith, only eight of the 18 Catholic clergy had been selected, and the Catholic bishop, Michael Anthony Fleming, had not been appointed to the St. John's board. Though Fleming was later placed on the board at the insistence of the other members, the damage had been done and the *Patriot* alleged that the appointments were influenced by "Tory advisers" of the governor, who was apparently absent at the time.[175]

Whether this decree was a calculated snub on the part of the

173 JHA 1836, 7, 24 Jan., 28 Mar., 8 Apr. 1836; 6 Wm. 4, cap. 13, An Act for the Encouragement of Education in This Colony (6 May 1836); £1,500 was granted to the elementary schools, £600 to existing institutions.

174 JHA 1836, 24 Feb. 1836.

175 *Patriot*, 9, 16 July 1836; The Rooms Provincial Archives Division, GN 2/1, J. Templeman to E. Wix, 8 July 1836.

Conservative Protestant council, or merely a reflection of their anti-Catholic prejudices, is not clear, but it certainly opened a way for the Protestant majorities on the boards, should they wish to do so, to bring undue influence to bear on policy decisions, since under the act boards could make their own bylaws. The opportunity was soon taken. On 8 August, two Protestant members of the board of Conception Bay, a fishing area adjacent to St. John's, the capital, proposed the division of their share of the grant between the Church of England, Roman Catholics, and Methodists. This was lost, but a resolution to adopt as a school book the Authorized Version of the Bible (to be read by Protestants "out of school hours") was adopted as the 11th bylaw. Four Catholic members immediately resigned, complaining to the governor that the clause was contrary to the Irish system and a diversion of public money to sectarian purposes.[176]

At the governor's suggestion, the Conception Bay board added the St. John's board seventh bylaw—which allowed ministers of religion to withdraw pupils of their communion for religious instruction, and which selected only unsectarian school books—to its regulations, but refused his request to expunge their own 11th rule. The governor, however, insisted that he could not sanction it. In October they went further and passed a resolution in favour of dividing the district grant between Protestants and Catholics; at the same time several members of the board expressed the determination of the Protestants of Conception Bay to withhold their children from schools in which the Bible was prohibited. Governor Prescott was undeterred, however, and on 11 November he announced that he would not sanction any expenditure of money except in accordance with rules approved by himself. The work of the board was effectively brought to a standstill and no meetings were held until the latter part of 1838.[177]

---

176 The Rooms Provincial Archives Division, GN 21/6, Proceedings of the Board of Education, District of Conception Bay, Minutes 1836–1841, 8, 9 Aug. 1836; JLC 1837, Appendix, D. Machin et al. to J. Templeman, 10 Aug. 1836.

177 JLC, E. Wix to J. Templeman, 15 July 1836; The Rooms Provincial Archives Division, GN 21/6, Board of Education Conception Bay, Correspondence Book (J. Templeman to J. Burt, 15 Aug., 1 Sept. 1836; J. Crowdy to J. Burt, 11 Nov. 1836), and Minute Book, 30 Aug., Oct. 1836–Nov. 1838.

The board of Trinity Bay, which contained no Catholic members, proposed to give religious instruction from the Authorized Version, though prohibiting books of a sectarian tendency. The members refused Governor Prescott's advice to drop the Bible, whereupon he attempted to conciliate them by suggesting that the rule concerning Bible reading be rescinded only if religious difficulties arose in practice; the board again refused to agree and he was forced to declare that "for the present" the district would be deprived of the benefits of the Education Act. Such being the case, wrote one of the commissioners, "the Board of Education for this district is now virtually dissolved."[178]

If Governor Prescott had acted decisively to uphold the principles of the act in Conception Bay, he temporized when faced with the intention of a third board, that of Bonavista, to flout the law. The board opted to use as school books those provided by the Newfoundland School Society, a militant evangelical missionary body. In a long correspondence with the governor's office, Bonavista made it clear that these books would include the Authorized Version, refusing the suggestion that they should adopt the non-denominational Irish National school books, which the chairman declared were "repugnant" and "hateful" to Irish Protestants. The governor allowed the board to proceed with its intentions on condition he reserved the right to rescind the rule concerning books, should it prevent Catholic children from participating in the benefits of the act. In the following year, the Board of Education for Twillingate, also on the northeast coast, joined the other boards by authorizing the New Testament as a reading book in their schools (with the proviso that Catholic children should read from parent-approved texts). The specific resolution was refused sanction by the governor. Though the responses of the four boards to the imperatives of the act were not uniform, all shared the sentiments expressed by a correspondent in the *Ledger*: "The great Protestant principle of education—putting into the hands of Protestant children, the Bible, the whole

---

178 JLC 1837, Appendix, G. Skelton to J. Templeman, 8 July, 12 Sept., 24 Sept., 4 Oct. 1836; The Rooms Provincial Archives Division, GN 2/1, J. Templeman to G. Skelton, 22 Aug., 19 Sept., 1, 8 Oct. 1836; "A Member of the Board," letter to the editor, *Ledger*, 11 Oct. 1836.

Bible and nothing but the Bible."[179]

The actions of the recalcitrant boards were in line with those of Protestants in other countries. In England, the Evangelicals of Liverpool were mounting a full-scale (and ultimately successful) assault against the local Council's non-denominational school system, and a similar campaign was being waged by the same forces in Australia. Few words, in any country, were spoken about the fate of the children whose schooling was at the mercy of theological disputations which disrupted school life in many parts of the colony. Governor Prescott stated in July 1837 that the operation of the Education Act had met with considerable impediments; one district was "entirely deprived" of its benefits, and in but few places was its operation "cordial and complete."[180]

• • •

Governor Prescott, as he later admitted, favoured non-denominational education and supported the Assembly's view on the matter; these sentiments were probably in his mind when in the following session of the Assembly he announced that he would "readily consent" to any educational measure that would assuage religious jealousies and promote universal instruction. He was taken at his word by Peter Brown, a radical Catholic from Conception Bay, who introduced "A Bill to Grant a Further Sum of Money and to Amend an Act for the Encouragement of Education in this Colony." Arguing that the 1836 act was a dead letter—religious differences had left most of the grant unappropriated—Brown proposed the exclusion

---

179 The Rooms Provincial Archives Division, GN 2/1, J. Templeman to H.J. Fitzgerald, 6 Sept. 1836; J. Crowdy to H.J. Fitzgerald, 5 Oct., 22 Dec. 1836; JLC 1837, Appendix, H.J. Fitzgerald to J. Templeman, 19 Aug., 19 Sept., 25 Nov. 1836; "Catholicus," letter to the editor, *Ledger*, 3 Oct. 1836; JHA 1838, Appendix, Twillingate: Education Report (23 Aug. 1837); J. Crowdy to Rev. Chapman, 12 Sept. 1837, and Chapman to Crowdy, 9 Oct. 1837; "Biblicus," letter to the editor, *Ledger*, 9 Apr. 1839.

180 J. Murphy, *The Religious Problem in English Education: The Crucial Experiment* (Liverpool, 1959); P. McCann and F.A. Young, *Samuel Wilderspin and the Infant School Movement* (London, 1982), ch. 12; see F.T. Whitington, *William Grant Broughton, Bishop of Australia* (Sydney, 1936); JHA 1837, 3 July 1837, Address to the Assembly.

of all "sectarian books" (the Bible presumably included), but permitted the introduction of those similar to the Irish National school books. With the acerbity of the controversy in mind, Brown inserted a clause allowing board members to sue and be sued. Finally, £750 was added to the existing annual grant.[181]

The bill, sent for approval to the Legislative Council, was promptly amended by that body. A conference was called, the outcome of which was entirely negative. The Council, in a lengthy statement, rejected the Assembly's arguments: the act had not been rendered inoperative, Council members declared, by dissensions on a few boards and the governor's refusal to sanction certain rules; the Assembly's proposals to restructure the boards would merely allow the views of the minority to predominate, the latter being entirely prejudiced in preventing those who wished to read the Bible to do so. The bill was rejected, joining the dozen or more, the *Patriot* noted, which had been "burked" by the Council.[182]

This was the first intervention by the (wholly Protestant) Council in the field of public education, and marked an intensification of Protestant opposition to non-denominational education. The *Public Ledger* continued to act as a focus of this opposition. In 1836 it had printed letters urging "No Bible—No Schools" and warning the governor of "a flame of opposition" that would teach him not to interfere with "our English privileges." In the following year the *Ledger* publicized opposition to the Irish National System, and published a plea for Protestants to support the Newfoundland School Society against "the designs of the enemy."[183]

The Newfoundland School Society, founded in 1823 by Newfoundland merchants and English Evangelicals, had established its own network of schools in Newfoundland, supported morally by the

181 *A Sketch of the State of Affairs in Newfoundland* (London, 1841), 60–61; CO 194/11, Prescott to Russell, 9 June 1841; JHA 1837, 26 Aug. 1837, Address to the Assembly; *Patriot*, 30 Sept., 21 Oct. 1837.

182 JHA 1837, 4 Oct. 1837, "Report of a Committee Appointed to Prepare Reasons to Be Offered at a Conference with Her Majesty's Council on Education Bill," "Report of Conference"; *Patriot*, 21 Oct. 1837.

183 "Z," letter to the editor, *Ledger*, 16 Sept. 1836; "A Protestant," letter to the editor, 23 Sept. 1836; "Z," letters to the editor, 5 Sept., 3 Oct. 1837.

British government. The Society's status was enhanced in 1839 when the first Church of England bishop of Newfoundland, the Evangelical Aubrey Spencer, became its vice-president. The Society, in fact, not only played a leading part in the fight against Catholicism and its support of non-denominational education, but also acted as a platform for Protestant and Conservative opinion. The annual meeting of the Society in London in 1838 extended a welcome to former Chief Justice Boulton, the hammer of the Catholic radicals, who reiterated the allegation that an attempt was being made in Newfoundland "to establish schools excluding the Bible," and declared that no system of education could be good that forbade the reading of the Scriptures. In the areas in which the Protestants kept their children from school, the Society collected subscriptions and set up temporary schools for "Protestant instruction." Opposition to the whole government scheme of education on the island, the Society stated unequivocally, was due to "the combined exertion of some influential persons, most of the clergy, some of the Wesleyan missionaries, and the entire body of your teachers."[184]

Despite the unpromising political climate, another education bill, again presented by the indefatigable Peter Brown, was put before the Assembly in August 1838 and, surprisingly, passed the Council, possibly influenced in this instance by Governor Prescott. Brown's intention was, as he declared at the committee stage, to remove from board members the power to obstruct the progress of education by empowering the governor to fill vacancies on the boards. The Council took the step (unexpected in the light of its previous opposition to non-denominationalism) of safeguarding the non-denominational status of schools by agreeing to forbid any minister to impart religious instruction therein, even adding a clause "or in any way to interfere in the proceedings or management thereof." Even more unexpectedly, it proposed a section forbidding the use of books inculcating "The doctrines or peculiar tenets of any particular or exclusive church or religious society whatsoever,"

184 *Record*, 3 May 1838; Proceedings of the Newfoundland and British North American Society for Educating the Poor (NBNASEP), 15th Report, 1838, 12.

a proviso which obviously excluded the use of the Bible. The act, passed on 25 October 1838, contained these clauses, plus the authorization of a special grant of £150 which was to be spent on the purchase of books used in Irish National Schools for school boards "who may approve the same." Finally, the boards of Conception and Trinity bays were ordered to expend the monies not disbursed in previous years to build or procure schoolhouses.[185]

The act undoubtedly strengthened the non-denominational nature of the system. Yet within less than a year Protestant forces contrived to nullify its most important provision—the exclusion of the Bible as a reading book. In order to better understand the atmosphere and context in which Protestants were able to achieve this success, a closer look at the ideology of international Protestantism in the late 1830s is necessary.

• • •

The worldwide expansion of the Protestant movement in the early Victorian era was a function of the expansion of Europe overseas. During the 19th century an estimated 8 to 9 million square miles of territory in North and South America and Australasia alone was occupied, within which the British Empire had expanded to 105 million people and 1,120,000 square miles by 1840.[186] Contemporaries saw the growth of British commerce and the extension of civilization as going hand in hand. To Protestants, the spread of the gospel, particularly to the "heathen" areas of the globe, was inextricably bound up with the progress of commerce. The providence of God, it was argued, had happily placed Britain in the position of acquiring power and territorial possessions, not for greed or self-aggrandizement, but to bring Christianity and civilization to heathen regions. The belief that its mission was a fulfilment of a divine providential plan gave Protestantism a confidence and sense

---

185 Assembly 29 Aug., *Patriot*, 1 Sept. 1838; JLC 1838, 11, 14 Sept. 1838; 2 Vic., cap. 5, An Act to Amend an Act Passed in the Sixth Session of the First General Assembly (25 Oct. 1838).

186 A.J. Youngson, "The Opening up of New Territories," in *The Cambridge Economic History of Europe*, Vol. VI (Cambridge, 1966), 139; "Extent and Importance of the British Colonies," *Colonial Magazine* 6, no. 23 (1841).

of superiority which inspired even its humblest labourer in the field. Only one power appeared to be able to challenge or frustrate the design—renascent Catholicism, directed from Rome. Protestants had watched the restoration of Pope Pius VII to Rome after the upheavals of the Napoleonic period, followed during the next decade by the revival of overseas missions, the re-establishment of the Jesuit Order and Propaganda Fide, and the founding of the Association for the Propagation of the Faith. The passing of the Catholic Relief Act by the British Parliament in 1829, which gave Catholics access to "offices, franchises, and civil rights," seemed to be the last straw. Beginning in Ireland, the long tradition of hostility to Catholicism was revived and intensified, and under the slogan of "No Popery" an international crusade was launched against Catholicism, depicting Catholics as deviant, superstitious, and irrational, and as likely to give their political allegiance to the pope as to the sovereign. Fanned by their dissemination of tracts and pamphlets, highly coloured "revelations" by renegade priests and the invective of Protestant divines, the crusade spread throughout the British Isles, to Canada, Australia, and the United States.[187]

The anti-Catholicism of the Protestants of Newfoundland thus did not spring entirely from local conditions, though the activities of the Irish Catholic community—political speeches from the pulpit by priests, rowdy marches and demonstrations at election times in which injuries were sustained, unrelenting radical policies in the Assembly—thoroughly alarmed the Conservative-Protestant elite. The "No Popery" crusade, however, with its stark division of the world into devious Catholics and heroic Protestants, strengthened and united all sects of the latter community; both the church and Dissenters, a leading Methodist, J. Pickavant, asserted, were aware of the necessity of saving Newfoundland from the influence of the agents of the Church of Rome.[188]

A united front of Protestants could only have been brought into being by the perception of a common danger. There was no natural

---

187 R.A. Billington, *The Protestant Crusade, 1800–1860* (New York, 1938).
188 MMS N. Am, Box 100, F10E, Newfoundland, J. Pickavant to Secretaries, 12 Sept. 1838.

sense of unity between the orthodox Anglicans, Evangelicals, and Methodists of Newfoundland. Bishop Spencer was opposed to any form of Dissent, and the Methodists complained of the encroachments of the Newfoundland School Society on what they considered "their" territory. The perceived threat from Rome, whipped up by "No Popery," temporarily united the different sects by making the defence of Protestantism seem more important than the interest of any particular group within it.[189]

Strengthened by this conviction, Methodists and Anglican Evangelicals acted together to attack the bastion of of non-denominational education, the 1838 Education Act. Four months after the 1838 act was passed, five members of the Conception Bay board resigned—Burt and Pickavant, Methodist ministers, and Stark, Ridley, and Stirling, the last three subscribers to the Newfoundland School Society. They informed the governor that they considered the act an "exclusive enactment" which penalized the Protestant majority and called for a division of the grant on religious lines. At the first opportunity Prescott filled the vacant places with Catholics, precipitating the resignation of the remaining Protestant, the Rev. Charles Blackman, a prominent Evangelical, who threatened that henceforward not a single Protestant child would be sent to school in the Conception Bay district.[190]

The tactics of resignation and the withdrawal of pupils were negative and ultimately self-defeating. A more positive and more adroit manoeuvre would be to attack the problem at its source by changing the law, or at least the interpretation of it, and this the Protestant majority on the Trinity Bay board proceeded to do—by calling the Protestant state to their aid. On 12 June 1839, the board declared the Authorized Version of the Bible to be unsectarian and submitted Section III of the act to the Attorney General and Coun-

---

189 A.G. Spencer, *A Brief Account of the Church of England* (London, 1867), 10; MMS N. Am., Box 103, F13E, Newfoundland, W. Faulkner to Secretaries, 4 Jan. 1843, and I. Sutcliffe to Secretaries, 20 Nov. 1843.

190 Proceedings of the NSS, 1833–1834, 1834–1844; JLC 1839, Appendix, J. Burt et al. to Colonial Secretary, 22 Nov. 1838; The Rooms Provincial Archives Division, GN 21/6, Board of Education, Conception Bay, Minutes, 18 Feb. 1839, and GN 2/2, C. Blackman to J. Crowdy, 2 May 1839.

cil member James Simms, requesting an opinion as to whether the Bible fell within its provisions. In a carefully worded but nonetheless remarkable judgment, Simms declared that he had "great doubts" as to whether the Bible inculcated the doctrines of any particular or exclusive church or society; he leaned toward the opposite inference—that it was not of a sectarian character. If that were so, then the boards were authorized "to choose and select such books as may be used in the schools." In other words, the Authorized Version of the Bible was a school book which the boards were legally entitled to select for use under Section III of the 1838 act. Though J.V. Nugent, one of the leading Liberal-Catholic politicians in the Assembly, in moving an address to the governor, described Simms's ruling as given in "great doubts and professed uncertainty," the judgment was allowed to stand.[191]

Did the Council (of which Simms was a member in 1838) have a possible future change of interpretation in mind when it added Section III to the Assembly's draft of the 1838 act? It is an attractive but unproven hypothesis. What is certain is that Simms's ruling had an immediate effect: Governor Prescott withdrew his objection to the use of the Bible, and sanctioned the rules and regulations to the Trinity board. Thus the tables were neatly turned against the Assembly on the most crucial issue which faced the educational system. Nugent gloomily predicted that if the system were broken down in Trinity it would eventually be broken down everywhere else.[192]

What effect did the three-year Protestant campaign have upon the schooling of children as envisaged under the education acts? Conception Bay was hit particularly hard; the withdrawal of Protestant children from school resulted in 7,000 to 8,000 children being deprived of schooling, according to Peter Brown in August 1838. The governor's restrictions on the operations of the Trinity Bay board, declared Richard Barnes, author of the 1843 Education Act, had left

---

191 JLC 1839, Appendix (W. Bullock to J. Crowdy, 12 June 1839), and Appendix (J. Crowdy to W. Bullock, 19 June 1839); 2 Vic., cap. 5, An Act to Amend an Act Passed in the Sixth Session of the First General Assembly (25 Oct. 1838); *Patriot*, 29 June 1839.

192 The Rooms Provincial Archives Division, GN 2/1, J. Crowdy to W. Bullock, 19 June 1839; *Patriot*, 22 June 1839.

everything "at a stand" in the district for two years. The Assembly later stated that the act was "inoperative in several districts" in 1837. When the Bible was introduced into the schools of Trinity Bay after the Simms ruling of 1839, Catholic children in attendance were kept at home by their parents as a consequence. After the assumption of office by Catholics on the Conception Bay board in February 1839, not a single Protestant child was sent to school in that region. The evidence is impressionistic, and though a small number of schools were in operation, it tends to confirm the governor's assessment of the position in 1843 that in nearly every district of the island the children either of Protestant or Catholic parents had been, at one time or another, excluded from the benefit of schooling. Expenditure on public elementary education, in fact, was $3,780 in 1836 and only $2,400 in 1841, as compared with $30,858 in 1846.[193]

In January 1840, Prescott made a last attempt to influence legislation by presenting to the Assembly, "as a model," the rules of the St. John's board which, as we have seen, forbade the teaching of sectarian tenets and enjoined the use of the Irish National school books. The following year the Assembly, heeding the advice, sent to the Council an education bill, one clause of which excluded the use of the Bible as a textbook. The Council, on the Assembly's refusal to withdraw the clause, put forward two proposals: either that no Catholic child should be compelled to read any book of a religious tendency; or, that the education grant should be divided on religious lines if parents could not agree to have their children educated in the same school. The Assembly rejected both propositions, the former on the grounds that it would allow Protestant doctrines to be taught in all schools to all the children, but for Catholics "the only return made them for the degradation was, that they should not be compelled to *read books* they disapproved of." After lengthy negotiations with the Council, the Assembly, anxious to place an act on the statute book before the original act of 1836 expired in May 1841, submitted a compromise proposal that would permit the in-

193 *Patriot*, 1 Sept. 1838; *Ledger*, 17 Mar. 1843; JHA 1841, 23 Apr. 1841, Address of the House of Assembly, and Address to Her Majesty; CO 194/117, Harvey to Stanley, 30 Nov. 1843; Blue Books, Newfoundland, 1836, 1841, and 1846. Figures converted from sterling at the rate of $4.8 to £1.

troduction of the Bible into "all the exclusively Protestant schools," provided "mixed schools" would limit "religious books" to those of the Irish National System.[194] The Council refused to agree to the Assembly's proposal and the bill was lost.

After the failure of the 1841 bill, the direction of Newfoundland popular education began to be influenced by political developments arising from the repercussions of the "No Popery" crusade on imperial policy. The British government had begun to take a close interest in Newfoundland affairs in the mid-1830s. In 1834 Governor Prescott had begun a clandestine correspondence with the Colonial Office in an attempt to persuade Rome to remove the Roman Catholic bishop Fleming, and from the mid-1830s onwards copies of the main St. John's newspapers began to be sent to London on a regular basis. Inflammatory articles from these papers were also reproduced (often with considerable embellishment) in Conservative and Protestant journals in Britain from the *Standard* to the Evangelical *Record*, from the *Protestant Magazine* to the Methodist *Watchman*, often utilizing material from the *Times* and *Ledger*. The Newfoundland press frequently reproduced this material as evidence of "respectable" British opinion. There was thus an intense two-way journalistic traffic across the Atlantic, embodying one persistent theme—that the "Popish hierarchy" in Newfoundland was fomenting "discontent, disorder, and ultimately rebellion."[195]

The Chamber of Commerce, representative of the merchant community, petitioned the queen for abrogation of the Representative Assembly, declaring they would not be ruled by those who paid no taxes nor owned any property. Other merchants in both Newfoundland and Britain made similar demands. Following a hotly contested and rowdy by-election in 1840, and a heated leading article in the *Times* in January of the following year which, significantly, compared Newfoundland to Ireland, prophesying that the "murdering and burning" of Catholic mobs in the former was but a foretaste of the fate of Protestants in the latter—the British gov-

194 JHA 1841, 29 Mar., 15, 21, 23, 24 Apr. 1841; JLC 1841, 19, 20, 23 Apr. 1841.
195 *Ledger*, 24 Feb. 1837, for suggestions of this process; *Record*, 20 Sept. 1838; "Popery in the Colonies," *Protestant Magazine* 1 (March 1839): 33–37; NBNASEP, 15th Report, 1838, 11; Gunn, *Political History*, 56.

ernment acted. The presentation of a petition from the St. John's Chamber of Commerce in the House of Lords by Lord Aberdeen—which again called for radical changes in the constitution which would give security of rights and protection of life—preceded a successful motion in the House of Commons for a Select Committee of Inquiry into the State of Affairs in Newfoundland. The selection of witnesses was somewhat partisan, the committee's report was never published, and the evidence suggested that principal merchants favoured the abolition of representative government. In September 1841 a new governor, Sir John Harvey, was appointed, who favoured an Amalgamated Assembly. In August 1842 the Newfoundland Act was passed, which raised qualifications for the franchise, abolished the Legislative Council and Representative Assembly and instituted an Amalgamated Legislature of 10 nominated and 15 elected members. In this Assembly, Catholic and Liberal politicians were in a minority.[196]

• • •

The way was now clear for changes in the educational system. Governor Harvey made an eloquent plea for an education act (without mentioning denominationalism) in his address to the Assembly in January 1843. The invitation was accepted by Richard Barnes, the member for Trinity, from the board of which, as we have seen, had come the successful breach of non-denominational schooling four years previously. Usually described as a Wesleyan, Barnes was, in fact, a deacon of the Congregational Church (to which Henry Winton, editor of the *Public Ledger*, also belonged). Barnes was also the treasurer of the Natives' Society, which stood for "the maintenance of constituted authority and order." His anti-Catholic credentials may be gauged from his conviction that "the strangers who

---

196 CO 194/101, Prescott to Glenelg, 24 Dec. 1838; CO 194/102, Address of Merchants, Traders and Shipowners of Conception Bay, 20 Feb. 1839; Addresses from Merchants in English Ports, 28 Feb., 7, 8, 12 Mar. 1839; *Times*, 11 Jan. 1841; Gunn, *Political History*, 77–78; Select Committee Appointed to Inquire into the State of the Colony of Newfoundland (1841); 5 and 6 Vic., cap. 120, An Act for Amending the Constitution of the Government of Newfoundland (Aug. 1842).

come amongst us [i.e., the Irish Catholics] and who are turning the country upside down with their accursed incantations, are more like fiends than men." He enjoyed the support of the new governor, Sir John Harvey, who admired him as a patriotic and respectable self-made man, "by no means unfavourable to the Church of England."[197]

Barnes's speech on the second reading of the bill was long, cogently argued, and well-researched. He claimed objectivity, but presented arguments and examples that reflected the standard Protestant line of the previous seven years, though no outsider would have guessed from his lengthy exposition that the situation he described had come about because of Protestant intransigence. He began by declaring that the lack of success of the system was due to no other cause than the fact that the people had no confidence in it; if the denominations met on common ground it would mean either the abandonment of religious principles or doing violence to religious feeling. Barnes's case for the division of the grant—which he presented as unavoidable—was based almost entirely on the presentation of Protestant and Evangelical materials, from the arguments of the Conception Bay Protestants in 1836 to a Methodist petition of 1843. Casting around for examples of denominational separation in education, he could find only New York and Prussia, though he argued that the principle would soon be admitted everywhere. He concluded with an ardent plea for an education which would lead to the creation of sober, upright, thrifty, industrious, and submissive working men.[198]

Barnes's eloquence and his display of a wide range of examples and statistics dazzled his audience and ensured a fairly easy passage for the bill. The Liberal-Catholic members did not speak out against the bill in committee and only one member—Charles Fox Bennett, a Protestant (and ironically a supporter of division when premier in the 1870s)—opposed the bill in principle. Barnes's speech was well received by both the Protestant-Conservative and Liberal-Catholic

---

197 JHA 1843, 17 Jan. 1843, Address to the Assembly; *Morning Courier*, 5 Sept. 1846; *Patriot*, 11 July 1840; *Ledger*, 22 Mar. 1836; CO 194/117, Harvey to Stanley, 30 Nov. 1843.

198 *Patriot*, 15 Mar. 1843; *Times*, 22 Mar. 1843.

press. The later circumstance may seem surprising, but Barnes's erudition, in an Assembly long accustomed to hearing pomposity and special pleading, had its effect. The Catholics and Liberals perforce had to accept the vote in favour of Barnes's bill with good grace; J.V. Nugent, one of the most radical Catholics in the Assembly, declared he would offer no "factious opposition" to a measure of such importance, as separate education was better than no education at all. Catholic members later declared that the act had been forced upon them, never having requested a division of the grant, a position confirmed by H.A. Emerson, a Protestant, in 1852.[199] Though in a sense the Catholic church benefited from the act, in that it obtained its own government-financed system of schools, Catholics as a body had certainly not asked for it. Both Bishop Fleming and his predecessor Bishop Scallan were in favour of a non-denominational system, partly from a sense of realpolitik, partly for the same reason as were the majority of Irish bishops—to provide literacy for the Catholic poor without compromising the faith.

The 1843 Education Act established separate Protestant and Catholic Boards of Education in each district and divided the education grant proportionately to the numbers in each denomination, with the Protestant boards appropriating monies for Methodist and Newfoundland School Society schools.[200] Governor Harvey justified it to the Colonial Office on the grounds that though "class legislation" of this kind normally perpetuated distinctions among colonial subjects, the "peculiar state of society" in Newfoundland justified such a "deviation." Lord Stanley, then Colonial Secretary, and architect of the non-denominational Irish system, was not satisfied, and suspended the act pending further reports from Harvey.[201]

The effect of the act, eventually allowed, was essentially divisive.

---

199 *Ledger*, 23, 28 Mar. 1843; see *Patriot*, 15 Mar. 1843; *Newfoundlander*, 16 Mar. 1843; *Times*, 22 Mar. 1843; J.V. Nugent, letter to the editor, *Times*, 22 Feb. 1851; J.L. Prendergast, *Express* (Extra), 27 Feb. 1852; G.H. Emerson, *Express*, 24 Mar. 1852; C. Benning, *Express*, 24 Mar. 1852, 7, 24 May 1853.

200 6 Vic., cap. 6, An Act for the Encouragement of Education in This Colony (22 May 1843).

201 CO 194/117, Harvey to Stanley, 26 May 1843; CO 195/20, Stanley to Harvey, 21 Oct. 1843.

By segregating into different schools Protestant and Catholic children, each would be taught that members of the opposing denomination were in error. Although children would not understand the theological position, the social lesson would be obvious. The new system thus helped to undermine the social and political solidarity of the fishery workforce which had been the basis of Liberal policies in the Assembly of 1837–1841. A process of dividing society according to religion was initiated which culminated in the "sharing of the spoils" in the 1860s, by which appointments and emoluments were made on a denominational basis rather than on merit. Educationally the act paved the way, in 1874, for the further division of the grant—between Church of England, Methodist, and Catholic congregations—with each allowed to pursue its own educational destiny, which led to duplication of schools and neglect of small communities.[202]

Though the Bible was the focus of contention, larger issues were also at stake. When the *Patriot* bluntly declared that "Bible-mania is one of those clap-traps got up to stultify the efforts of the legislature to ameliorate the state of the country,"[203] it pointed toward the political dimensions of the controversy over the schools, even though it simplified both the issues and the motives of the protagonists. The denominational issue touched on wider questions: for whose benefit were the schools to be organized, and in what kind of state? Merchants were certain that the polity should safeguard their commercial interests, and this meshed with the Protestant desire for ideological and political supremacy. Securing Protestant control of their own schools—even at the cost of allowing Catholics the same privilege—seemed the logical outcome.

Neither in the subdivision of the education grant in 1874 nor in the turbulent events preceding the 1843 act can any extensive evidence of popular preference for segregated schooling be discerned, as was later alleged. Undoubtedly large numbers of parents

---

202 An estimated 77 per cent of the electors in Conception Bay in 1836 voted Liberal, though only 43 per cent were Catholic (calculated from statistics in the *Patriot*, 15 Oct. 1836); S.J.R. Noel, *Politics in Newfoundland* (Toronto, 1971), 23–25.

203 *Patriot*, 8 Dec. 1838.

of both denominations often kept children away from school in the seven years preceding 1843. Although the inspiration for acts of civil disobedience undoubtedly emanated from the religious and secular elite, nevertheless the "No Popery" crusade did strike a chord among many Protestant parents insofar as they were willing to obey the initiatives of their pastors and keep their children from attending school. But this was hardly the same as a spontaneous grassroots uprising against the system of 1836. The contention of Richard Barnes that a system of non-denominational education was not a viable proposition for Newfoundland failed to take into account that the system had never really had a chance to work before the Protestant elite's employment of anti-Catholic propaganda, the promotion of civil disobedience, and the solicitation of intervention from the state in both Newfoundland and Britain worked toward its destruction.

CHAPTER 5

The Grammar Schools at Carbonear and Harbour Grace

> Thou hast most traitorously corrupted the youth of the realm in erecting a grammar school ... thou hast caused printing to be used ... thou hast built a paper mill.
>
> —William Shakespeare, *Henry VI*, Part 2, 4.7

In 1843 the Newfoundland legislature passed two acts establishing interdenominational grammar schools in the towns of Carbonear and Harbour Grace. These institutions rarely receive a mention in histories of Newfoundland education; they are not only interesting in their own right but also stand in contradiction to the received view that the Newfoundland educational system, from the early 19th century to the end of the 20th century, was essentially denominational. The author and journalist Philip Tocque, for example, writing in 1845, believed that the system was "wholly denominational," and in 1971 the historian S.J.R. Noel described it as "totally church-controlled." F.W. Rowe, in *The Development of Education in Newfoundland*, refers to the two grammar schools but ascribes their establishment to a governmental desire to keep secondary education undenominational; he goes no further in explanation of "this unusual procedure."[204]

An approach to understanding the origin and purpose of the grammar schools has to embrace a social and historical dimension. The schools were not an aberration but were in large part due to the

---

204 P. Tocque, *Kaleidoscopic Echoes* (Toronto, 1895), 21; Noel, *Politics in Newfoundland*, 21; F.W. Rowe, The *Development of Education in Newfoundland* (Toronto, 1964), 66.

long-term efforts of the Reform movement, associated with William Carson, Patrick Morris, and John Kent, to achieve an extension and improvement of education as part of the struggle for self-government.

The Reform movement dated from 1812 with the publication of the Scottish doctor William Carson's pamphlet *A Letter to the Members of Parliament of the United Kingdom*, an attack on the tyranny of the naval governors and surrogate courts which included a petition praying for, among other things, the endowment of a seminary "for the education of our youth." In another pamphlet, in 1813, Carson argued that "[t]he happiness, prosperity and freedom of this island will depend upon the virtue, industry and knowledge of the people, above all others, it is a paramount duty to attend to the education of the youth." Patrick Morris declared in 1821 that the real wealth of the island lay not in the capital of the merchants but in the skill and industry of the inhabitants. A public meeting of the Reformers in St. John's in 1822 reiterated their position, emphasizing that only a popular government "would foster the resources of the country" and "educate and civilise the people."[205] This education, Morris emphasized, would not have a religious content.[206] In short, the Reformers' position was representative government, resource development, and popular education without religion.

After 1832, with the achievement of representative government, the Reformers—Liberal-Catholics and some Protestant allies—were able to influence legislation. On 24 February 1836 Carson read to the House of Assembly the report of a Select Committee on Education which, citing examples of European countries as to the social benefits of education, outlined the structure of the subsequent act establishing interdenominational public elementary schools. The motion to pass the bill for the act was also proposed by Carson. This initial Assembly was "of Protestant and mercantile aspect";

---

205 W. Carson, *A Letter to the Members of Parliament of the United Kingdom* (Greenock, 1812), 33, and *Reasons for Colonising the Island of Newfoundland* (Greenock, 1813), 22; *A Report on Certain Proceedings* (St. John's, 1821), 78; PP, 1824, XVI, Papers and Accounts Relating to the Island of Newfoundland, No. 41, "A Report of the State of Newfoundland, for the Information of the Right Honourable Earl Bathurst," 6 Dec. 1822.

206 Morris, *Remarks on the State of Society*, 21, 23, 42.

the second Assembly of November 1836, however, contained only four mercantile seats with a large contingent of Liberal-Catholics, but it was dissolved on legal grounds; in the election of June 1837 Reformers "swept the board," and remained in a majority until the dissolution of 1841.[207] In the years of the Reformers' domination of the Assembly the foundation of the two grammar schools was laid.

According to Arthur Barnes, educator, Minister of education, and historian, the term "grammar school" was used in a generic sense by merchants and the local elite to describe any middle-class school. The two schools were certainly not copies of the traditional English grammar school, which taught mainly Latin and Greek language and literature. They had more in common with the private schools and academies founded in England by Protestant Nonconformists in the late 18th and early 19th centuries. These institutions taught a commercial-scientific curriculum for the sons of tradesmen and professional men.[208] These schools could have been known to merchants and to educated middle-class immigrants to Newfoundland. Far from being an anomaly, grammar schools were part of the drive of the Reformers for an educational system catering to all classes of the community and free from any church interference. The outcome of their efforts to establish grammar schools completed a three-tier system of education—an academy for the middle classes of St. John's (1845–1850); grammar schools for the commercial element of the two largest outports (from 1844); and elementary schools for the children of fishing families (1836–1843). During those dates, all were interdenominational.

HARBOUR GRACE GRAMMAR SCHOOL: THE FIRST DECADE, 1845–1856

Dr. William Carson's landmark speech on education to the Assembly in January 1836 not only set forward the cause of higher education in St. John's but also found an echo outside the capital. Dr. Barnes wrote that the citizens of Harbour Grace were inspired by Carson's

207 JHA 1836, 24 Feb. 1836, Report of Select Committee on Elementary Schools; JHA 1836, 11 Apr. 1836; Gunn, *Political History*, 14, 33–36.

208 B. Simon, *Studies in the History of Education 1780–1870* (London, 1960), 102–17.

words and, believing that they were as equally entitled as St. John's to the means of educating their youth, "took some steps to assert their claim." This was understandable. Harbour Grace was the principal port of Conception Bay and a growing commercial community engaged in the cod and seal fisheries. In 1845 it deployed 76 sealing vessels and nearly 400 fishing boats.[209] Its citizens felt the need for educational progress commensurate with their community's growing demographic and economic importance, and in public meetings and letters to the press they urged the formation of an institution of higher education.

In 1835 the *Star and Conception Bay Journal* had advocated "a good English Grammar School" in every populous harbour as a preliminary to the encouragement of education. The following year a correspondent in the *Conception Bay Mercury* suggested that "the most advantageous spot" for an academy would be Harbour Grace, which was centrally situated and more salubrious than St. John's and free from "the noises, bustle and ... vices" of a large town.[210] These proposals, however, did not come to fruition. Barnes suggests that the representatives of Conception Bay at that time—Peter Brown, James Power, John McCarthy, and A.W. Godfrey—did not exert themselves to secure for their constituents "what must have been an useful necessity," possibly because they felt that the majority of the voters believed that the school was intended for the rich man's child. On 24 February 1836, a House of Assembly Committee under Carson reported that an annual grant should be made for the immediate establishment and future support of a grammar school in Harbour Grace.[211]

No further steps were taken for the next seven years. In the Legislature of 1837–1841 opposition from the Council frustrated the

209 For Barnes, cf. E. Dawe, "In Search of Dr. Arthur Barnes," unpublished manuscript, ASCD (n.d); ASCD Coll. 057, Arthur Barnes papers; A. Barnes, *A History of Education in Newfoundland*, "The Establishment of Harbour Grace Grammar School," 8; Abstract, Census and Return of the Population of Newfoundland, 1845.

210 *Star*, 10 Feb. 1835; "Philomath," letter to the editor, *Patriot*, 9 Feb. 1836.

211 Barnes, *History*, "The Establishment of Harbour Grace Grammar School," 9; JHA 1836, 24 Feb. 1836.

Reformers' persistent efforts to legislate for an interdenominational classical academy. Early in 1843, however, the question of such an academy in St. John's was being seriously debated in the Amalgamated Assembly. Harbour Grace lost little time in putting forward its own claims. On 3 February 1843 a public meeting was held in the town's courthouse, chaired by Dr. William Stirling. He put a resolution to the meeting which pointed out that Harbour Grace, because of its central position and healthy situation, was "the most desirable place in Newfoundland for a Public Academy," which would offer a "superior education ... embracing nautical science." The meeting decided that a petition on these lines should be presented to the government. Less than three weeks later Thomas Ridley, a leading merchant of the town and a member of the House of Assembly, presented the petition:

> That the inhabitants of the District of Conception Bay have hitherto been without the means of giving their children any instruction in classical knowledge, and the higher branches of literature; that the central position of Harbour Grace, in reference to the other parts of the District, and its healthy and pure air, render it peculiarly eligible for the establishment of a Public Institution, and praying the House to grant them the means of supporting such an Institution at Harbour Grace.[212]

According to the *Times*, Ridley assured the House that if land could not be procured for the school he would himself "give a piece," a gesture which the *Times* somewhat hyperbolically considered a "noble and disinterested profession of *True* patriotism," by which "the best interests of Newfoundland are *sure* to be promoted and advanced."[213] The bill passed the Assembly apparently without opposition on 8 April. The act established a school for the instruction of youth "in the several branches of scientific and classical learning," and £400 was granted to build a school house and to provide

---

212 *Herald*, 17 Sept. 1845; JGA 1843, 22 Feb. 1843.
213 *Times*, 29 Mar. 1843.

"a Library, and sufficient Astronomical, Nautical, and Mathematical Instruments for the same." Seven commissioners were assigned to manage the school, appoint a master or masters, fix their salaries, introduce branches of learning other than those prescribed, settle fees and attendance times, and make rules and bylaws. Classics, mathematics, and navigation were to form the core of the curriculum, and no books were to be used which did not have the commissioners' approval. The masters' salary, paid by the government, was fixed at £150 per annum, plus pupils' fees, and the master had the responsibility of keeping a report and a register book and transmitting annual reports to the governor. There was no reference to religion or religious teaching in the act; the school, in the words of the *Newfoundlander*, was to be based on "the principles of amalgamation and non-compulsion." This was consonant with the view of the Harbour Grace merchant John Munn, who became a mainstay of the school; shortly before the passing of the act he had stated to the Assembly that he had been educated in a Scottish seminary where no religion was permitted.[214]

On 1 July 1843, Governor Harvey appointed Thomas Ridley, John Munn, J.L. Prendergast, Peter Brown, William Stirling, Alfred Mayne, and Daniel Green as commissioners of Harbour Grace Grammar School—a nice admixture of Protestants and Catholics, Liberals and Conservatives. At the first meeting of the board, Ridley read the governor's commission, and under its authority the commissioners elected William Stirling, a 30-year-old Scottish-educated doctor, as chairman. The main object of the board in the summer of 1843 was to obtain a suitable site for the school. A piece of ground to the west of the courthouse was chosen by the commissioners and sanctioned by the governor.[215] A contemporary photograph of the school shows a wooden, two-storey rectangular building, with five windows on the upper floor and a large entrance porch, fronted by a

214 5 Vic., cap. 7, An Act for the Establishment and Support of a Grammar School at Harbour Grace (22 May 1843); *Newfoundlander*, 30 Mar. 1843; House of Assembly 18 Feb., *Times*, 1 Mar. 1843.

215 *Gazette*, 4 July 1843; ASCD Coll. 057, Barnes Papers, Minute Book of the Board of Commissioners for the Harbour Grace Grammar School 1843–1877, Minutes, n.d. [18 July 1843]; *ENL*, s.v. "Stirling, William."

white wooden fence.[216]

The directors then turned to the issue of securing a suitable master. A notice was placed in local papers, and also in those of London, Dublin, and Edinburgh, these last via the good offices of the London-based merchant firm of Robinson and Brooking:

> **WANTED**
> FOR the HARBOUR GRACE GRAMMAR SCHOOL, a MASTER capable of Teaching the Classics, Mathematics and Navigation, in addition to such other branches of learning as shall hereafter be prescribed by the Directors of the said School.
>
> Salary granted by the Government £150, Stg., per annum, together with a House.—Applications and testimonials will be received by the Subscriber until the 10th day of May next.
>
> W. STIRLING, Chairman
> Harbour Grace
> 24th Jan. 1844[217]

Eighteen replies were received; six made the shortlist, and John Irving Roddick was elected (by a majority of one).[218] Roddick was a man of some distinction in his native Scotland. Born in Dumfriesshire in 1810, he was the cousin of the famous preacher Edward Irving and a friend of the illustrious Thomas Carlyle. Initially intended for the ministry, he had received a solid classical education, as was common in Scotland of the time, and eventually took up teaching. At the time of his appointment he was a teacher of classics in the High and Lower School of the Liverpool Mechanics' Institute. His grandfather, Martin Roddick, had owned a fleet of ships that traded largely with Newfoundland, and this connection may have influenced his

216 *ENL*, s.v. "Harbour Grace."
217 ASCD Coll. 057, Barnes papers, Minutes of Harbour Grace Grammar School, 19 Jan. 1844; *Ledger*, 6 Feb. 1844.
218 ASCD Coll. 057, Barnes papers, Minutes of Harbour Grace Grammar School, 19 Jan. 1844; *Ledger*, 28 May 1844.

grandson's decision to accept the appointment. Roddick sailed for Newfoundland in John Munn's brig *Alert*, arriving in the summer of 1844.[219]

What type of school had the legislature and the board of directors brought into being? Dr. Arthur Barnes was critical of the educational orientation of the directors, feeling that they had, "with characteristic conservatism," an exaggerated respect for British middle-class schools. The Newfoundland merchants, he maintained, brought to the island the curriculum and methods of the English model for the children of the rich, but little for the poor. Many merchants sent their sons and daughters to England to be educated, while others employed private tutors; both these courses were expensive, so elements of the merchant class began to favour a home-based higher education for their sons, particularly if government paid the teachers' salaries. The smaller planters and the fishing families, "from whose industry and drudgery the few obtained princely fortunes," were thus left with the rudiments of education. Furthermore, in Barnes's opinion, politicians and those in charge of the school were woefully ignorant of the "magnificent and far-reaching" theories and practices of European and American educators—Pestalozzi, Fellenberg, Herbart, Froebel, and Horace Mann. They had little excuse, for these educators' achievements could be found in the English papers "which came as regularly as the vessels came."[220]

The grammar school reflected the growing importance of the town in which it was established. In the 1840s and 1850s Harbour Grace had developed into a commercial town second only in importance to St. John's. Tocque called it "the Brighton of Newfoundland" on account of its beauty; at the centre of its rise was "two of the most enterprising, as well as the largest mercantile establishments in Newfoundland owned by Ridley and Munn."[221] British-born Thomas Ridley established a flourishing business in Harbour Grace, engaging

219 *ENL*, s.v. "Roddick, John Irving"; H.E. MacDermot, *Sir Thomas Roddick* (Toronto, 1936), 1; Barnes, *History*, "Principal Roddick and Opinions of His Work," 2.

220 Barnes, *History*, "Harbour Grace Grammar School," 10–12.

221 Tocque, *Newfoundland: As It Was, and as It Is in 1877* (Toronto, 1878), 112, 115. Brighton is a picturesque English seaside resort.

in the seal hunt and carrying on extensive operations in Labrador, but his repressive practices made him unpopular with the fishing community. He was elected to the Amalgamated Legislature in 1842 and sat on the Executive Council from 1843 to 1848. John Munn, a Scottish Presbyterian, came to Newfoundland in 1825, first working as a bookkeeper. In 1833 he set up in business with William Punton, and under Munn's direction the firm expanded to become the largest general and mercantile business outside St. John's, and active in the seal and Labrador fisheries. One of the most powerful men in Harbour Grace (often referred to as "Munnsborough"), he sat in the Amalgamated Legislature from 1842 to 1848 as a Conservative, and was a member of the Legislative Council from 1855 to 1889. He took over Ridley's business when the latter went bankrupt in 1870. He became chairman of the board of directors of the grammar school in 1854 when Stirling retired because of ill-health.[222]

The school owed much of its success to the interest taken by these two merchants. It is undeniable, however, that both men's concern for education was largely self-serving. Under their guidance the school came to function as an essentially vocational institution, serving the interests of the merchant class. Shortly after it opened, Bertram Jones, the first government inspector, noted that the course of instruction, which included bookkeeping, geometry, navigation, and geography, was "eminently suited to the requirements of a community where commercial pursuits constitute the main occupation of the people."[223]

Harbour Grace Grammar School opened on 3 February 1845, and 33 pupils were admitted in the first quarter, increasing to 54 by the end of the year, a number which Roddick felt "quite sufficient to keep one usefully and constantly employed." The school was divided into three classes. The first class (numbering seven pupils at the beginning) was the classical department; they studied the works of the Roman historian Cornelius Nepos, Ellis's Exercises, and Latin grammar. A second group of nine worked on mathematics (mainly geom-

---

222 *DCB*, s.v. "Ridley, Thomas" and "Munn, John"; ASCD Coll. 057, Barnes papers, Minutes of the Harbour Grace Grammar School, 5 Mar. 1854.
223 JGA 1846, Report upon the Inspection of Schools in Newfoundland by Bertram Jones, Esq. (27 Dec. 1845).

etry) and navigation, in three sections. The third component, numbering 37 pupils in five classes, was engaged in mathematics, reading, and spelling. The fees, graded according to class, were fixed at 70, 50, and 30 shillings per annum. Teaching aids—globes and maps—were provided. On 3 September Roddick advertised that he had vacancies for two boarders; in order to make his house "an agreeable home," every attention would be paid to their comfort.[224]

Roddick put into practice some innovative teaching methods. He was particularly keen on the technical aspects of the English language, and every scholar was grounded in English grammar "in such a manner as that he can apply its rules to the parsing and analyzing of sentences in whatever form they may be presented to him." Etymology—"the chemistry of languages"—was taught together with grammar, as was reading and spelling, and a voluntary elocution class met twice a week. Writing (i.e., penmanship) and composition, particularly letter writing, was given due importance. Geography was taught to the whole school with the help of "two splendid globes" and a number of skeleton maps. Roddick was able to devote only one hour per week to the many divisions of physical science, but he encouraged the boys to discover the truth of various facts by experiment: "my object being rather to create, than satisfy a desire for scientific knowledge." In 1851 a grant from the legislature enabled the school to purchase a selection of "Philosophical and Mathematical Instruments," including a theodolite, a sextant, an air-pump receiver, a microscope, a model of a steam engine, and several other pieces of apparatus. The library had been increased to 110 volumes.[225]

The catalogue of books to be used in the school—advanced texts issued in Britain—covered a wide range: seven in English and English grammar, three in geography, three in arithmetic, two in navigation, three in mathematics (algebra and geometry), five in German,

---

224 JGA 1846, Appendix, Report of the Harbour Grace Grammar School, 1845, and Appendix, Report of the Commissioners of the Harbour Grace Grammar School (16 Mar. 1846); Rules and Constitution of the Harbour Grace Grammar School, *Herald*, 2 May 1849; *Herald*, 24 Sept. 1845.

225 JGA 1846, Report of the Harbour Grace Grammar School, 1845; JHA 1852, Report of the Commissioners of the Harbour Grace Grammar School for 1851.

eight in French, five in Spanish, 28 miscellaneous volumes (including works on ethnology and classical history), and, strangely for a school with a commercial orientation, 18 Latin and 14 Greek texts. The pupils could draw upon this list of nearly 100 volumes, purchasing the relevant books for their area of study.[226]

Books used in the schools, including texts, had to be scrutinized by the commissioners before adoption. One text was Pinnock's *History of England* (not included in the above catalogue), and its use led to a situation similar to that experienced by the Carbonear school, coming under the proscription of the local Roman Catholic hierarchy.[227] According to Barnes, a "hot discussion" arose, but the commissioners did not oppose the church and blacked out certain alleged offensive passages in the book, and Roddick, unlike O'Donovan of the Carbonear Grammar School, apparently acquiesced. The predictable result was that the paragraphs were deciphered by the pupils, many declaring that they were the only passages in the book which they knew thoroughly. The incident gave rise to a long and satirical letter to the *Herald* from a member of the public, ridiculing the commissioners' action.[228]

The school appeared to have reached a peak in the late 1840s and early 1850s. It was praised as the best school on the island in both press and Assembly.[229] If the report of the public examination of 1847, for instance, was any indication, "this increasingly useful and respectable seminary" enjoyed public support and esteem. The reporter recognized "a number of the principal inhabitants of this town" who were gathered in the spacious and well-ventilated schoolroom adorned with maps and globes. Among them were four directors—William Stirling, John Munn, J.L. Prendergast, and Alfred Mayne—three ministers of religion, a dozen or so prominent citizens, and other interested individuals. "It was difficult to say which elicited most applause," the report continued, "the unwearied ac-

226 "Rules and Constitution of the Harbour Grace Grammar School," *Herald*, 2 May 1849.

227 Cf. next section "Carbonear Grammar School 1843–1866."

228 Barnes, *History*, "Harbour Grace Grammar School," 14–15; "Pasquin," letter to the editor, *Herald*, 7 Apr. 1852.

229 *Courier*, 27 June, 1 July 1848; *Herald*, 10 Apr. 1850, 5 Feb. 1851.

tivity and energy of the Principal, or the animation, readiness, tact, and uncommon precocity evinced by the boys." The report for 1854 claimed that the school had never been "in a more efficient or prosperous condition," with an average daily attendance of 50 pupils, accommodated in an enlarged schoolroom—for which the Commissioners went into debt for the sum of £52; only the library remained to be extended. Reports from the 1850s show that the number of pupils who attended fluctuated around 50 and that the curriculum remained the same.[230]

Roddick had taken on a herculean task in teaching single-handedly such a wide variety of subjects to an average of 50 pupils. Though some of his teaching, as we have seen, was based on explanation, with emphasis on practical application, for most of the time he unavoidably had to fall back on memorization methods. The boys learned much of geography, history, and even grammar by recitation from a textbook while other classes were silent.[231] "Principal Roddick was a disciple of the old school," wrote Barnes, "and reigned like a king over his pupils." To maintain "discipline" Roddick adopted "the greatest misery principle," and employed two of the least admirable weapons in a teacher's armoury—corporal punishment and sarcasm. He made free use of a whip,[232] even for the most trivial misdemeanours; for serious offences a boy would be whipped so severely that he would be absent from school for a week. His charges were subject, on the slightest provocation, to "a withering sarcasm," which they disliked more than corporal punishment. Pupils in mathematics who failed to give correct solutions after a demonstration of the principles were treated to "a dissertation on their mediocrity" rather than sympathy; boys who dared to ask questions in search of knowledge were often snubbed. Barnes summed up his methods as "cruel and harsh."[233]

---

230 *Herald*, 22 Dec. 1847; JHA 1855, Report of Commissioners of the Harbour Grace Grammar School (7 May 1855); JHA 1857, Annual Report of the Grammar School at Harbour Grace (3 Jan. 1857).

231 Barnes, *History*, "Principal Roddick," 6.

232 Possibly a tawse, a leather strap divided at the end into narrow strips, used frequently by Scottish teachers.

233 Barnes, *History*, "Principal Roddick," 6–7.

Roddick was, however, praised as "efficient" by his superiors.[234] This efficiency enabled the school to produce, during his tenure (he taught until 1876), a sufficient number of pupils qualified in the subjects required by the mercantile community. There was, for instance, a constant demand in the commercial offices of Harbour Grace, Carbonear, and St. John's for young men who could conduct correspondence in Spanish and act as interpreters on the many Spanish vessels which plied the fish trade between Newfoundland and Spanish ports. In the mid-1850s, half the pupils of Harbour Grace Grammar School were studying Spanish. Bookkeeping was also in demand, as were navigation, trigonometry, and geometry by those who wished to qualify for a captain's certificate.[235]

CARBONEAR GRAMMAR SCHOOL 1843–1866

Carbonear Grammar School, during its relatively short life, was enmeshed in a complex interplay of educational reform, denominational politics, and social change to a greater extent than almost any institution of its time. Born in a period of social and educational reform, it expired in an atmosphere of conservative reaction. During the years of its greatest success, however, the school pioneered an innovative and forward-looking type of teaching that was unequalled in the colony.

Although the act founding the school was passed in 1843, its origin went back to 1838, when the Committee of Supply in the House of Assembly, then dominated by the Liberal-Catholic Reformers, allocated £100, for three years, "towards supporting a Grammar School at Carbonear," naming as a board of directors Robert Pack, John Walsh, MD, William Bemister, and Felix McCarthy, members of the merchant-professional elite of the town.[236] The following year the Committee of Supply reappropriated the 1838 grant, added to it a further £100, and named a new board of commissioners: William Brown, Thomas Newel, James Power, John Elson, and John Walsh.

---

234 ASCD Coll. 057, Barnes papers, Minutes of the Harbour Grace Grammar School, 3 Jan. 1857.

235 Barnes, *History*, "Principal Roddick," 5, 6; JHA, Report of Harbour Grace Grammar School, 1856.

236 JHA 1838, 25 June 1838, Report of the Committee of Supply.

The course of instruction was to comprise Greek, Latin, English, bookkeeping, mathematics, and the 3Rs. The bill was printed and a copy attached as an addendum to the Select Committee on Newfoundland of 1841. An amount of £300 was allocated to establish the school, and the master's salary was set at £100 per annum, plus two-thirds of the fees. A clause excluded "the spiritual teacher of a congregation or a clergyman in holy orders" from becoming a teacher and forbade religious instruction and reading of books "having a tendency to teach any particular form of religion."[237] Later in 1839, the Assembly, in an Address to the Queen, stated that the council had rejected the bill.[238] The £400 allocated by the Committee of Supply in 1838 and 1839 remained unexpended.

Action on a grammar school for Carbonear was not taken for a further five years. Eventually, in February 1843, J.L. Prendergast, the Liberal-Catholic member for Conception Bay, playing the expected role of securing benefits for his constituents, introduced a bill in the Assembly for a grammar school in Carbonear. The act, when passed, granted £400 (the unexpended monies of 1838 and 1839) "towards purchasing, building, or leasing … and furnishing" a schoolroom, and for providing a library and astronomical, nautical, and mathematical instruments. The wording of the act concerning the remuneration of the teacher was not precise, and caused difficulties later. The master was to receive "independently of any amount of fees which he may receive by virtue of any provisions of this Act," a salary "not exceeding in the whole One Hundred and Fifty Pounds per Annum." The directors were given the power "to appropriate the … Fees to the purposes of this Act." Classics, mathematics, and navigation were to form the basis of the curriculum, with the seven commissioners given power to prescribe additional subjects. The clauses in the bill prohibiting religious orientation were dropped, but the commissioners were to approve of all books used, and the

---

237 JHA 1839, 6 June 1839, Report of the Committee of Supply; CO 194/11, 23 Apr. 1841, Select Committee on Newfoundland: Acts of the Legislature of Newfoundland.
238 House of Assembly, "Address to the Queen," *Patriot*, 19 Oct. 1839.

school remained interdenominational.[239] The board of commissioners consisted of Edmund Hanrahan, Robert Pack, James Power, John McCarthy, W.W. Bemister, George Forward, and Wright, of whom Hanrahan, Power, and McCarthy were identifiable as Catholics.

As soon as the act became law on May 1843, the directors convened a special meeting at which they resolved "to procure a Professor competent to teach Classics, Mathematics and Navigation." Alexander O'Donovan, an Irishman, was appointed; he arrived in Newfoundland in October 1843. As no school was then erected, a room was rented at £1 per month and O'Donovan began teaching 24 pupils. Fees for classics and French were set at £3 per annum, commercial subjects £2-10, and geography, English grammar, history, and writing £1-10. Tenders were then put out for a piece of land on which to build the school and a house for the master. A site in the centre of the town was secured for £100, which was underwritten by the legislature. A contractor, Robert Ayles, was engaged to construct "the exterior of a Grammar School House" for the sum of £400. The directors, however, estimated a sum of £300 would be necessary to complete the work.[240]

In the event, the legislature granted £200, which enabled a contractor to complete the school and a residence, except for two rooms. On 1 November 1845 O'Donovan and his family moved into the residence, and on the same day the school opened in the new schoolroom. Thirty pupils attended, of whom 23 were taking subjects with a commercial application—geometry, algebra, navigation, mensuration, and bookkeeping. In January 1846 Bertram Jones, the first inspector, visited the school, and found 30 pupils in attendance. Observing that an English-type grammar school with a classical curriculum was unsuitable for Newfoundland outports, he described the Carbonear School as "partaking more of the character of that which

---

239 6 Vic., cap. 8, An Act to Authorize the Governor to Appoint Commissioners for the Appropriation of Certain Monies Granted to Her Majesty for the Establishment of a Grammar School at Carbonear, and Remaining Unappropriated, and to Make Further Provision for the Support of the Said School (22 May 1843); *Gazette*, 4 July 1843.

240 JGA 1845, Report of the Board of Directors of the Carbonear Grammar School for the Year 1844.

in England is to be found in Commercial Schools." Jones considered O'Donovan to be "a very superior instructor," although he was hampered in his teaching by the difficulty or impossibility of obtaining sufficient books, maps, and other apparatus. Jones was not flattering O'Donovan. He had excellent qualifications; a graduate of Trinity College Dublin, he had been head of the English department at Belfast Seminary and a teacher of classics, French, and history at Carlow College.[241]

Three years after its opening, Carbonear Grammar School appeared to be thriving. In August 1848, however, several correspondents in the press drew attention to a set of circumstances which threatened the future of the school and O'Donovan's career as its master. The correspondents alleged that O'Donovan was withholding pupils' fees, and that in August 1848 the board had given him four months' notice to quit his post. O'Donovan stated that he would be willing to enter into a new arrangement. It was revealed, however, that Edmund Hanrahan had originally engaged the matter on the assumption that he could add fees to his salary.[242] O'Donovan retained his post, and the episode did not affect the progress of the school. By the beginning of 1851 the number of pupils on the roll had increased to a peak of 40; 11 were studying languages and 25 taking commercial subjects.[243]

O'Donovan was one of the few teachers of his time to give his teaching a theoretical basis. His pupils were encouraged to draw diagrams, solve problems, and answer questions on the previous day's lecture. English grammar was taught by parsing and analyzing sentences, augmented by frequent reference to appropriate texts. He also

---

241 JGA 1845, Report of the Board of Directors for the Carbonear Grammar School for the Year Ending 31 Dec. 1845; JGA 1846, Report upon the Inspection of Schools in Newfoundland by Bertram Jones, Esq; JGA 1845, Report of the Board of Directors of the Carbonear Grammar School for the Year 1845.

242 "Pacificator," letters to the editor, *Newfoundlander*, 10, 17 Aug. 1848; *Herald*, 17 Aug. 1848; R. Ayles, Secretary to the Board, letter to the editor, *Newfoundlander*, 7 Sept. 1848; "Mediator," letter to the editor, *Herald*, 20 Sept. 1848.

243 JHA 1851, Report of Alexander Donovan, Principal of the Grammar School, Carbonear, for the Year Ending Jan. 1, 1851.

gave a weekly lecture to 10 or 12 selected pupils on natural philosophy (i.e., science). By 1848 O'Donovan had acquired a large variety of English textbooks on all subjects. In a later report he regretted the lack of sufficient mathematical and mechanical instruments to enhance his teaching; these would have enabled him "to impress by ocular proof, generally more convincing than auricular on the minds of his pupils those truths of which, so circumstanced, he could only convey the theory."[244]

It became customary for the school to hold a public examination of the pupils in the spring and at Christmas each year, in which the master put the pupils through their paces in front of an audience of parents and guests. Reports show that O'Donovan used the occasions to elaborate on the theoretical underpinning of his teaching. In 1851 he began by propounding his view of education; he contended that it was a continuous process of successive small efforts and that the learner should proceed "step by step—link by link." Judicious attendance at lectures, plus questions and private study, would enable a pupil to develop powers of which he was unaware, and insensibly lead him to the acquirement of knowledge which, O'Donovan observed, "is often a cause of astonishment to himself."[245] His method of teaching arithmetic was to explain its principles in a manner that required reasoning by the pupil (rather than a reference to a rule) and applying previously learned principles. Geography lessons had a particular interest for him:

> In Geography, by not confining the pupils rigidly to the authors which they had studied; but by frequently varying the ordinary questions; by starting others, grammatical, historical or geographical, which may be suggested by the answers on these; by comparing the moral, political and social condition of the different countries on the globe; by judiciously

---

244 JHA 1848–49, Appendix, Report of Carbonear Grammar School (10 Feb. 1848); JHA 1851, Appendix, Report of Alexander O'Donovan, Principal of the Grammar School, Carbonear, for the Year Ending Jan. 1, 1851.

245 *Herald*, 30 Apr. 1851, spring examination, Carbonear Grammar School; *Newfoundlander*, 16 Jan. 1854, Christmas examination, Carbonear Grammar School.

> blending historical facts with those more properly belonging to Geography, the study has been rendered a pleasure not a toil, as would inevitably be the case, were the usual routine pursued of enumerating a catalogue of capitals, capes, islands, &c.

In history, pupils were taught to take "a concentrated view of the entire, and to acquire … an acquaintance with the morals and the minds of men, according to the ages in which they flourished, the circumstances under whose control they acted, and the external causes which gave rise to these circumstances."[246]

• • •

In 1852 O'Donovan became embroiled in another altercation, this time with the Catholic church. On 14 March 1852 Fr. John Dalton, in the pulpit of the Catholic chapel, read a letter from John Thomas Mullock, the Roman Catholic bishop, condemning the use of Pinnock's *History of England* and a Scotch *Reading Book* in the grammar schools of Carbonear and Harbour Grace. Dalton denounced the parents who allowed their children to read them and ordered the offending books to be removed from the schools, on the grounds that they were heretical and subversive of the Roman Catholic religion. To this piece of attempted clerical censorship O'Donovan replied in two letters to the *Weekly Herald*. In the first, he recalled that two years earlier, in a report of the school's public examination, he had criticized Pinnock's *History* for its occasional obscurity, inaccuracy, inappropriateness, and offensiveness, but he still considered that it was superior to any other book on the same subject. While a teacher in Catholic schools in Ireland he had untrammelled use of the book without objection by eminent Catholics. The question, he declared, resolved itself into "History or no History?" The "ayes" would be for history even with faults, he asserted with confidence, subject to the inspection and explanation of the teacher. In his second letter, O'Donovan expressed his amazement that he had aroused

246 *Herald*, 31 Dec. 1851, Christmas examination, Carbonear Grammar School; *Herald*, 3 Apr. 1850, spring examination, Carbonear Grammar School.

"the storm that burst upon [him] yesterday in the chapel of Carbonear from the lips of the Rev. Father John Dalton." He claimed that the priest had resorted to quoting isolated passages to condemn him, and he rebutted the charges that he had stated that the bishop was in error, or that as a teacher he was a corrupter of youth who possessed "ulterior motives." In the chapel he had been at a disadvantage, with no right of explanation or response. Nevertheless, he concluded, the study of history in his school would not be discontinued because a book "did not on every point agree with the ideas of his lordship."[247] O'Donovan's dignified and independent defence of his integrity was unprecedented in the Newfoundland of his day, when obedience by teachers to the clergy was almost universal.

O'Donovan continued to teach throughout the 1850s, but the strain on his health, not alleviated by an apparently insufficient salary, forced him to apply to the Assembly for an increase in salary at the end of the decade. Edmund Hanrahan, then the surveyor general in Philip Little's Liberal government, presented a petition on O'Donovan's behalf on 23 March 1858. Hanrahan stated that the principal had been existing—"he would not say living"—on a salary of £150 per year, "which was totally inadequate for the support of his position, and a very ill recompense for his services and ability." O'Donovan, he continued, was well known as a scholar and a gentleman; he had struggled on, but now had a large family. J. Hayward, the Liberal member for Harbour Grace, supported the petition; in his opinion O'Donovan, as a teacher, was "inferior to none in the whole island." E.D. Shea (Liberal, Ferryland) felt it was "the worst description of bad management" that O'Donovan should be allowed to exist upon such a pittance and hoped that his salary would be "respectably and liberally increased."[248] These statements suggest that after the 1848 dispute and O'Donovan's agreement with the directors, he did not receive any fees.

O'Donovan's position was not eased by developments in the political situation. At the beginning of the 1860s public affairs took a

---

247 *Herald*, 3 Apr. 1850, spring examination, Carbonear Grammar School; O'Donovan, letters to the editor, *Herald*, 17, 31 Mar. 1852.

248 JHA 1858, 23 Mar. 1858, Petition of O'Donovan; House of Assembly 23 Mar., *Courier*, 27 Mar. 1858.

dramatic turn to the right.[249] On 28 February Governor Bannerman, taking offence at critical remarks aimed at him by the leader of the Liberal government, John Kent, declared, "I must dispense with the services of yourself and your colleagues, and that you hold office only until a new government shall be formed …" Bannerman then ordered Hugh Hoyles, the Conservative leader, to form a government. When the Liberals won a vote of no-confidence against Hoyles, Bannerman dissolved the Assembly, an action praised, almost inevitably, by Bishop Feild. In the election that followed 14 Conservatives were returned without a contest, but Hoyles won a majority only by disenfranchising two districts, Harbour Grace and Harbour Main, in which destructive clashes had occurred. When the Assembly met in May 1861, an angry crowd of some 5,000 gathered outside the Colonial Building. Troops were called out, met by a volley of stones. Orders were given to open fire, and three people were killed and several injured, including a Catholic priest. Hoyles continued as head of government. Thus began five years of Conservative rule, notable for a series of authoritarian measures to counter disorder and assert conservative values, including a ban on mumming.[250] The whole situation was to have significant consequences for Carbonear Grammar School.

Evidence was accumulating that the school was beginning to decline. School reports for the early 1860s showed that attendance had slumped from 28 at the beginning of 1860 to 13 in December. O'Donovan attributed this to pupils leaving for business, for college, or to reside in Harbour Grace; many were withdrawn for work in the Labrador fishery. Though attendance improved to 21 in 1861, the following year it was 14. Moreover, the fabric of the building was deteriorating, as O'Donovan reported in 1861:

> The school-house is sadly in want of repairs. The rain pours literally in two cuts through the roof, wetting the floors and causing the ceiling to fall. A portion of the house (the best

249 The following paragraphs rely on E.C. Moulton, "Constitutional Crisis and Civil Strife in Newfoundland, February to November 1861," *Canadian Historical Review* 48, no. 3 (1967): 251–72.
250 Gunn, *Political History*, 157ff.; Noel, *Politics in Newfoundland*, 23ff.

> part of it) has never been finished, left unboarded and unceiled, and an entire floor (the garrett) 40' by 40' requires flooring. Two stoves are required …[251]

Whether the deterioration was due to the reasons adduced by O'Donovan or to his own failing powers (perhaps not helped by having to live on "a pittance") were moot points. O'Donovan struggled on, but the "genial and intelligent Irishman," as Tocque called him, died on 16 September 1864, leaving a widow and six children.[252]

Even before O'Donovan's decease there had been opposition to the school. The Methodists of the town, their confidence bolstered by increasing numbers and the establishment of the Methodist Academy in St. John's in 1858, felt strong enough to found their own academy in Carbonear in 1863. The Protestant inspector of schools described it as "what might be termed a Grammar School," with a highly competent teacher. It accommodated 20 pupils of "advanced age," who paid fees of £4 per annum. John Webb was appointed principal and prominent Methodist worthies served as directors. A year after the establishment of the academy, John Rorke, the MHA for Carbonear, increased the pressure by presenting a petition from the town's Methodists praying for the repeal of a section of the Grammar School Act and the appropriation of a portion of its endowment to support the Wesleyan Academy. He alleged that the grammar school had dwindled and was now virtually a failure, whereas the academy was in a prosperous condition.[253]

Rorke was born in Ireland in 1807; a Methodist in religion and a Conservative in politics, he had by the 1830s become a substantial merchant with interests in the Labrador trade. In 1863 he was elected as Conservative member for Carbonear, replacing the Liberal-Catholic Edmund Hanrahan, and was appointed to the board

251 JHA 1863, Return of Grammar School, Carbonear, 1860, 1861, 1862.
252 Tocque, *Kaleidoscopic Echoes*, 119; *Gazette*, 27 Sept. 1864.
253 JHA 1863, Report of the Protestant Inspector of Schools 1863, 38–39; B.V. Manning, "Education in Carbonear to 1875: A Historic and Religious Perspective" (MA thesis, Bishop's University, 1990), 110–11; House of Assembly 15 Feb., *Ledger*, 1 Mar. 1864.

of directors of the grammar school in 1848.[254] In many ways Rorke was symbolic of the rise of Methodism, both in the island generally and Carbonear in particular. The Methodists had doubled their numbers in the population from 14,000 in 1845 to 29,000 in 1857, or one-sixth of the population of the island; by 1857 there were 1,859 Methodists in Carbonear, making them virtually equal in numbers to the Catholic population; the Church of England counted a mere 895 adherents.[255]

It was clear that Rorke and the Methodists were staging an attack on the grammar school, and in 1865 and 1866 the battle was fought on the floor of the House of Assembly, with the Liberal-Catholics opposing the Methodist case.[256] The issues raised did not concern education per se, but had everything to do with denominational rights and privileges. Kent, with some exasperation, declared that he thought that the subject "had been definitely settled a quarter of a century ago." On 6 March 1865 both Kent and Rorke presented petitions to the Assembly. Kent's petition, from Roman Catholic inhabitants of Carbonear, prayed that a majority of Catholics should be appointed to the board of Carbonear Grammar School; Rorke urged that the grant for Carbonear Grammar School be divided, giving a proportion to the two Protestant denominations, plus an additional sum to enable them to provide an academic education for their youth. This was somewhat in advance of his previous position on the issue.

Kent's petition had been prompted by the action of Hoyles's government. Hoyles, whose view of the grammar school was exceedingly negative—he maintained that it had been a continual source of trouble to the government, that it was "of a most worthless character," and that any further expenditure on it would be "an abuse and waste of public money"—stated that on the death of O'Donovan the

---

254 *ENL*, s.v. "Rorke, John"; "Hon. John Rorke," in *Newfoundland Men*, by H.Y. Mott (Concord, 1864); *Courier*, 13 July 1848.

255 Abstract, Census and Return of the Population, &c., of Newfoundland, 1845, 1857.

256 Unless otherwise stated, the following paragraphs are based on House of Assembly 6 Mar., *Ledger*, 2, 5 May 1865; Assembly 8 Mar., *Ledger*, 9 May 1865.

government considered it a fitting opportunity to place the school under "proper management." A group of Roman Catholics had voted that the chairman resign, and appointed a new teacher. The government could not countenance this and, "in order to prevent similar occurrences," appointed two Protestants to fill vacancies on the board caused by the deaths of two members. He added that when the school was established there was a majority of Roman Catholics in the population of Carbonear, and consequently there was a majority of Catholics on the board; in Harbour Grace the board had a majority of Protestants, in keeping with the town's religious composition. But he emphasized that the government's appointment of the two Protestants to the Carbonear board was not made on that account but to prevent the board from any further "intermeddling" with the school until the matter was settled by the legislature. Hoyles repudiated the view held, for different reasons, by both Protestants (Rorke) and Catholics (notably Kent and Thomas Talbot) that the Carbonear Grammar School and the Harbour Grace Grammar School were by "tacit understanding" respectively Catholic and Protestant institutions; this notion did not appear on the record and therefore could not be considered. H. Renouf (a Liberal-Catholic) named the Protestant appointees as McNeill and Hawker, and the teacher appointed by the Catholics as Laurence Mackey, a former pupil of O'Donovan. He was replaced by John Webb, who was the first principal of the Methodist Academy.

Ambrose Shea, the veteran Liberal reformer, condemned Rorke for reviving sectarian animosities and Hoyles for claiming that Protestants had a majority in Carbonear, which, he declared, was not justified by figures in the last census. (In fact the census of 1857 showed that the Protestants outnumbered the Catholics by 69, hardly an overwhelming majority.)[257] John Bemister, a Methodist, made the case that, in the previous 20 or 30 years, Protestant numbers in Carbonear had increased considerably while Catholic numbers had decreased, so it was "quite right" that the former should have a majority on the Carbonear board; the division of the grant, he added,

257 Abstract, Census and Return of the Population, &c., of Newfoundland, 1857.

would put an end to the difficulty. The arguments of both sides were repeated heatedly before Hoyles concluded the debate by denying that the Carbonear school should be under the control of the Catholics, and reiterating that the best solution was the division of the education grant.

There the matter rested until the first legislative session of the following year. At the end of 1865 the Hoyles government had been succeeded by the Conservative administration of Frederick Carter, with Kent and Shea as co-opted members. Once again the affairs of Carbonear Grammar School were on the table.[258] On 5 March 1866, Thomas Talbot, the Liberal-Catholic member for St. John's West, presented a petition from Mackey seeking payment of his salary as principal of the grammar school from January 1865. The government, stated Talbot, had disallowed Mackey's appointment and refused to pay his salary, although he continued to conduct the school and had brought it to "an admirable condition," with increased enrolment. According to Carter, however, Mackey had been appointed when the chairman of the board, Captain Pike, had been absent, so the government had repudiated the procedure as irregular. Renouf denied this, stating that Pike had resigned, McCarthy had been elected chairman, and Mackey had been appointed without dissent, four members being present.

John Bemister, now the Colonial Secretary, reminded members that, before O'Donovan died, the government, following complaints from the populace, had appointed a Commission of Inquiry to examine the state of the school, but that the attitude of the directors was entirely at variance with its contents. The details are obscure, but apparently the commission's report was not implemented. Kent took the view that the board's attitude to the commission laid the foundation for the appointment of the two Protestants to the board, a situation which had ignited the whole controversy. But Kent, now a member of the Carter government, modified his previous views and argued that the best solution to the problem was the division of the grant for the school between Catholics and Protestants. Carter

258 The following paragraphs are based on House of Assembly 5, 20 Mar., 22 Apr., *Express*, 12, 23 Mar., 8 May 1865.

concluded that the best course would be the introduction of a separate bill.

Five days later Rorke did what the Methodists and the Conservatives had been threatening to do all along—he introduced a bill for the repeal of the Carbonear Grammar School Act.[259] He justified it on the grounds that its necessity would be known to members, and that the government had proposed "reasonable and highly satisfactory terms," which would meet the views of members opposite, and would be productive of much advantage to the youth of his district. Carter stated that the government had increased the appropriation to the school from £200 to £300, to be divided between Catholics and Protestants according to population; he thought the school itself might be converted into a courthouse and lockup. The bill was accepted by both Protestant and Catholic members. Little that was new was heard at the committee stage of the bill, though Carter added an additional sum of £70, to be disposed of by a committee for the construction of a courthouse and lockup. Rorke made an eloquent plea for a lockup to meet the need to incarcerate prisoners. The bill was read a third time and passed and then passed by the council without a debate.

The act repealed the act of 1843 and apportioned $1,200 equally each year between the Protestant and Catholic communities of Carbonear according to population, for the support of their schools. Commissioners were to be appointed to manage such schools and prescribe their rules and regulations. The building reverted to the government, "to be appropriated to such public purposes as the Governor in Council shall determine."[260] Thus an experiment in interdenominational education was ended, to be replaced by two denominational institutions.

The question remains—why did the Harbour Grace Grammar School continue to flourish, whereas its counterpart in Carbonear came to an end after 23 years? Part of the answer lies in the difference between the two masters. O'Donovan was an advanced education-

---

259 The following paragraphs are based on House of Assembly 25, 27, 28 Apr., *Express*, 9, 11 May 1866.

260 29 Vic., cap. 17, An Act to Repeal the Carbonear Grammar School Act, and for Other Purposes (1 May 1866).

ist who believed in encouraging his pupils' potential. Furthermore, he possessed an independent spirit, which led him to challenge the school's board on the question of fees and to stand up to priests of his own religion when he felt that his integrity as a teacher was challenged by church intervention. Roddick, on the other hand, acquiesced to the Catholic church's position on school books, displayed a minimal amount of educational theory, and generally kept his pupils under a harsh disciplinary regime, reinforced by verbal and physical abuse. Classed by his superiors as "efficient," Roddick delivered a curriculum suitable to a mercantile milieu. Furthermore, Harbour Grace Grammar School had the backing of the two leading merchants of the town, John Munn and Thomas Ridley. Their wealth and enterprise as merchants, socio-political dominance, and determination to maintain a school advantageous to the merchant elite were essential to the prosperity of the town's grammar school, and found no counterpart in the neighbouring community.

The overriding factor in the demise of the school was the change in the religious and political climates. Following the 1843 Education Act, and the machinations of Bishop Feild, denominationalism in education had spread rapidly, notably in the tripartite division of St. John's Academy; furthermore, the upsurge of Methodism culminated in the establishment of Methodist academies in St. John's and Carbonear. Politically, the advent of Hoyles's Conservative government in 1860, and its unprecedented hostility to Carbonear Grammar School, and the failure of the Liberals to provide resolute opposition to the government's determined attack on the school, created an atmosphere inimical to the existence of an independent progressive educational institution. In the event the Methodists, under the leadership of Rorke, joined forces with Hoyles's and Carter's Conservatives to legislate Carbonear Grammar School out of existence.

CHAPTER 6
The Amateur Theatre

> The Stage is one great source of public amusement, not to say instruction. A good play, well acted, passes away a whole evening delightfully at a certain period of life, agreeably at all times; we read the account of it next morning with pleasure, and it generally furnishes one leading topic of conversation for the afternoon. The disputes on the merits or defects of the last new piece, or of a favourite performer, are as common, as frequently renewed, and carried on with as much eagerness and skill, as those on almost any other subject … plays … are "the brief chronicles of the time," the epitome of human life and manners. While we are talking about them, we are thinking about ourselves. They "hold the mirror up to Nature"; and our thoughts are turned to the Stage as naturally and as fondly as a fine lady turns to contemplate her face in the glass. It is a glass, too, in which the wise may see themselves; but in which the vain and superficial see their own virtues, and laugh at the follies of others.
>
> —William Hazlitt, *A View of the English Stage* (1808)

THE GEORGIAN THEATRE AND ARMY AND NAVY THEATRICALS

"The most brilliant period that the stage in our land has yet experienced," wrote one historian of the Georgian theatre. Extending from the mid-18th century to the 1830s, it was the age of Peg Woffington, Sarah Siddons, David Garrick, Edmund Kean, the Kemble family, and a host of other celebrated actors.[261] These thespians flourished in an era of hedonism and display. For the middle and upper ranks the stage was a metaphor for the theatricality of late Georgian so-

261 W.S. Scott, *The Georgian Theatre* (London, 1946), 4, 25.

ciety, a world where performance, display, and spectatorship were essential components of the functioning of the social mechanism. The elite of society flocked to see, and be seen at, productions in the theatre, at Vauxhall and Ranelagh pleasure gardens, coronations, processions, military displays, and sporting spectacles.[262]

The reign of the four Georges, from 1714 to 1830, was also an age of paradox. The later Georgian period saw the beginnings of the Industrial Revolution, the rise of a factory proletariat, the disruption of the old agricultural economy, poverty and unemployment, widespread civil unrest, and repression of working-class political activity by a ruling class fearful of the spread of the ideas of the French Revolution.

The economic and social turbulence of the Midlands and the North did not, however, affect the London theatrical scene, which was dominated by two large theatres, Covent Garden and Drury Lane, each having an audience capacity of over 3,000. Under the Licensing Act of 1737 they had been given the appellation of patent theatres as the sole legal sites of drama and comedy, and for many years, as Jane Moody points out, they stood unchallenged as England's national theatres, "the cultural Parliament of the nation," with a repertoire that embraced Shakespeare, Goldsmith, Sheridan, and popular dramatists of the day. Toward the end of the 18th century, the growth of working-class and artisan districts outside the bounds of Westminster and the patent theatres, were fertile grounds for the rise of so-called minor theatres, which, debarred from presenting "legitimate" drama, put on illegitimate productions—extravaganza, burlettas, and melodrama. Minor theatres such as the Coburg (popularly known as "the Blood Tub" because of its many gory productions), the Surrey, and Sadler's Wells offered cheaper seats which attracted plebeian audiences of shopkeepers, artisans,

---

262 G. Russell, *The Theatres of War: Performance, Politics and Society, 1793–1815* (Oxford, 1995), 7, 22; G. Rudé, *Hanoverian London, 1714–1808* (Stroud, 2003), 64ff.

apprentices, and all ranks of seamen.[263]

The Georgian theatre as a whole worked under severe restrictions. The censorship or banning of plays by the Lord Chamberlain, which had been in operation since 1737, was aimed at suppressing political or socially subversive content, and resulted in few controversial or important subjects reaching the stage. "[F]or every *School for Scandal*," writes a historian of the period, "hundreds of musical burlesques and sentimental comedies were staged that made no demands on the facial muscles whatsoever." Shakespeare's plays were produced, but bowdlerized by Garrick.[264]

The theatre of the late Georgian period operated in a wartime setting. The Revolutionary and Napoleonic wars (1792–1815) were the backdrop to the rounds of pleasure. As a result, army and navy personnel became a familiar feature of the social landscape, and acquired a prominent position in society. This was strengthened by one of the lesser-known characteristics of army and navy personnel—their addiction to theatricals; all ranks were caught up in the surge of enthusiasm for amateur theatre which swept polite society in the late 18th and early 19th centuries. The social elite were increasingly withdrawing from attendance at the patent theatres (where they suffered the gaze of plebeian members of the audience and interruptions from the gallery) and devoting themselves to private theatricals at their country seats. Jane Austen, in *Mansfield Park*, gives an amusing but probably authentic account of young people of the gentry class rehearsing Kotzebue's *Lovers' Vows*. Thespian activity in the army was mainly the province of the officer class in fashionable regiments, particularly the Brigade of Guards, which were officered by the higher echelons of society, members of which would have had experience of theatricals in the family, in academies or at public schools. Acting thus offered the officer class an entry to

---

263 J. Donohue, introduction to *The Cambridge History of British Theatre*, Vol. 2, ed. Donohue (Cambridge, 2004), 222–28; J. Moody, "The Theatrical Revolution, 1776–1843," in *British Theatre*, 199–205; M. Slater, *Douglas Jerrold 1803–1857* (London, 2002), 37–40; J. White, *London in the Eighteenth Century* (London, 2012), 302ff.

264 V. Gattrell, *City of Laughter: Sex and Satire in Eighteenth-Century London* (New York, 2006), 62–63; Scott, *Georgian Theatre*, 14.

public society, with all the consequent advantages.[265]

Amateur theatricals also flourished in the navy. The difference between the amateur theatricals of the army and navy reflected the different roles of the two services. The navy was seen as the defender of British imperial and commercial interests and a bulwark of the island's security; it was "a closely knit and complex fighting unit with its own rituals language and costume," a wooden world of which civilians knew little.[266] A ship provided a meaningful venue for amateur theatricals. The first recorded performance of *Hamlet* took place on the East India ship *Red Dragon* off Sierra Leone in 1607. The dramatist Douglas Jerrold, author of *The Mutiny at the Nore* and the enormously popular naval drama *Black-Eyed Susan*, had served in Nelson's navy in his youth. As a "Volunteer Class 1" in the *Namur*, captained by Jane Austen's brother Charles, Jerrold took part in amateur theatricals, acting in *Macbeth* and a play called *The Iron Chest*.[267]

When ashore, sailors found attendance at the theatre was the most accessible form of entertainment after the public house, and they made the gallery largely their preserve, from which they made their presence felt, often against the effusions of patriotic officers. Service actors put on plays in theatres hired for the occasion. The hierarchy of box, pit, and gallery of the Georgian theatre was accepted, along with the adoption of a prologue and the production of playbills. One of the most important purposes of service theatricals was the support of charitable causes. The donation of profits to the poor enhanced the worth of the army and navy in society and deflected criticism from the church and others opposed to the theatre. Charity also linked the services to local philanthropy, a significant force in Georgian society. In this way charity was not only done but was seen to be done.[268] On 24 November 1800, the *Portsmouth Telegraph* reported:

---

265 Russell, *Theatres of War*, 122–25, 133–35; Jane Austen, *Mansfield Park* (Folio Books 1984), 103ff.; Moody, "Theatrical Revolution," 212.

266 Russell, *Theatres of War*, 139.

267 J. Armstrong, *The Arden Shakespeare Miscellany* (London, 2011), 41; Slater, *Douglas Jerrold*, 23–25.

268 Russell, *Theatres of War*, 98, 110, 136–38, 159–60, 163.

> On Tuesday the two favourite pieces of *Bon Ton* and *High Life Below Stairs* were performed by the Officers of the Somerset Militia, for the laudable purpose of applying the receipts of the House to relieve the distressed Poor of that Place.

In a similar vein the *Hampshire Telegraph*, in February 1805, announced that "the Charity Play by the Military Officers at Chichester, will take place on Tuesday next …" Military theatricals, consequent upon the roles of the services in Britain's wars, had a global dimension, played wherever in the Empire the army or navy was posted or engaged. Soldiers and sailors took comedy and drama to the West Indies, North America, India, the Iberian peninsula, South Africa, and Australia. This export of culture, Russell argues, reinforced British colonial control, in the form of soft power which strengthened the sinews of Empire.[269]

An account of the Amateur Theatre in St. John's shows that the institution was not an isolated phenomenon but part of a long tradition of army and navy theatricals enacted by officers and men throughout the Empire. The St. John's theatre had all the main features of service theatricals elsewhere—amateur talent, much the same repertoire of plays, and service in the cause of charity. But the St. John's theatricals were almost certainly the most well-established and long-lasting of them all, and were another important channel by which the island was brought within the orbit of British imperial culture.

THE AMATEUR THEATRE

On 18 March 1817, Mr. Wakeham of HMS *Pike*, a member of the naval squadron stationed in St. John's, stepped on to the stage of the newly founded Amateur Theatre to deliver an address of welcome to the "crowded and respectable" audience, the first part of which began:

> Now when stern winter bids the Tempest rave,

269 Russell, *Theatres of War*, 133, 136, 158–59.

And binds in frozen chains the torpid wave;
While crystal masses o'er the Ocean glide,
And isolate us from the world beside,
In this lone spot we would your smiles engage …

The second part, addressed "To the Ladies," ended with the lines:

We here to night, the mimic Scene prepare,
And if our humble Efforts may succeed,
This cause to aid we'll think our brightest meed,
Or should they fail, our only hope will be
To see our faults conceal'd by gentle CHARITY.

Wakeham was introducing the first production of the theatre, *The Fair Penitent*, "a celebrated tragedy" by Nicholas Rowe. The venue was a store lately occupied by the merchant W.B. Rowe, with tickets at 5 shillings.[270] The organizers of the first production were three members of the Society for Improving the Condition of the Poor, William Thomas, Thomas Williams, and James Blaikie, and the patrons were "the Worshipful the Magistrates."[271] Three weeks later a second play was produced—"the much-admired Melo-Drama" *Point of Honor*, followed by a farce entitled *Bon-Ton: Or High Life above Stairs*, repeated on the following evening. The *Gazette* noted that "a considerable sum of money has been raised … for the distressed objects of the Town—the community has been highly gratified and amused, and the Gentlemen who were the actors have given scope to their talents …" Unfortunately, not six months after the opening of the theatre a devastating fire swept St. John's and there were no performances during 1818.[272]

Following the rebuilding of the city after the fire, performances at the theatre recommenced in 1819. The governor, Sir Charles Hamilton, was now the Patron, and performances were scheduled to begin "precisely at ½ past Six"; the venue presumably was the

270 *Gazette*, 14, 25 Mar. 1817.
271 P. O'Neill, *The Oldest City: The Story of St. John's, Newfoundland* (Portugal Cove-St. Philip's, 2003), 178; *Mercantile Journal*, 4 Apr. 1817.
272 *Gazette*, 1, 18 Apr. 1817; O'Neill, *Oldest City*, 178.

renovated Rowe's store, but the theatre now boasted a gallery.[273] The early days of the theatre were described by a naval officer, Captain William Glascock, stationed in St. John's during 1818–1819:

> the expenses ... including decorations, scenery, stoves, property, puffing, wigs, wardrobe, lights, scene-shifters, theatrical-tailors, and midshipmen's, milliners, were entirely defrayed out of the profits of the first month's performances.

He noted, however, that the profits were diminished by the extravagant charges made by the town's shopkeepers and tradesmen. The live-wire of the company was the deputy stage manager, a former marine, whose many duties included deputizing for absent actors, issuing stage directions (in the language of the lower deck), and instructing his charges to recite their lines with great rapidity, with some tolerance of ad-libbing and improvisation. Soldiers of the garrison and sailors of the squadron were allowed free admission to the dress rehearsals, with the predictable result that ribald commentaries greeted the appearance of the officers disguised as women when recognized by the men.[274]

The opening performance of the 1819 season was heralded by an announcement in the *Mercantile Journal* of a sale of tickets at the House of Messrs. Perkins and Winter. The first play was "the much admired comedy," George Colman the Younger's *John Bull; Or the Englishman's Fireside*, followed by "the Popular Farce" *A Miss in Her Teens*.[275] At the performance of the latter piece an incident occurred, typical of the period when interventions and noisy interruptions by the audience were considered part of the theatre-going experience. The most extreme example had occurred in London in 1808 on the opening of Convent Garden after rebuilding; playgoers objected to the rise in prices and demonstrated inside and outside the theatre

273 *Mercantile Journal*, 18 Feb. 1819.
274 Captain W.N. Glascock, *Naval Sketch Book* (London, 1826), 2:158–61, 163–65.
275 *Mercantile Journal*, 4, 18 Feb. 1819.

for 67 consecutive nights.[276] Nothing like these "Old Price Riots" happened in St. John's, but halfway through *A Miss in Her Teens* a member of the audience rose in his seat and loudly denounced the acting of a Mr. Marcus, following this up by leaping onto the stage and dealing the actor several "knockdown blows." Marcus was defended by a correspondent in the *Mercantile Journal* who deplored the insult to the actor when he was "gratuitously exerting his best efforts." The incident caused ripples among the citizens of the town; a young merchant, George Niven, was led to deny that he was the culprit, naming as the perpetrator one A.Z., who had been "kicked out of the theatre," and who fought a duel the same night with, it was speculated, Mr. Marcus.[277]

Despite, or perhaps because of, this incident, the 1819 season proceeded successfully. *The Poor Gentleman*, a comedy (with "new music, scenery and decorations"), was succeeded by Goldsmith's *She Stoops to Conquer*. John Tobin's comedy *Honey-Moon* ran for two nights and realized receipts of £48, which was immediately handed over to the secretary of the Society for Improving the Condition of the Poor. In the early summer of 1819 the well-known stock-piece Thomas Morton's *Speed the Plough* was offered twice, followed by a performance of *The Rivals* and a revival of *John Bull*, each followed by a short farce.[278] From the point of view of theatrical quality, the 1819 season was a success, and must have made heavy demands on the management, staff, and performers.

In 1822, after two further seasons of well-known comedies and tragedies—to the acclaim of the press—the directors improved the appearance of the auditorium: the front of the theatre had been newly decorated with "Characteristic Devices," so as to give the stage "a very pleasing effect"; this was done to showcase an old favourite, *John Bull*. The quality of the next offerings was quite high—two per-

---

276 M. Baer, *Theatre and Disorder in Late Georgian London* (Oxford, 1992), 135.

277 "B," letter to the editor, *Mercantile Journal*, 25 Feb. 1819; George Niven, letter to the editor, 3 Mar. 1819; "Crito," letter to the editor, 11 Mar. 1819; "Lucius O'Trigger," letter to the editor, 25 Mar. 1819; O'Neill, *Oldest City*, 180.

278 *Mercantile Journal*, 25 Feb., 11, 19 Mar.; 1, 8, 15 Apr.; 13, 20 May; 2 June 1819.

formances of *The Merchant of Venice*, a production of John Home's tragedy *Douglas*, preceded by a comedy, *A Cure for Heart Ache*.[279]

At the end of the 1822 season it was, however, becoming evident that the existing building was inadequate for the type of plays presented and the audience they attracted. On 7 October 1822 Newman Hoyles, in his capacity as chairman of the theatre committee, wrote to Governor Hamilton requesting the grant of a piece of land for a new theatre, stressing that it would be for the benefit of the poor. Hamilton promptly agreed to grant a plot at the corner of Duckworth Street and Queen's Road and advanced a loan of £50. H.P. Thomas then issued a notice for contracts to build a theatre 56 feet long and 41 feet wide.[280]

The foundation stone of a new theatre was laid on 8 November 1822, preceded by a procession of the officials of two masonic lodges, carrying a mallet, a sword, a vase, goblets, square, compasses, and other masonic paraphernalia, accompanied by constables, magistrates, members of the theatrical committee, and a guard of the military. Officials assembled on a platform, the military band played some national airs, and the treasurer deposited beneath the foundation stone a flask containing a scroll commemorating the event.[281] The proceedings, in almost every detail, were similar to the laying of the foundation stone of the new Convent Garden theatre in London in 1808. The new structure, which cost £300 to build, was a rectangular saltbox with four windows, and equipped with a gallery and boxes. A visitor further described it as "a small timber and shingled building, not 30' high—it is used occasionally during the winter season, but never in the summer ..." The future of the Amateur Theatre was now secure; it had a purpose-built home and government and civic support. A new season opened on 17 February 1823 with a performance of Matthew Lewis's *The Castle Spectre*, for which the theatre had been furnished with "Entire New and Appropriate Music, Scenery, Dress and Decorations"; nevertheless,

---

279 *Mercantile Journal*, 8, 22 Mar. 1821; 7, 14, 28 Feb., 28 Mar., 11 Apr. 1822.
280 The Rooms Provincial Archives Division, GN 2/2, Hoyles to Hamilton, 7 Oct. 1822, and GN 2/1, Proclamation of Governor Hamilton, 10 Oct. 1822; O'Neill, *Oldest City*, 183; *Mercantile Journal*, 24 Oct. 1822.
281 *Mercantile Journal*, 14 Nov. 1822.

during performances, hot wax from the chandelier often dripped on the heads of those in the audience sitting beneath it.[282]

The extant playbills of the productions of the first six years of the theatre's existence show that the plays were of a popular rather than a challenging nature. The majority were comedies, plus a few melodramas and two or three productions that could be described as dramas, including Shakespeare's *The Merchant of Venice*. Samples of the offerings for the remainder of the 1820s show a similar pattern: melodrama—*Rob Roy*, *Guy Mannering*; comedy—Cumberland's *West Indian*, Colman's *John Bull*—and undemanding fare in the manner of *A Cure for the Heart-Ache, The Way to Get Married*, and *Love à la Mode*.[283] The reason for these offerings was not far to seek—from the beginning the productions of the Amateur Theatre fed upon the London stage; all the presentations were those which had enjoyed successful runs in the various theatres of the capital. The Amateurs, in fact, based their productions on playbooks such as *The London Edition of Plays*, several numbers of the *English Theatre*, and an edition of *Plays* containing the current London successes.[284] The result was a diet of what today we would call middle-brow entertainment, not inferior to that playing in London. The Amateurs, in fact, were aiming high in reproducing in St. John's what theatre-goers in London took for granted.

The theatre was seen by the populace as an enjoyable evening's entertainment and often an occasion for audience participation. In February 1824 the management had to issue a warning:

> That any persons found annoying the audience, or the performers, by cheering, calling out names, or in any way interrupting peace and good order, will occasion the performance for the evening to stop.

This was accompanied by a prohibition that "no calls on the Band

282 O'Neill, *Oldest City*, 184; ASCD MF89, letter of Phoenix Fire Co., 8 Nov. 1845; *Mercantile Journal*, 13 Feb. 1823.
283 *Mercantile Journal*, 10 Apr. 1823; 5 Feb., 4 Mar. 1824; 23 Feb. 1826; 18 Jan., 5 Apr., 27 Feb. 1828; 4 Mar. 1830.
284 *Mercantile Journal*, 1 Mar. 1827.

for particular tunes will be attended to."[285] But the management also lost few opportunities to remind the patrons of the underlying charitable purpose of the theatre—the first performance of the 1823 season had been preceded by an address, 40 lines long, written by the Rev. Blackman and delivered by Mr. Harvey, which began:

> Friends of the Cause, which Charity sustains
> To soothe pale Hunger and Afflictions pains!
> I come to bid you welcome to a stage—
> The pride and credit of a generous age.

It ended with a plea for "the cause which gives the poor RELIEF." The evening concluded with several popular songs, one of which, composed and sung by Mr. Hogsett, extolled the virtues of charity. Stressing the necessity of charity was no doubt occasioned by the severe economic crisis in the fishery of the early 1820s. The theatre had established a Charity Committee which operated in much the same way as that of the Benevolent Irish Society. The five-member committee—Francis Forbes, John Boyd, William Thomas, C. Acherly, and James Clift—was authorized to distribute the profits of the theatre's productions to the poor, and the Amateurs were requested to supply the names of deserving persons, who received bread, fish, and molasses on a weekly basis. During the first quarter of 1824, £105 was expended in this way.[286]

The theatre contrived to present the usual number of plays throughout the 1830s. There was, however, a noticeable tendency for the management to put on items thought to have a more popular appeal—melodramas, comedies, "laughable after-pieces," and repeat performances—*The Castle Spectre* appeared at least half a dozen times.[287] But did this satisfy the playgoers of the period? Toward the end of the 1830s, there is some evidence that audience enthusiasm for plays acted by amateur gentlemen, male and female parts alike, was cooling. In January 1837 a correspondent wrote to

285 *Mercantile Journal*, 5 Feb. 1824.
286 *Mercantile Journal*, 29 Mar. 1821, 20 Feb. 1823, 27 May 1824.
287 *Ledger*, 1830–1839.

the *Times* urging "amateur gentlemen" to get up a play or two, presumably to fill a gap in production. In the same year the *Times* had urged respectable inhabitants to look more favourably on the theatre, and a correspondent later requested them not to hold balls and routs on the evening of a performance.[288]

Whatever the case, in 1841 the management decided on a radical revision of policy—they broke with tradition and invited professional touring companies to perform in the theatre. This led to changes in its whole orientation. Whereas the staple formula had been a full-length play accompanied by a short piece, acted entirely by men, the professional companies introduced female actors to the stage and included in the program songs, dances, monologues, and impressions—in effect, an added concert. This resulted in concerts in their own right becoming a popular form of entertainment in the capital.

• • •

The turning point in the character of the Amateur Theatre can be dated to August 1841 with the arrival, for an extended tour, of a group of professional players known as the Davenport family. Thomas Davenport, a former Edinburgh lawyer, had taken his family troupe across Britain and North America, with his daughter Jean, a 12-year-old child prodigy, in the starring role. The family was granted the use of the Amateur Theatre, with appropriate compensation being made to charity. The Davenport family stayed in Newfoundland for over a month, during which Miss Davenport fulfilled a hectic program, and received more publicity than any other performer of the century. She made her debut on 2 August in the title role of Shakespeare's *Richard III*, "as acted by her in London, Edinburgh, Dublin, New York, Boston, &c." This was followed by a piece entitled *The Manager's Daughter*, in which she took seven parts, including American, Scottish, Irish, and French characters, interspersed with singing and dancing. Her Richard III was declared "critically true to nature" and the applause was "loud and long." She

288 "A Theatrical Admirer," letters to the editor, *Times*, 25 Jan., 29 Mar. 1837; "Foster," letter to the editor, 14 Feb. 1838.

repeated this to an overflow audience two days later, followed with a reading of Shylock from *The Merchant of Venice*, plus "a laughable piece" *Actress of All Work*, with songs and dances, including "one of the most popular dances of Europe"—the Cachoucha.[289]

From Miss Davenport's arrival to her farewell performance, the theatre management and the St. John's press (with one exception) indulged in what can only be described as Davenport mania, an enthusiasm which also communicated itself to the audiences. A guinea was offered for a seat at some of her performances, and her portrayal of Shylock was greeted "with such cheers as have never before been heard in our Theatre." She was described as an actress who "seems to set all juvenile competition at an immense distance"; the first juvenile actress of the day, capable of "astonishing performance ... beyond belief" and similar expressions of acclaim. A lengthy valedictory poem printed in the *Times* and *Ledger* began:

> Fair child of genius! If, to say "farewell!"
> Alone, might disentwine the magic spell
> Which thou hast woven with mysterious art,
> Thro' charmed eyes, and ears, around the heart ...[290]

Did she deserve such unrestrained adulation? The editor of the *Patriot* R.J. Parsons, an unconventional Liberal and ardent Newfoundland patriot, did not think so. Following a critical letter from one "Scipio," the paper argued that the press had given too high an estimate by far of the dramatic talents of the young lady (which allegedly exceeded those of Edmund Kean, Mrs. Siddons, and the dancer Taglioni) and exaggerated the public reaction. The portrayal of Richard III by a 12-year-old, the paper maintained, could not have reached the standard in the commonest English provincial theatre. Admittedly "she is very clever, but nothing more," and was competent, but not above mediocrity, in masculine impersonation. This not unreasonable criticism brought forth an expostulation from the *Public Ledger*, which printed an indignant letter from Thomas

289 *Ledger*, 30 July, 3, 6 Aug. 1841; *Patriot*, 28 July 1841.
290 *Ledger*, 6 Aug., 30 July, 14 Sept., 29 Oct. 1841; *Express*, 29 July 1841.

Davenport condemning the "unmanly and insidious attack" on his daughter, and the "moral turpitude" of its author who, Davenport alleged, had never seen her perform. The *Patriot* defended itself in acrimonious terms.[291] The Davenports, however, extended their stay in St. John's. Miss Davenport starred in *Rob Roy* and also in "the Romantic and Historical Play" *Wallace*, and gave two benefit concerts, one for herself and the other for her mother. In the former she acted a "monopologue," comprising a history of her life and public career;[292] in the latter she played the breeches role of Sir Peter Teazle in Sheridan's *The School for Scandal*. In early September she concluded her stay with a portrayal of Richard III for two nights at the Court House, Harbour Grace.[293]

In November 1841, shortly after the Davenports' departure, a professional troupe from Halifax under the management of H.W. Preston took over what then became known as St. John's Theatre. The ground for actresses having been broken by Jean Davenport, the company included four females—Mrs. Preston, Mrs. Chapman, Mrs. Wilson, and Miss Hildreth, plus four men—a company "selected with care from the principal Theatres on this and the other side of the Atlantic." Preston was determined to improve both the amenities and attractions of the theatre and to raise the quality of the drama. He informed the public (via a correspondent in the *Ledger*) that the stage was to be "handsomely carpeted" and "fashionably furnished" and the scenery repainted. More importantly, the cast was to be reinforced with the addition of "Ladies and Gentlemen of the highest theatric talent," in order to encourage the establishment of "pure dramatic taste" in the town. These improvements would, it was hoped, enable the theatre to be "as well adapted for dramatic presentations as any to be found in British America."[294]

Did Preston and his company succeed in establishing "pure dramatic taste" in St. John's? Between the end of 1841 and shortly be-

291 *Patriot*, 18, 25 Aug. 1841; *Ledger*, 20 Aug. 1841.

292 *Ledger*, 10 Sept. 1841. Monopolologue (properly monopolylogue): "An entertainment in which a single performer sustains many characters" (*NSOED*).

293 *Ledger*, 14, 21 Sept. 1841.

294 *Ledger*, 9, 23 Nov. 1841; "Theatricus," letter to the editor, 11 Feb. 1842.

fore the Great Fire of June 1846 they certainly presented a repertoire of high-quality dramatic works: Bulwer-Lytton's *The Lady of Lyons*, Dion Boucicault's *London Assurance*, *Macbeth* (twice), *Hamlet*, *Richard III*, plus a clutch of "sensationalist" melodramas, mainly for the actors' benefit nights.[295] (The actors were not paid a salary but given a benefit night during the season and were allowed to pocket the proceeds.)

The Great Fire devastated all of downtown St. John's, including the Amateur Theatre. It could not, however, kill the desire of its citizens for theatrical entertainment, possibly stimulated by Preston's efforts. Out of the ashes of the conflagration arose another amateur theatre. Known as the Garrison Theatre, it was located in the British Hall on Prescott Street, and the actors were a company of officers and men of the Royal Newfoundland Corps, who carried on the tradition of the former Amateur Theatre, and donated the proceeds to charity. During the early 1850s they put on a varied programme of current popular pieces: *Don Caesar de Bazan* ("successfully produced on the English and Irish boards"), Payne's *Charles II or The Merry Monarch*, Gore's *King O'Neill*, Lover's *Rory O'More*, and many others.[296]

The theatre's clientele was largely defined by the price of tickets. By 1822 these had settled at 2 shillings for the pit and 3 shillings for the boxes. In 1841 they were increased to 2 shillings and sixpence and 5 shillings respectively, but reduced two years later, by popular demand, to 2 shillings and 3 shillings and ninepence.[297] These prices were high enough to exclude poorer fishers and labourers. Neither was the theatre patronized by the elite. In the words of Captain Bonnycastle in 1842, "the taste for this amusement is not great among the wealthy classes, who do not mingle very frequently in public." Glascock observed that the theatre-going fraternity mainly consisted of "the middle orders." These citizens, Bonnycastle noted, were respectable and well dressed; each man wore "a blue jacket and trousers, of good cloth, and a low-crowned glazed hat." The pit of

---

295 *Ledger*, playbills 1841–1845.

296 *Express, Newfoundlander, Courier, Ledger*, playbills 1854–1855.

297 *Ledger*, 30 July 1841, 24 Nov. 1843; *Mercantile Journal*, 20 Feb. 1822.

the theatre was usually filled with these people, and "not a word nor an indication of row or noise occurs"[298]—a change from a generation earlier.

Did the theatre affect the social consciousness and worldview of the people of St. John's? For those attending the theatre—mainly the middle ranks—it was, at the simplest level, a means of escape from the chores of everyday life into a world of make-believe. Melodrama, which made up a great part of the repertoire, offered colourful settings, sensational action, dramatic reversals, and the triumph of virtue over vice. The celebrated English theatre critic William Hazlitt underlined its appeal: "The common people like that which strikes their imagination. They like the dazzling and the wonderful."[299] But did the audiences of St. John's take away from the theatre any perceptions beyond those stimulated by dramatic action? The radical German playwright Bertolt Brecht argued that, whether good or bad, any stage presentation made some impression on the spectators—political, moral, and aesthetic influences all radiated from the theatre; "[t]here is no play and no theatrical performance which does not in some way or other affect the dispositions and conceptions of the audience." The modern British theatre critic J.S. Bratton observed that "[p]erformances enter the consciousness of an audience at several levels. It can influence their construction of the world and affect the way they see themselves and other people or how they think about their world and their place in it."[300]

Without documentation it is not possible to judge the meanings which playgoers in St. John's absorbed. There were, however, two ideological strands running through most of the presentations they attended—racism and patriotism—which possibly made an impression. Racist and nationalist attitudes toward "the other"—

298 Bonnycastle, *Newfoundland in 1842*, 2:120–22; Glascock, *Naval Sketch Book*, 2:166.

299 W. Hazlitt, *A View of the English Stage* (1808; London, 1906), 281.

300 B. Brecht, "Is It Worth Speaking about the Amateur Theatre?" in *Brecht on Theatre*, ed. J. Willett (New York, 1964), 150–51; J.S. Bratton, introduction to *Acts of Supremacy: The British Empire and the Stage*, by Bratton et al. (Manchester, 1991), 1.

whether Catholic nations, "inferior" races of the Empire, or foreigners in general, were endemic in early 19th-century Britain, and influenced the theatre, among other genres. The Irish, in particular, were a prominent target for playwrights and actors. The stage Irishman, with a shillelagh in one hand and a keg in the other, was a stock character of comedies and farces.[301] Comic Irish names, in plays performed in St. John's, delineated the type: Fergus O'Bothermen, Larry O'Gig, Thaddeus O'Transit, and Dennis O'Glib. "Irish comedies"—*The Irishmen in London*, *The Irish Lion*, *King O'Neil*—also depicted the Irish as figures of fun. Actors such as Mr. Kennedy and Thomas Prescott built their reputations on "broad Irish character" performances.[302]

If the Irish were mocked, African-Americans suffered a double insult in that they were caricatured by white people with blackened faces, in the so-called nigger minstrel shows and slave plantation idylls which emerged in early-19th-century America and Britain. The stereotype of the "nigger minstrel," with wide mouth and frizzy hair, perpetually wise-cracking, dancing, and strumming a banjo, entered popular consciousness in the early 19th century and remained throughout the Victorian period. A typical example of this caricature was the slave plantation idyll "Carolina Slaves upon a Holiday" included in the concerts brought to Newfoundland by the Harmoneum family in May 1845. Shows such as this helped to associate blackness with fecklessness, deviousness, and social and cultural inferiority and emphasized the superiority of the imperial white race.[303] The extent to which the citizens of St. John's absorbed these sentiments is problematic, but they could not have been unaware of them, particularly as they were presented as a natural part of the cultural universe. There was no evidence of overt racism, however, in Newfoundland of the time.

During the 1840s and early 1850s, public opinion was moving

---

301 R.G. Cave, "Staging the Irishman," in *Acts of Supremacy*, 1–15.

302 *Ledger*, 18 Feb. 1840; 30 July, 14 Sept., 16 Nov. 1841; 5 Jan. 1844; *Mercantile Journal*, 8, 16 Mar. 1820; *Express*, 8 Oct. 1853; *Newfoundlander*, 27 Apr. 1854.

303 M. Pickering, "Mock Blacks and Racial Mockery: The Nigger Minstrel and British Imperialism," in *Acts of Supremacy*, 176–236.

toward what I have termed (in chapter 13) "a species of displaced patriotism," namely an acceptance of the power and mystique of the British Empire and reverence toward Queen Victoria as its head. These sentiments would have received reinforcement from the content of the melodramas and quasi-melodramas of the period. Warfare and the Empire were redesigned as spectacle, with adventurers and sailors—the gallant few—as heroes; they were shown as naturally superior to those of other races and destined to rule the subjects of the Empire. "At the Coburg," writes Jane Moody, "spectators saw British imperial ambitions dramatized as an heroic crusade for liberty against usurping tyrants and barbaric native customs." The iconic hero was "Jack Tar," the intrepid sailor, who achieved an almost mythic identity as the essence of British bravery and patriotism.[304] An illustration, in *Acts of Supremacy*, of an incident in Edward Fitzball's *Floating Beacon* shows Jack Tar leaping aboard a ship, having rescued the heroine, and bellowing at cowering enemies: "Mayhap, you don't know I'm an old cruiser, and not without my bull-dogs for foreign varment like you." *The Floating Beacon* was shown in St. John's in 1844, billed as an "Extraordinary Attraction."[305] From the mid-1840s, it was *de rigueur* to add the phrase "God Save the Queen" or "Vivat Regina" to concert and drama playbills.[306]

A recent historian of the theatre has suggested that the theatre in England in the late 18th and early 19th centuries was a significant element in the formation of national identity; Edmund Burke, Sir Walter Scott, and William Hazlitt were cited to the effect that the theatre was a school of morals—to be interpreted as patriotism, the refinement of manners and consciousness of the historic achievements of the nation.[307] A single theatre in St. John's could hardly have made the same impact. But it can be argued that the effect of theatrical performances on the conceptions and dispositions of thousands of individuals broadened out toward a collective devel-

304 Bratton, "British Heroism and the Structure of Melodrama," in *Acts of Supremacy*, 34–40; Moody, "Theatrical Revolution," 205.
305 Bratton et al., *Acts of Supremacy*, 37; *Ledger*, 9 Jan. 1844.
306 *Courier*, 12 May 1845; *Ledger*, 5 Oct. 1852; *Evening Post*, 1 Nov. 1853; *Express*, 25 Aug. 1855.
307 Baer, *Theatre and Disorder*, 177ff., 192ff.

opment of social citizenship. Bonnycastle, as we have seen, noticed a generational change in social attitudes by the 1840s. Seen in this light, the theatre played a small but significant part in moulding a community of immigrants into a viable polity.

CHAPTER 7

*"Rollicking Boys": Mumming in St. John's and the Outports**

> That exactly in the ratio as they worked long and monotonously, the craving grew within them for some physical relief—some relaxation, encouraging good humour and good spirits, and giving them a vent—some recognized holiday, though it were but for an honest dance to a stirring band of music …
>
> —Charles Dickens, *Hard Times* (1854)

"A performance of a (traditional) masked mime." The dictionary definition of mumming captures the essential features of the folk art. It was brought to Newfoundland by immigrants in the early 19th century and continued to flourish in its traditional form until the latter part of the century in both St. John's and the outports. Mumming was an example of an art form which originated among the masses and was regularly practised by them. At Christmas time, plays and parades were eagerly awaited events for workers in St. John's, as were house visits to fishing families in the outports. Mumming was a genuinely popular activity outside the orbit of commercial entertainment, distinguished by an organic relationship between performers and audience, based on communities bound together by ties of kinship, neighbourhood, and work.[308]

Mumming came to Newfoundland from England, with some admixture from Ireland, and its structure and much of its content

---

* I have followed H. Halpert and G.M. Story, *Christmas Mumming in Newfoundland* (Toronto, 1969), in using the word "mumming" rather than "mummering."

308 *NSOED*; A.E. Green, "Popular Drama and the Mummers' Play," in *Performance and Politics in Popular Drama*, ed. D. Bradby et al. (Cambridge, 1980), 139–66.

followed models current in the British Isles. The most common form of English mumming was the hero/combat play. Its dramatic core was a combat between two of the performers, one of whom was killed and then restored to life by a wonder-working doctor. There were many variations, in time and place, but the essential features were stable. R.J.E. Tiddy, in *The Mummers' Play*, summarized them:

> The typical Mummers' Play opens with a naive induction in which one of the performers craves the spectators' indulgence, asks for room, and promises a fine performance. When this is concluded the two protagonists appear, and after each has boasted of his valour they fall to fighting. In this duel one or other is wounded or killed. A doctor is then summoned who vaunts his proficiency in medicine and proceeds to revive the fallen hero. Here the main business of the play ends. It is now the turn of minor characters to enter and provide irrelevant amusement of a simple sort. One of them collects money and the performance finishes with a song.[309]

E.K. Chambers, in *The English Folk Play*, outlined a normalized (British) text. It begins with a speech by the Presenter, St. George ("a man of courage bold"), who then fights and slays the Turkish Knight. The latter is revived by a doctor, speaking nonsense verse. Big Head then leads some singing and dancing and is followed by various minor characters delivering rhymes, after which a collection is taken.[310]

Mumming plays bear a distant kinship to traditional English folk festivities, specified by the cultural historian C.L. Barber as

---

309 The other main types are the Wooing Play and Sword Dance ceremonies. A. Helm, *The English Mummers' Play* (Woodbridge, 1981), 1, 11ff.; R.J.E. Tiddy, *The Mummers' Play* (Oxford, 1923), 73.

310 Chambers defines the play as one "put together, as far as possible, from constantly recurring formulas, and represents the general succession of incidents and run of dialogue which one may conceive to lie behind the widely variant versions" (E.K. Chambers, *The English Folk Play* [New York, 1964], 6–9).

"morris dances, sword dances, wassailings, mock ceremonies of summer kings and queens and lords of misrule, mummings, disguisings, masques—and a bewildering variety of sports, games, shows and pageants ..." All were pursued enthusiastically by the peasantry and opposed with vigour by church and state. Recently it has been suggested that mumming came into prominence in England in the early 19th century, the era of agrarian and industrial revolutions, and the advance of capitalist social relations and production for the market in countryside and town, and that agricultural workers and people in small towns or industrial villages created or re-created the folk dramas.[311]

Mumming also took root in Ireland. Plays of the hero/combat type, were brought over from England by settlers and reworked into a distinct Irish tradition. By the 19th century mumming was practised in at least 10 counties, and texts of hero/combat plays survive from Wexford, Dublin, Antrim, Derry, and Fermanagh. Of these, three were of English origin, one showed Scottish influence, and that of Wexford was a development from an older type found in Ulster, where southern English influences were strong.[312]

Irish mummers went in noisy procession from house to house, as did their successors in Newfoundland. The men were dressed in sleeveless coloured shirts (usually green) gathered at the waist and wore conical hats made of rushes. After knocking to gain entrance to a house, they assembled at the end of the kitchen farthest from the hearth. Each man then stepped forward to deliver a speech or take part in the combat and resurrection. The householders tried to guess some identities, but this was not an important part of the visit, which concluded with music, singing and dancing (with the girls looking out for possible husbands), the consumption of food and drink, and the taking of a collection. Most of the plays includ-

---

311 C.L. Barber, *Shakespeare's Festive Comedy* (Princeton, 1959), 5; K. Thomas, *Religion and the Decline of Magic* (London, 1991), 74ff.; R. Williams, *The Country and the City* (Oxford, 1973), chs. 10 and 17; A.E. Green, "Popular Drama and the Mummers' Play," in *Performance and Politics*, 139–66; J.M. Golby and A.W. Purdue, *The Civilisation of the Crowd* (London, 1984), ch. 1, 143; R. Hutton, *The Stations of the Sun* (Oxford, 1996), 72ff.

312 A. Gailey, *Irish Folk Drama* (Cork, 1968), 11–12, 17–62.

ed, in addition to traditional characters, those associated with Irish history and legend—St. Patrick, Oliver Cromwell (with a copper nose), Daniel O'Connell, Jack Straw, and Miss Funny, who collected the money. Prince George and St. Patrick were usually the antagonists. Gailey states that "the plays most easily recognisable are in Newfoundland" and were "an amalgam of folk drama material that originated mainly in south-west England and in Ireland. The Newfoundland plays, however, are specific to the island." A. Helm, another historian of mumming, confirms this transference: the English mummers' play travelled in two steps—first to Ireland, then to Newfoundland.[313]

MUMMING IN ST. JOHN'S

St. John's in mid-century was a bustling commercial town with a population of nearly 25,000 inhabitants. During the 12 days of Christmas mumming provided a welcome break from the drudgery of commerce and the toil of the fishery, in which pursuits the great majority of the population were engaged.

Charles Dickens, with characteristic perspicuity, expressed the need of workers to counteract drudgery with gaiety:

> That exactly in the ratio as they worked long and monotonously, the craving grew within them for some physical relief—some relaxation encouraging good humour and good spirits, and giving them a vent—some recognised holiday, though it were but for an honest dance to a stirring band of music …[314]

In St. John's, mumming provided the "honest dance" which its plebeian citizens craved, and the mummers' parade and the acting of a play became the showpieces of the Christmas period, with Water Street, running on an east-west axis parallel to the waterfront, providing the route for the parade. Mumming was a Christmas cus-

---

313 H. Glassie, *All Silver and No Brass: An Irish Christmas Mumming* (Bloomington, IA, 1975), 18–30, 43–47, 60, 78–87; Gailey, *Irish Folk Drama*, 14–17, 99, 36–38, 54–56, 68; Helm, *English Mummers' Play*, 31.

314 Charles Dickens, *Hard Times* (Penguin Classics edn., 2003), 30.

tom in St. John's at least from the 1830s and almost certainly earlier. In December 1833 a correspondent in the *Ledger* gave a colourful, if critical, account of the rite:

> It is an old but senseless practice with a certain portion of the inhabitants of this town to *celebrate* the Christmas holidays, by dressing themselves up in the most ludicrous, the most fantastic shapes under the character of "mummers" and parade the public streets, carrying with them all kinds of offensive and defensive weapons.[315]

A more sympathetic observer, visiting geologist J.B. Jukes, writing of the early 1840s, observed that during the latter part of December and the whole of January, the lower orders ceased work and, during Christmas, amused themselves with an old English custom in which

> [m]en, dressed in all kinds of fantastic disguises, and some in women's clothes, with gaudy colours and painted faces, and generally armed with a bladder full of pebbles tied to a kind of whip, paraded the streets, playing practical jokes on each other and on the passers by, performing rude dances, and soliciting money or grog. They called themselves Fools and Mummers.

In 1842, Captain Bonnycastle, noting that "the working classes are every year adding to their numbers and respectability," described mumming as "a sort of saturnalia" of these classes.[316]

These were incidental observations by outside observers. Mumming in St. John's, however, received its chronicler in the person of William Whittle, a Newfoundlander domiciled in Boston.[317] The 1842 parade, he wrote retrospectively, brought together up to 300

---

315 "A Lover of Peace," letter to the editor, *Ledger*, 24 Dec. 1833.

316 J.B. Jukes, *Excursions in and about Newfoundland* (London, 1842), 1:221; Bonnycastle, *Newfoundland in 1842*, 2:120, 129.

317 Unless otherwise stated, the following paragraphs are based on W. Whittle, "Christmas Customs," *Evening Telegram*, 24 Dec. 1885.

young men—"the most stalwart fellows who ever trod the deck of a ship"—who arrayed themselves in costumes similar to those of pantomime clowns, wearing trousers or pantaloons of blue broadcloth with red stripes down the sides and white shirts adorned with ribbons, lace, or artificial flowers. On their heads were large cocked hats made of paper, ingeniously and artistically decorated with ribbons and plumes and sometimes topped with a model of a full-rigged sailing brig. All, except the captain and his assistants, wore masks, usually of a grotesque nature. The men completed their dress with a sword hanging at their sides, loaned from the barracks for the occasion. They would also follow the fashion of the day by smoothing bear's grease into their hair and covering their clothes and handkerchiefs with a liberal supply of scent. Women were excluded, but represented by youths with painted faces, wearing silk dresses donated by ladies of rank. These cross-dressers, known as oonchooks, spoke in falsetto voices and ran at spectators with "Indian yells," wielding inflated bladders. As G.J. Bond noted, however, they were recognized as a legitimate part of the show.[318]

Preparations for the parade involved many of the community, and the costume to be worn was discussed for weeks in homes, at parties, and on street corners. "No belle over dressed for the 'Irish Ball'," observed Whittle, "that had as many come to criticise her taste or admire her appearance as a 'fool' had." It was a point of honour for each mummer to try to keep secret the outfit in which he was to appear. Those taking part in the procession gathered at the Custom House on Water Street,[319] and anyone who has participated in street marches in the 20th century[320] can imagine the tension, the barely suppressed excitement, and the good-natured banter that took place as the participants lined up, with the captain and his assistants at the head. No doubt there was some impatience to be moving, as the weather would be cold, likely with snow on the ground. Once

---

318 Bonnycastle, *Newfoundland in 1842*, 2:139; Devine, *In the Good Old Days!*, 54; Prowse, *History of Newfoundland*, 402; G.J. Bond, "Old Christmas Customs," *The Book of Newfoundland* (St. John's, 1937), 2:259.

319 Now the site of the Sir Humphrey Gilbert Building.

320 As did the author in anti-nuclear marches in these streets in St. John's in the 1980s.

started, the parade proceeded along Water Street, Duckworth Street, and other thoroughfares, ending up at the house of Bill Cody, at the junction of what is now Hamilton and Patrick streets, where the wassail bowl provided much-needed hot refreshment. On their way to their destination, however, the mummers called at Government House (the residence of the governor) and at the homes of local notables. In the houses to which they were admitted, unmasked mummers (presumably a small group of the parade) performed a play of the hero/combat type.

There are two extant descriptions of the play which the mummers performed, both dating from the early 1840s. One is a short summary by Bonnycastle:

> They perform, at those houses which admit them, a sort of play, in which the unmasked characters only take a part, and which is very long and tiresome after once hearing. It is a dialogue between the captain and a sailor, and commences with Alexander the Great, and continues down to Nelson and Wellington. They are both armed with swords, and a mock fight goes on all the while, till one is supposed to be slain, when the doctor is called in to bring him to life again.

Bonnycastle's description closely resembles the text of an Irish play of 400 lines from County Wexford transcribed by Gailey, which features a captain, a fight, Alexander the Great and Nelson, and the stock figure of a doctor. Another play, known as "The Tragedy of St. George," selected verses of which were set down by Whittle, was performed in St. John's in the early 1840s. It is not unlike the play described by Bonnycastle, and thus similar to the Wexford drama. Its cast of characters included St. George (not Prince George as in Ireland), St. Patrick, the Turkish Knight, Alexander Czar of Russia, the Doctor, Dan Donnelly, Valentine and Orson, and Father Christmas as Presenter. The first five of these characters appear in the Wexford play, but the action in "The Tragedy" is different in that St. George is wounded by St. Patrick. Dan Donnelly, who speaks one verse, was a celebrated Irish prize fighter. Father Christmas was an interpolation from English West Country plays.[321]

Parades and mumming plays, with some variations, continued to be performed in the 1850s, as the *Ledger* observed. Although the basic hero/combat structure was maintained, in a sense the drama was recreated every year, with the addition of new characters, additional rhymes, and modified resuscitation themes. This is evident from two accounts from the 1850s. Admiral Sir Cyprian Bridge, son of the Rev. T.F.H. Bridge, recalled in his memoirs that he watched a parade as a boy about the year 1850. He distinguished between mummers and masked "Fools," who traversed the streets making "pretended assaults" on bystanders with bladders or a cow's tail fastened to a cudgel. The recipients received these blows good-humouredly; prominent people, significantly, were let off with a single stroke. The mummers were dressed in white shirts, dark trousers, and a beribboned hat, each carrying a sword and led by a hobby-horse and a dragon. They visited the larger houses, always in the daytime, and performed a play in which St. George killed the dragon; other combats ensued, the dead being restored to life by a surgeon, uttering the words:

> I have a little bottle of ellicampaine
> If a man is dead let him rise and fight again.[322]

In the late 1850s, Alex A. Parsons witnessed the parade as a boy. His account shows several of the features familiar to the early 1840s. The parade passed along Water Street, halting at the foot of Market House Hill (now the site of the Court House). The mummers, "in all kinds of fantastic dress," were led by a hobby-horse, "nodding and ges-

---

321 Bonnycastle, *Newfoundland in 1842*, 2:140; Gailey, *Irish Folk Drama*, 17–30; Halpert and Story, *Christmas Mumming*, 189, 194–202; Father Christmas is the Presenter in English plays from Dorset, Somerset, and Cornwall (Tiddy, *Mummers' Play*).

322 *Ledger*, 16 Dec. 1853; Admiral Sir Cyprian Bridge, *Some Recollections* (London, 1918), 26–27. I was alerted to this account by Dr. Hans Rollmann's article "Christmas Mummering in St. John's," *Evening Telegram*, 24 Dec. 2006. Ellicampaine (properly elecampane) was a well-known remedy of the period for pulmonary complaints, derived from the root of the plant of that name (*NSOED*).

ticulating wildly," while masked members of the troop chased spectators and struck them with whips. Parsons recognized Father Christmas and St. George, and several characters in "feminine apparel."[323]

Thus, for the Christmas period, the popular masses in the mid-19th century made the principal streets of the city their own. Whittle viewed the mumming displays as a form of licensed disrespect for authority—a reversal of customary social roles, tolerated by the upper ranks. "The labouring classes," he observed, "had enlarged privileges granted to them, if not by positive law, at least by well-established custom." This position was strongly defended by the mummers themselves. In 1842 a case of alleged assault by a mummer was brought before the magistrates by Pascoe Carter, a master cooper. He claimed that a mummer named James Walsh had dealt him a blow on the head with a "swat" or bladder attached to a stick, knocking him to the ground; a scuffle ensued, Walsh lost his mask, and Carter retired from the fray. Both men were coopers and, according to Carter, had previously quarrelled over work hours; consequently he felt that Walsh had "a revengeful feeling" toward him. The authorities convicted Walsh and fined him £2.10 and costs, or one month's imprisonment in default of payment. The magistrate added that many persons "assuming the dress and disguise of 'mummers' are by no means so inoffensive as they and their friends would have it believed," and often wreaked vengeance on those they deemed or believed "personally or politically opposed to them."[324]

This was the official version. Mummers and their supporters were having none of it, and dispatched to Governor Harvey a petition containing 52 signatures.[325] From "time immemorial," the petition stated, it had been usual for young lads, principally natives of Newfoundland, to commemorate "the joyous season of Christmas" by appearing in the costume of mummers, and amusing themselves and the inhabitants generally by indulging in "innocent pas-

---

323 A.A. Parsons, "Memoirs of Christmas—How the Great Festival Used to Be Celebrated," *Holly Leaves*, Christmas Number 1817.

324 Whittle, "Christmas Customs"; The Rooms Provincial Archives Division, GN 2/2, Carter and Simms to Crowdy, 6 Jan. 1842.

325 The Rooms Provincial Archives Division, GN 2/2, "The Respectful Memorial of the Undersigned Inhabitants of St. John's" (n.d.).

time"—a practice derived not only from the customs of England, Ireland, and Scotland but still used generally in every country on the continent of Europe. The petition concluded that Walsh was convicted for the offence, "if offence it was," of striking Carter with a blown bladder, but it was impossible to prove it was actuated by malice, so it was better to prosecute "real offenders" than a poor innocent lad of excellent character who helped support his family; the governor, therefore, should exercise pardon for the accused, who lay in jail. This defence of Walsh apparently had some effect, for Pascoe requested the magistrates to remit the remaining part of Walsh's sentence on assurances that he would not in future molest or threaten him.[326]

• • •

Although the characters and verses of mummers' plays remained essentially stable, with variations around central themes, they accumulated over the years fragments from drama, mythology, folklore, hymns, and popular songs. According to Chambers, some of the most enduring elements of the English folk play came from chapbooks. These were small folded pamphlets, almost always illustrated by woodcuts, which sold at one penny and were distributed across the country by itinerant chapmen; chapbooks formed the staple reading of the working poor during the 18th and early 19th centuries. These cheap booklets covered a wide variety of subjects, from ballads to prophecy, but their content was more traditional than the topical themes of other street literature, often including short versions of medieval romances.[327]

Among the most popular of these were *The Seven Champions of Christendom*, *Guy of Warwick*, and *Valentine and Orson*. John Simons, in his *Guy of Warwick and Other Chapbook Romances*, follows Chambers in affirming that these stories, and in particular *The Seven Champions*, were "a formative influence on the texts of the English Mummers' plays." The major part of this last text, put

---

326 The Rooms Provincial Archives Division, GN 2/2, Carter and Simms to Crowdy, 12 Jan. 1842.
327 Chambers, *English Folk Play*, 11, 38, 61, 154, 179; V.E. Neuberg, *Popular Literature: A History and a Guide* (Harmondsworth, 1977), 102–22.

together by Richard Johnson in 1596, concerned St. George, a legendary soldier-saint and Christian martyr, probably of Middle Eastern origin. In the Middle Ages he was adopted as a patron saint by many European countries and cities; his status as the patron saint of England probably dated from the 14th century.[328] His exploits as a dragon slayer and smiter of foreign foes coloured his legend with a distinct patriotic appeal during the developing course of English nationhood, immortalized in the rallying cry of Shakespeare's Henry V at Agincourt: "Cry God for Harry! England! and St. George."

St. George became the key character in mummers' plays of the early 19th century as the embodiment of English virtue who overcomes the personification of foreign evil in the shape of the Turkish Knight.[329] In these dramas St. George is rarely portrayed as overcoming the dragon, his legendary opponent, though the following verse is found in certain English texts:

Here am I, St. George, that worthy champion bold,
And with my sword and spear I won three crowns of gold,
I fought the fiery dragon and brought him to the slaughter,
And by that I won fair Sabra, the King of Egypt's daughter.

A version of these lines occurs in both the so-called Change Islands and Salvage plays which, as will be shown, were popular in the outports. Guy of Warwick, another epitome of English knightly bravery (and also a dragon slayer), the eponymous hero of a chapbook romance, also appears in the Salvage play. Orson, twin brother of Valentine, appears in another chapbook romance of French origin, *Valentine and Orson*; the latter was separated from his brother and brought up in the woods by a bear. He makes an entrance in the St. John's play as "the wild man of the wood" and recounts the story of the romance:

First I was taken by a wondrous bear,
And was fed by him for many a long year.

---

328 J. Simons, ed., *Guy of Warwick and Other Chapbook Romances* (Exeter, 1998), 26; S. Riches, *St. George: Hero, Martyr and Myth* (Stroud, 2000); G. Morgan, *St. George* (Edison, NJ, 2006); Chambers, *English Folk Play*, 170ff.
329 Morgan, *St. George*, 134; Riches, *St. George*, 33.

Then I was taken by Prince Valentine,
And little I thought he was a brother of mine.
To prove the truth of what I say,
My brother Valentine is here today.[330]

The influence of chapbook romances on mummers' plays is an interesting example of the convergence of two plebeian art forms—popular literature and folk drama.

In the early 19th century when mummers' plays were developing and flourishing, the texts took a contemporary turn. The traditional nationalism embodied in the exploits of the heroes of romance took on a sharper edge, reflecting the surge of popular patriotism and the growing sense of identity of Britain as a Protestant country opposed to Catholic and foreign "others," inspired by Britain's victories in the Napoleonic wars and her increasing dominion over alien races in her expanding colonial possessions.[331]

The mummers' plays current in Newfoundland during the 1840s and 1850s conveyed to spectators, explicitly and implicitly, a sense of England's imperial power and the inferiority of the foreign "other." The plots revolve around St. George (King or Prince George as he became under the Hanoverians), the Valiant Soldier, Jack Tar, the perennial avatar of naval supremacy, Sir Guy, and other heroic stereotypes, who warded off threats by infidel orientals to England's taken-for-granted overlordship. In the Change Islands play King George stands for "old England," a monarch who has won wealth and women from the Orient and believes himself superior to any other man in the world—the king of Egypt is his "armour bearer"; he denigrates the Knight as "you Turkish dog," vowing that "no Turk stand on this English land." In the Salvage play King George again boasts of his conquests, and opposition to the Turkish Knight, and the Valiant Soldier fights the "Turkish dog" to "maintain King

330 Halpert and Story, *Christmas Mumming*, 196, 198, 203; "The History of Guy, Earl of Warwick" (prose version), in *Guy of Warwick*, ed. Simons, 54–68; "The Famous History of Valentine and Orson, the Two Sons of the Emperor of Greece," in *Guy of Warwick*, ed. Simons, 138–50.

331 L. Colley, *Britons: Forging the Nation 1707–1837* (London, 1993), 364–75.

George's rights."[332]

In the same play, Sir Guy, described by Simons as a knight who "fought to spread the name of England as a country of heroes and … to save the land from foreign invaders,"[333] announces himself as

> … Sir Guy, a man of mighty strength,
> Who slew down Duncow, eighty feet in length;
> Is there anyone here holds King George a spleen,
> I'm resolved to conquer, it's for King George I'll die.

Oliver Cromwell appears, to boast that he has conquered many nations. Ireland is not spared; in the St. John's play King George denigrates St. Patrick as a cowardly "stable boy" not worthy of a fight. These nationalist stereotypes and racist undertones were entirely compatible with the times in which the plays were performed.[334] The extent to which these prejudices affected popular feelings cannot be ascertained. It is probable that the appeal of mumming lay largely in spectacle rather than in content, and the plays described above, which were popular in the outports, provided as much colourful incident as could be desired.

MUMMING IN THE OUTPORTS

> Christmastide was … mummering time. Long before Christmas, considerable time was spent on designing costumes and fantastic rigs, … and for a whole fortnight, the night air was tortured by the inarticulate cries peculiar to "jannies." The mummers went around in groups of various numbers touring the village from one end to the other … There was a heroic folk-play brought by the Irish immigrants from the "Old Country" that used to be performed by the young men during the Christmas holidays. The ac-

332 Bratton, introduction to *Acts of Supremacy*; Halpert and Story, *Christmas Mumming*, 198, 199, 203, 206.

333 Simons, *Guy of Warwick*, 20.

334 Halpert and Story, *Christmas Mumming*, 194, 203, 206. The reference to St. Patrick also appears in an Irish mummers' play from County Fermanagh (Gailey, *Irish Folk Drama*, 55); cf. ch. 6.

tors personated some of the great heroes of history, Napoleon Bonaparte, Alexander, Doctors Faustus, Sir Isaac Newton, St. George, St. Patrick.[335]

Thus did the folklorists Lawton and Devine describe mumming in Old King's Cove in the mid-19th century. The outport was one of many hundreds scattered along the island's extensive coastline—usually small communities, with square wooden houses clinging to the cliffs above coves or stretched in a line along the shore. Life in the outports revolved around the catching and curing of fish, mainly cod, from May to October. Both tasks were arduous and time-consuming. Patrick O'Flaherty has written that life in the outports was one of endless repetitive labour, overshadowed by "ignominious dependence upon fickle nature and merchant credit."[336] But the people who did the real work of the country also knew how to relax when the fishery was over. During the 12 days of Christmas labour could be transformed into joyous release, and mumming, together with indoor and outdoor games, provided the means of transfiguration.[337]

One large outport, King's Cove, was notable for its violin band, a dozen strong. On Christmas Eve they paraded through the community, accompanied by performers on a drum (a sawn-off barrel with goatskin heads), cymbals (two pot covers), a tambourine (a metal tray), and a triangle (a pair of tongs). Dances were a feature of life in most outports. One of the most popular dances, held at the largest house in the community, was the cotillion, followed by the couples dancing an intricate "single step." The cotillion consisted of time-beating in the centre of the floor, followed by swinging and a grand chain. Custom demanded that on the final beat of the last bar the dancers should stamp both feet with as loud a "whelt" as possible. Other dances were the eight-handed reel and the kissing dance.

Quilting and matting parties were frequent; weddings were a

---

335 J.T. Lawton and P.K. Devine, *Old King's Cove* (n.p., 1944), ch. 4.

336 O'Flaherty, "Looking Backwards: The Milieu of the Old Newfoundland Outports," *Journal of Canadian Studies* 10, no. 1 (1975): 3–10.

337 The following is compiled from Lawton and Devine, *Old King's Cove,* and Devine, *In the Good Old Days!*

signal for celebration, begun by firing sealing guns over the heads of the bride and groom; and raffles were held for the benefit of widows or poor fishers. The articles raffled might be a gun, a watch, a violin, a sheep, or a goat, and would be won by the person scoring the highest number in three throws of the dice for a fee of a shilling.

Indoor games were legion and usually demanded alertness and quick wits. In forfeits, each player deposited an article with the Master of Ceremonies, and an Oracle had to decide, by observation, the owner of a selected item and the unfortunate person then had to undertake a unique or difficult task. "The Birds and the Fishes" and "The Priest and his Boots" were guessing games, depending on local lore and knowledge. A more physical entertainment was "Start the Cask out of the Cargo," a tug-of-war without a rope. Outdoor games were also played: "Hurley," a form of hockey; "Cat," similar to the British "rounders," an ancestor of baseball; "Quoits"; and many others with curious names and rules of play. These various indoor and outdoor diversions were an attraction for gathering of families and friends in and around the home; the young men displayed their prowess in the noisy and community-wide festival of mumming. The earliest record of mumming in the outports was made by Lewis Anspach, the Swiss-born missionary of the Society for the Propagation of the Gospel in the Conception Bay area from 1807 to 1812. He wrote that men and women would don disguises and go from house to house "singing and dancing" for the reward of food, an activity apparently confined to immigrants, which was resented by the settled inhabitants. Tocque recalled that when he was a boy at Carbonear in the 1820s there were both day and night mummers; the former were dressed in beribboned white shirts and fancy hats, the latter wore humpbacks or cowhides with projecting horns. Apparently a traditional play was performed by one of the groups, for Tocque remembers acting as Oliver Cromwell, with his friend John Bemister (later an MHA and Minister) taking the role of Wellington.[338] In January 1831 two Harbour Grace magistrates investigating

338 *DCB*, s.v. "Anspach, Lewis Amadeus"; L.A. Anspach, *A History of the Island of Newfoundland* (London, 1819), 475–78; Tocque, "When I Was a Boy," *Evening Telegram*, 15 Feb. 1897. Cf. M. Doyle, *Newfoundland in Exile: The Life and Times of Philip Tocque* (Halifax, 1997), 8.

the case of a group of men disguised as mummers entering a planter's house party, assaulting guests, and breaking furniture, stated that "mumming has for many years prevailed here and Carbonear particularly, also in other parts of Conception Bay."[339] Six years later a respectable citizen of Carbonear complained to the *Public Ledger* that "fools, with their faces masked" were "infesting" the streets, despite the orders of magistrates prohibiting it. Prowse records that Christmas in the outports was enlivened by "a carnival of dancing, mumming and, of course drinking," with masked mummers going from house to house, and often ending the evening with a fight.[340]

On 6 January 1858, Henry Lind, the Evangelical missionary at Sandy Point, Bay St. George, recorded in his diary: "I am sorry to find that a majority of the young people (and some of the married ones) are busy in dressing up to act as 'Mummers,' commonly and properly called 'Fools.'" He added, on the following day: "This evening had a good company to practice singing, such I fear is the feeling or want of feeling among these people that singing or playing fools is treated with the same indifference." At about the same time, a young assistant in a St. John's merchant store took part in mumming "in a distant outport." Dressed in buskins and a beribboned white shirt and disguised with a canvas mask, he watched a mummers' troop, with hobby horses, "yelling and prancing like Kickapoo Indians" before setting off. In the houses they visited they started "hooting and prancing," flicking the inhabitants with switches, and pulling people from hiding places. After the mummers were unmasked, glasses of spirits were provided and the visit ended with dancing to the sound of a fiddle.[341] The anecdotes suggest that mumming was a feature of outport life from at least the second decade of the 19th century. The usual procedure was a noisy procession from house to house,

---

339 The Rooms Provincial Archives Division, GN 2/2, Danson and Buckingham to J. Campbell, Pro-Secretary, 20 Jan. 1831. Cf. L. Little, "Plebeian Collective Action in Harbour Grace and Carbonear, Newfoundland, 1830–1840" (MA thesis, Memorial University, 1984), 77–83. Little sees the incident as an attack against "respectability." No one was apprehended.

340 "An Observer," letter to the editor, *Ledger*, 13 Jan. 1837; Prowse, *History of Newfoundland*, 451.

341 ASCD, OMF-002, Ms. Diary of Henry Lind, 1857–1864; J.T.W., "An Old-Time Christmas," *Christmas Greeting* (1893): 17–20.

entry into the kitchen, the reciting of lines in turn by the mummers followed by dancing, eating, and drinking, on the pattern common in England and Ireland.

The hero/combat play was the staple presentation, and its performance has been reported from 14 communities, mainly on the East Coast: Brigus, Boxey, Burgeo, Change Islands, Fortune Harbour, Greenspond, Herring Neck, North River (C.B.), Renews, Salvage, Sop's Arm, Tilting, and Trepassey. Six include a text, there are four fragments, and four reports of plays. Other fragments are known from Twillingate and Burgeo. P.K. Devine remembered a play (apparently acted in the outports in mid-19th century) containing the roles of St. Patrick, St. Michael, St. George, Hector, and Alexander. A more detailed example was given by Devine and O'Mara, editors of the *Christmas Review* of 1892, who recalled the "days of yore" (the 1840s) when the yule log was dragged along the highways of the "fairly populated" outports, and a pantomime was played "under the mummer's mask," in which St. George, the Dragon, Father Christmas, St. Patrick, Dr. Foster, Piscator, Mephistopheles, and St. Andrew were impersonated by Newfoundland fishers. "Fancy the sealing gaff giving place to the crozier," exclaimed the writers, "the 'sculping knife' to the sword, and the hundred and one incongruities of this *olla podrida*."[342]

The strongest evidence for the performance of mummers' plays outside the capital is the surviving texts of two plays, one at the beginning of the 19th century, the other near the end. The earliest play of which there is record is known as "The Salvage Play" acted, according to tradition, by the first settlers in Newfoundland. It has some affinities with Chambers's normalized English text, in which King George slays the Turkish Knight. In the Salvage play, however, King George slays the Grand Turk, who is resuscitated by the Doctor. "The Valiant Soldier" then wounds the Turkish Knight. English characters are introduced—Dim Dorothy (presumably Dame Dorothy of West Country plays) and Sir Guy. Oliver Cromwell (with

---

342 *ENL*, s.v. "Folklore"; Halpert and Story, *Christmas Mumming*, 184; Devine, "Quaint Christmas Customs," *Christmas Bells* (1901); M.A. Devine and M.J. O'Mara, eds., *Christmas Review* (1892), 1.

a copper nose) is a character from Irish plays. "The Change Islands' Play" was reputedly brought to Newfoundland by an English schoolmaster in the 1880s. It is largely a contest between the Turkish Knight and King George; both are wounded, but are revived. Some characters of apparent English provenance then recite their lines—Beelzebub, Hercules, Jack Tar, and Pickedy Wick.[343]

The English and Irish both brought their cultural traditions to Newfoundland, which influenced the form and content of the mummers' plays. It was, however, the English form of these dramas which had the greater impact on those performed in Newfoundland. The English immigrants from the southwest—Devon, Dorset, and their hinterlands—would have known of the plays current in their areas in the early 19th century. One of these appears in a surprising source—the Dorset novelist Thomas Hardy's *The Return of the Native.*

Hardy's preternatural powers of observation and memory, recalling the folk plays of his youth and the tales of local inhabitants, make it likely that the excerpts of the St. George play in the novel are accurate. In 1920 Hardy supplied Wessex mummers with the script of *The Masque of St. George*, with instructions that it was to be performed precisely as done in Dorset villages 70 or 80 years earlier,[344] that is, the 1840s and 1850s—the dates of the action in *The Return of the Native.*

In the novel *The Tragedy of St. George* was performed by a group of 15 to 20 young men.[345] Their dress, as later described and illustrated by Hardy himself, was a white tunic tied around the waist by a strap, and they wore helmets shaped like a tea cozy with a tuft at the top—not unlike those worn later in Ireland. In the novel the players' womenfolk decorated the costumes with "coloured loops and bows of silk and velvet." The men carried a wooden sword in their left

343 Halpert and Story, *Christmas Mumming*, 190, 197–207; Cromwell appears in most Irish texts (Gailey, *Irish Folk Drama*).
344 E. Brennecke, *The Life of Thomas Hardy* (New York, 1925), 79, 82; M.A. Zeitler, *Representations of Culture: Thomas Hardy's Wessex and Victorian Anthropology* (New York, 2007), 86.
345 Unless otherwise stated, the following paragraphs are based on T. Hardy, *The Return of the Native* (Oxford World's Classics edn., 2005), 118ff.

hand, and in their right hand a 6-foot-long staff, with transverse sticks at the top holding paper tassels, which they would clash together to punctuate their speeches. At the rehearsals the older men would give advice on gesture and gait and prompt the words from memory. The troupe would perform at four or five houses in an evening, getting ale and money after each performance. This is similar to the practice of mumming in Newfoundland at the same period. When the text of Hardy's play is compared to that of the same name performed in St. John's, the correspondence is even more striking; the main characters are the same—St. George, the Turkish Knight, the Doctor, Father Christmas—and the wording of the speeches is similar. Father Christmas's introduction is exactly the same in both plays:

> Make room, make room my gallant boys,
> And give us space to rhyme;
> We've come to show St. George's play,
> Upon this Christmas time.[346]

The four lines of the Turkish Knight's entrance speech differ in only two words from Hardy's version (apart from "come" for "comes" in line 1):

> Here comes I, a Turkish Knight,
> Who learned in Turkish lands to fight;
> I'll fight this man with courage bold;
> If his blood's hot, it will soon run cold.

A few other lines comparable to those given by Hardy are found in the two other hero/combat plays in Newfoundland for which there are texts—from Salvage and Change Islands—and include King George, Father Christmas, the Valiant Soldier, the Turkish

---

346 Hardy to A. Hopkins, 20 Feb. 1878, in *The Collected Letters of Thomas Hardy Volume 1, 1840–1892*, ed. R.L. Purdy and M. Millgate (Oxford, 1978), 54–55; Halpert and Story, *Christmas Mumming*, 194; Hardy, *Return of the Native*, 131.

Knight, and the Doctor, with similar combats and revivals.[347]

How to account for these cultural transfers? Hardy either consulted a text or, more likely, relied on his memory when writing the mummers' lines in the late 1870s (*The Return of the Native* was published in 1878). The text of *The Tragedy of St. George* was repeated to William Whittle in Boston in 1885 by an old Newfoundlander who remembered its performance in St. John's in the early 1840s before the Great Fire of June 1846,[348] that is, at the time when it was being performed in Dorset villages. Verses and characters of the play came to Newfoundland, almost certainly brought by Dorsetshire immigrants, perhaps before the 1840s.

As a coda to mumming in the outports, there is the very different thesis of Gerald Sider, an American Marxist scholar, who sought an explanation of mumming in the dominance of merchant capital and the workings of the social relations of production. Undoubtedly there was a temporal coincidence between the hegemony of the merchants and the flourishing of mumming, but Sider fails to provide evidence of any necessary or causal connection. Equally unsupported is his contention that mumming played a crucial role in the reorganization of work relations in the fishery, the house visit providing a framework for the discussion of the makeup of work units.[349] There is no empirical evidence to support this contention. Possibly some informal conversation of this kind occasionally took place at the Christmas period as at other times, but this is not the same as saying that mumming provided the only occasion for it. Sider places the era of mumming in the context of the dominance of merchant capital (which, unlike most historians, he analyzes fully) but he does not explain why mumming should thrive in this economic system rather than in any other.

• • •

Mumming had flourished in Newfoundland since the begin-

347 Halpert and Story, *Christmas Mumming*, 196–202; Hardy, *Return of the Native*, 131–32.

348 Halpert and Story, *Christmas Mumming*, 193.

349 Sider, *Culture and Class*; "Christmas Mumming and the New Year in Outport Newfoundland," *Past and Present*, no. 11 (1976): 102–105.

ning of the 19th century, but in the years 1860 to 1861 several events occurred which conspired to end the practice in its traditional form. In the Christmas festivities of 1860 in St. John's, there was a clash between mummers and spectators, in which the latter came off second best. Mr. Justice Carter, a stipendiary magistrate, in late December 1860 ordered St. John's to be plastered with posters prohibiting masked men to appear in the streets of St. John's. A correspondent in the conservative *Times*, assuming the mantle of "well-disposed citizens," applauded this curtailment of mumming "with its disgusting attendants—rioting, drunkenness and profane swearing." The proclamation had no immediate effect; from 1 January 1861, the mummers were on the streets again "in pretty considerable force," and some shopkeepers put up shutters to cover their glass windows.[350] But the action of the magistrate was a warning signal to mummers that official tolerance of their actions was beginning to wear thin. In the following year the whole position of mumming in society changed dramatically.

Over the Christmas holidays of 1860–1861 a tragic incident occurred in Bay Roberts which ultimately led to the demise of mumming. Although the *Standard and Conception Bay Advertiser* had in early December cautioned mummers to be peaceable and careful because "people now-a-days always carry firearms," a scuffle reportedly occurred when "some scoundrels disguised as mummers" attacked Isaac Mercer, who was returning from the woods; he died from his injuries the following day.[351]

The Clerk of the Peace and Superintendent of Police were dispatched to Bay Roberts to investigate. The *Standard* advised "an augmentation of the police force, and a strict system of discipline." Bannerman issued a proclamation (signed by John Kent, Colonial Secretary) urging citizens to assist the authorities in apprehending the "person or persons at present unknown" who had murdered Mercer, and a £100 reward was offered to the informer. The *Times* wondered why the attackers had not been arrested at once, as they

350 Whittle, "Christmas Customs"; M.A. Devine, *Notable Events in the History of Newfoundland* (St. John's, 1900), 234; *Telegraph*, 26 Dec. 1860; *Times*, 22 Dec. 1860; *Ledger*, 4 Jan. 1861.

351 *Standard*, 19 Dec. 1860; *Express*, 3 Jan. 1861; *Gazette*, 8 Jan. 1861.

must have been well known to the inhabitants of the town.[352]

At this point the issue was raised to a new level by the intervention of the Church of England in the person of its bishop, Edward Feild. Declaring himself outside party politics and merely seeking to uphold the cause of "religion and righteousness," he wrote a long letter to the *Telegraph*, recounting the circumstances of Mercer's death, the results of the inquest, the questioning of some mummers without result, and the tearing down of government proclamations, including one on the Protestant schoolhouse, which was subsequently broken into and damaged. The death of Mercer, the bishop was "led to suppose," resulted from "the senseless, savage sports of the parties who infest our streets at Christmas, glorying in the name and dress and actions of 'Fools.'" Shortly afterwards, however, in a letter to the *Express*, he admitted, "from fuller information," that he was "led to hope the assault committed on Mercer … was not premeditated, or at least that no such extreme violence was intended or desired."[353]

This retraction was obscured in the commotion which followed the publication of the first letter. Attention was focused on an extraordinary paragraph in which Feild appeared to condone in advance a possible act of revenge for Mercer's murder: "But blood cries from the ground," he fulminated, "and however much such a feeling may be deplored and deprecated, it is feared that, if other means are not used to bring the offenders to justice, an opportunity will be taken by the young men in the Harbor to avenge Mercer's death."

The rest of Feild's letter, and a subsequent letter to the *Express*, was designed to demonstrate that "the general disordered state of the country," particularly in Harbour Grace, Carbonear, and St. John's, had one basic cause—the "infliction" of representative government upon a country which was entirely unsuited to it. Feild's intervention ignited a press controversy which continued for several weeks. Opinion divided along the traditional lines of Conservative-Prot-

---

352 *Gazette*, 8 Jan. 1861; JHA 1861, 5 Jan. 1861, Bannerman to Colonial Secretary, 5 Jan. 1861; *Standard*, 9 Jan. 1861, cited in *Times*, 16 Jan. 1861; *Gazette*, 15 Jan. 1861; *Times*, 16 Jan. 1861.

353 Feild, letters to the editor, *Telegraph*, 13 Jan. 1861, and *Express*, 14 Feb. 1861.

estant versus Liberal-Catholic. The *Ledger* delivered a steady drumbeat of anti-mumming comments, attacking the *Newfoundlander*, attempting to link J.L. Prendergast, then the Liberal MHA for Harbour Grace, to the alleged murderers, and asserting that "low, savage, Roman Catholic blackguards" were terrorizing Harbour Grace. Correspondents in the *Ledger* and *Times* followed suit; terms such as "ruffians," "blackguards," and "fiends" were freely used.[354]

The *Patriot*, on the other hand, impugned Feild for his "lugubrious verbiage" and "exaggerated views," particularly his denunciation of responsible government as the source of all social evils. It found "most extraordinary," however, what it called Feild's "undisguised incitement to violence," coming as it did from one who professed to preach peace and goodwill. The *Newfoundlander* also refuted at some length Feild's allegations of "disorder" arising from responsible government, while attempting to put the Mercer affair in perspective:

> But suppose it at its worst—with all the blackness of wilful murder on its face, it would be but a solitary and exceptional instance of crime, having no possible link or reach beyond the small and comparatively obscure locality where it was perpetrated. It is impossible, having regard to the time and occasion, to assign to it a wider range or significance than this.[355]

Some aspects of the situation were unclear. The *Gazette* stated that the perpetrators were "disguised as mummers," and Feild admitted that some genuine mummers were out that day who had no connection with the incident. Moreover, he added, there was bad feeling in Harbour Grace "arising out of election matters." The fact that Mercer was a Protestant suggested that sectarian animosity may have been an issue. In June, when two citizens of Harbour Grace "supposed to have been connected with" the Mercer affair were arraigned before the Supreme Court, Judge Little declared that "no

---

354 *Ledger*, 18, 29 Jan., 15 Feb. 1861; "A Lover of Truth," letter to the editor, *Ledger*, 29 Jan. 1861; "Colonus," letter to the editor, *Times*, 2 Mar. 1861.
355 *Patriot*, 18 Feb. 1861; *Newfoundlander*, 25 Feb. 1861.

malice prepense was shown to exist between the accused and the deceased," and ordered them discharged on bail; Judge Robinson concurred.[356]

The Conservative-Protestant press began to use the Mercer incident to condemn the practice of mumming in general. The *Times*, for instance, pressed for guilt by association. As Mercer was slain by men in the guise of mummers, it thundered, "so every man [mark!]—*every* man, we say, who appeared in the same costume at Bay Roberts when the murder was committed will be looked upon with suspicion (to apply no stronger phrase)." The tolerance shown to mumming by the middle and upper ranks in previous decades was disappearing. The social and political situation was changing, and not to the advantage of the working class and its public revels. In St. John's the lower middle and middle classes were increasing in numbers and respectability; in the words of George Story, "as the values of the burgeoning middle class made themselves felt, the increasingly stuffy tone of the capital was no longer congenial to traditional festivities."[357] The growing influence of the Newfoundland School Society's Evangelicals, who were opposed to any sort of frivolity, was also modifying attitudes. But political events were ultimately decisive in the future of mumming.

The year 1860 had opened with Bannerman's dubiously legal dismissal of Kent's Liberal government. The following general election was won by Hugh Hoyles's Conservatives (with several seats in dispute). The government, once established, passed a series of measures which strengthened authority; with regard to mumming it saw its chance and took it. A clause restricting the activities of mummers was hastily added to a bill for the prevention of nuisances (mainly filth in the streets). When the bill was debated in the Assembly during the summer, condemnation of mumming was almost unanimous, echoing the tone of an earlier debate in January, when Kent alone demurred.[358] In the debates of June, Mercer's mur-

356 *Gazette*, 8 Jan. 1861; Feild, letter to the editor, *Telegraph*, 13 Jan. 1861; *Daily News*, 21 Feb. 1861; *Post*, 23 Feb., 19 June 1861.

357 *Times*, 13 Feb. 1861; G. Story, "Mummers in Newfoundland History," in *Christmas Mumming*, ed. Halpert and Story, 178.

358 Gunn, *Political History*, 160ff., 176; Assembly 21 Jan., *Express*, 31 Jan. 1861.

der was condemned in terms exceeding those concerning almost any other murder of the time—no doubt a stick with which to beat mumming, to which authority seemed determined to put an end.

The only member of the Assembly or Council to defend mumming was the veteran Liberal R.J. Parsons, who declared that people had little amusement, and that mumming was "one of the old customs of the country," similar to dancing round the maypole in England. The rest condemned Mercer's murder as "this horrible deed," "that diabolical act," "this diabolical deed," and so on, and urged prohibition or varying degrees of restriction or regulation. Mummers were likened, without evidence, to barbarians, molesters of women, wielders of dangerous weapons, and potential murderers. Patrick Kough believed that mumming had degenerated from an orderly and respectable amusement since "the lower classes with masks" had taken it up. The general feeling against mumming in both Houses cut across political and religious lines. The Liberals Kent and Morris made some protest against the prevailing tide of opinion, but voted for the bill in the end.[359] Clause VII of the act was a draconian measure:

> VII—Any Person who shall be found, at any Season of the Year, in any Town or Settlement in this colony, without a written Licence from a Magistrate, dressed as a Mummer, masked, or otherwise disguised, shall be deemed to be guilty of a Public Nuisance, and may be arrested by any Peace Officer, with or without a Warrant, and taken before any Justice of the Peace, in the District or Place where such Person may be found; and on conviction, in a summary manner, before such Justice, may be committed to Gaol for a Period not exceeding Seven Days, unless he shall pay a Fine not exceeding Twenty Shillings; such Licence to be numbered, and a corresponding Number worn by the Person so licensed, on a conspicuous part of his Dress.[360]

359 Assembly 18 June, *Express*, 2 July 1861; Council 15 June, *Courier*, 3, 6 July 1861.

360 24 and 25 Vic., cap. 3, An Act to Make Further Provision for the Prevention of Nuisances (25 June 1861).

According to the *Ledger*, 150 licences were issued at Christmas 1861–1862. Apparently some unlicensed youths also joined the activities. This did not satisfy the government; in March 1862 a further act to abate nuisances was passed, which included Clause VII of the 1861 act but omitted the words "without a written license from a magistrate." A ban on mumming was thus made absolute. At Christmas 1862–1863 notices banning the use of firearms and forbidding mumming were placed around the city. Nevertheless, the mummers came out again; "numbers of rollicking boys" were on the streets, but they confined their activities to "serenading the town's people every night." It was the best mummers could do in the circumstances, but it was not the mumming of yore. In 1864 there were no celebrations on the streets. The two acts had effectively put an end to street parades in St. John's.[361]

Mumming, however, continued in the outports, particularly north of Conception Bay—in, for instance, Brigus, Conception Harbour, Harbour Main, and Holyrood. But before the end of the century, the presentation of plays by troupes, which had its heyday during the period from the 1830s to 1860, had all but disappeared, superseded by the house visit, with its emphasis on disguise, questioning, and disclosure.[362]

Mumming in Newfoundland, in its authentic form of parades and the presentation of plays in houses, was a popular social rite until the early 1860s. But it was over 100 years later before a scholarly attempt was made to restore it to its rightful place as a form of popular folk drama. Halpert and Story's *Christmas Mumming in Newfoundland* (1969) retains its place as the pre-eminent study of

---

361 *Ledger*, 10 Jan. 1862; 25 Vic., cap. 4, An Act to Amend the Laws Now in Force for the More Speedy Abatement of Nuisances (27 Mar. 1862); C. Byrne, "Some Comments on the Social Circumstances of Mummering in Conception Bay and St. John's in the Nineteenth Century," *Newfoundland Quarterly* 77 (1981): 3–6; "Musty Past," 6 Jan. 1864, in *Evening Telegram*, 14 July 1883; Story, "Mummers in Newfoundland History," 179.

362 Byrne, "Some Comments," 6; M.R. Robertson, *The Newfoundland Mummers' Christmas House Visit* (Ottawa, 1984); J.F. Szwed, "The Mask of Friendship: Mumming as a Ritual of Social Relations," in *Christmas Mumming*, ed. Halpert and Story, 106–18.

mumming and the starting point for further research.

• • •

Mumming invites understanding in the wider context of the human propensity for play—in the broadest sense that includes dance, theatre, rituals, revels, and the carnivalesque. Johan Huizinga, in his classic *Homo Ludens*, calls play "an absolute category of life," a voluntary activity distinct from common reality; it is never imposed by physical necessity or moral duty, and arouses in its participants a devotion that can pass into rapture. Seen in this light, mumming, as an expression of play, was a recreation which became "re-creation," freeing its participants from conformity to rigid social roles—men became women, neighbours became strangers, the strong and silent, vociferous actors. In dressing up, the "extraordinary" nature of play reached perfection, observed Huizinga, "the disguised or masked individual 'plays' another part, another being. He is another being." Devine had made the same point about Newfoundland outport mummers half a century earlier:

> After a hard season's work at the fishery, the harmless sports and relaxation of the Christmas season made new men of them … Phlegmatic and silent fishermen, who had not a word to say all the year round, now blossomed into Grand Knights of St. Patrick, St. Michael and St. George, Hector, Alexander, etc., and gave out their heroic speeches in verse as they went in fantastic mumming costume from one neighbour's house to another.[363]

More recently, Terry Castle, in *Masquerade and Civilization*, has offered a socio-psychological analysis of masking and disguising in relation to the carnivalesque, which attempts to reveal their meaning to the individual and the group. Masks and disguises, Castle argues, are "an intoxicating reversal of ordinary sexual, social and metaphysical hierarchies," bringing about "both a personal abdi-

---

363 J. Huizinga, *Homo Ludens* (Boston, 1955), 1–14; Devine, "Quaint Christmas Customs," *Christmas Bells* (1901).

cation from the responsibilities of identity and a group abdication from the strictures of the social order itself." In mumming, as we have seen, personal liberation expressed itself in verbal and physical form—extravagant acting, "Indian yells," "carnival blows," general horseplay, and the occasional fight. The social order, from which mumming was an unauthorized release, appeared as regulated labour (with long hours and few breaks) and the imposition from above of a restrictive social morality enshrining conformity to social norms. As mumming was exclusively the territory of the "lower orders," it appeared to the upper ranks of society as a potentially dangerous affirmation of class interest.[364]

Rex Clark, in an analysis of Newfoundland mumming, sees it as a manifestation of class struggle. Outport fishers, he maintains, were sensible of their exploitation by merchant capital, and produced "forms of collective, class-based resistance." In mumming, culture was enlisted on the side of the oppressed, as a form of struggle which asserted their interest and identity, primarily vis-à-vis the merchant class, which they perceived as exploiters. Cyril Byrne, in his survey of 19th-century mumming, suggests that it had "a dimension of political statement and protest about it," adding that

> the incidents involving violence are all related to political events and to the uneven distribution of wealth and political power in early 19th century Newfoundland and to the increased awareness of that fact after organised forms of political life were introduced to the island early in the 19th century.[365]

Two questions arise. Did such rituals of disorder actually or potentially disrupt social structures, or did they function as safe-

---

364 T. Castle, *Masquerade and Civilization* (Stanford, 1986), 6, 73; R. Malcolmson, "Popular Recreations under Attack," in *Popular Culture Past and Present*, ed. B. Waites, T. Bennett, and G. Martin (London, 1982), 20–40; Golby and Purdue, *Civilisation of the Crowd*, ch. 2.

365 R. Clark, "Romancing the Harlequins: A Note on Class Struggle in the Newfoundland Village," in *Contrary Winds: Essays on Newfoundland Society in Crisis*, ed. Clark (St. John's, 1985), 7–20; C. Byrne, "Some Comments," 6.

ty valves that reaffirmed the status quo by returning regenerated and reinvigorated workers—"new men"—to the labour force for another year of exploitative tasks? I tend to agree with Castle that the "safety valve" theory fails to consider the seriousness which the ruling powers in society viewed mumming and similar rituals; historically, such rituals have been linked to actual rebellion.[366]

For the "stalwart fellows" of Newfoundland who took part in mummers' parades and the presentation of plays in houses, mumming was in one sense a pleasant outing. But they were also aware that it was a gathering of their own class, and that as a class they were flouting conventional rules of dress and behaviour; at the same time they were immersing themselves in a literary, historical, and dramatic culture (albeit in a somewhat elementary form) that the class structure, particularly in the outports, ordinarily denied them. During its heyday mumming offered fishers and workers an opening into political and cultural assertion. Governmental beheading of mumming in 1861–1862 was one of the more discreditable pieces of class legislation of the century.

366 Castle, *Masquerade and Civilisation*, 88. Cf. P. Burke, *Popular Culture in Early Modern Europe* (New York, 1978), 199–204, for a summary of the debate.

CHAPTER 8
Entertainment and Society, St. John's 1840–1855

> The history of human pleasures—of festivity, games, jokes, and amusements—has seldom met with the same dignified attention accorded the history of human suffering. Wars, plagues, and collective miseries of all kinds have always been conventional historical and philosophical topoi; laughter … has not. This imbalance reflects a standard interpretation of experience: that suffering is perpetual, fundamental to human life, and hence worthy of discourse. Pleasures, felt to be discontinuous and fleeting (not to mention morally and theologically problematic), remain trivial.
>
> —Terry Castle, *Masquerade and Civilisation* (1986)

ST. JOHN'S

"That Paris is France," observed Governor Sir John Harvey in 1844, "may be applied with at least equal truth to the City and District of St. John's in relation to Newfoundland."[367] Three years earlier a previous governor, Sir Thomas Cochrane, had informed a British Select Committee that the capital had a population of about 13,000 and was the residence of all the merchants and "a certain number of men of intelligence."[368] Both statements place St. John's as a commercial town and a centre of administration and culture distinct from the outports. The city had been expanding following the resumption of trade with the US after the ending of the American War, and the Napoleonic War period of 1793–1815 led to further development of the city as the migratory fishery declined. "Politically, the most important change that took place in Newfoundland

367 CO 194/20, Harvey to Stanley, 9 Jan. 1844.

368 Select Committee Appointed to Inquire into the State of the Colony of Newfoundland (1841), Minutes of Evidence, Sir Thomas Cochrane, 4. Cochrane underestimated the size of the population; it was nearer 20,000.

during the Napoleonic wars, wrote S.J.R. Noel, "was not the increase of population as such but its concentration in St. John's, which emerged as the island's first town."[369]

As one approaches St. John's by sea, the entrance to the harbour—a channel aptly called the Narrows—is almost hidden by towering, nearly vertical, cliffs. The sight impressed J. Mullally, a visitor in the mid-19th century: "it appears as if the mountains had been torn apart, leaving a safe passage open to the harbour, where, even in the most violent storms, the waters are hardly ever agitated above a ripple. The city is built on the side of a hill … it overlooks the harbour, which is a little over a mile in length, and a quarter of a mile in width; and which is one of the best harbours in the world …"[370]

In 1804 Governor Gower gave a brief description of the state of the city:

> [T]he North side of the harbour is now taken up with merchant stores, wharfs, etc. for the purposes of trade and the fishing stages with many of the flakes and other erections for curing fish removed to make room for them … It is to be regretted that along with the buildings required for this trade, the seaside is crowded with Dwelling Houses, Retail Shops and Public Houses with various artificers who, however, necessary to the general convenience of the trade and fishery, are not engaged in carrying on either, & many of them might therefore, with equal advantage thereto, dwell at a greater distance from the Waterside and by that means have more space for the Trade and fishery … The increased population of St. John's which has naturally accompanied the increase of trade, being scarcely able to find lodging in the houses now built and rents are so exorbitant that a labouring fisherman or artificer can seldom obtain a small part of a miserable hovel for the shelter of his family for less

---

369 Cadigan, *Newfoundland and Labrador*, 76, 82, 97; Noel, *Politics in Newfoundland*, 5.
370 J. Mullally, *A Trip to Newfoundland* (New York, 1855), 36–37.

than £8 or £10 per annum.

In 1813 Governor Keats reported that St. John's had become "the Emporium of the island ... with a population of nearly 10,000 inhabitants [and] seems to have grown out of its character from a fishery to a large commercial town ..."[371] The Napoleonic War period witnessed several important developments in the fishery—the North Shore fishery boomed and extended its operations to Labrador, and the seal hunt began to develop as a large-scale commercial enterprise. Other changes worked to the advantage of St. John's, and the capital consolidated its position as the centre of trade and commerce, leading to competition between merchant firms in the capital and those in the outports. St. John's merchants began to supply smaller outport firms, which in turn supplied fishing families. During the 1830s, as fish production stagnated or declined, several outport firms became insolvent. By the end of the 1840s trade and commerce was centralized in St. John's.[372] Parallel with the concentration of economic power in St. John's was the centralization of administration in the capital. The isolation of the outports and their largely cashless economy, which precluded direct taxation and inhibited local government, meant that St. John's was the fountainhead of the island's administrative system, embodied in the governor, the Legislative Council, and the House of Assembly. The link between the capital and the electoral districts was the member of the House of Assembly, whose duties were multifarious.

By the 1840s, observers had begun to notice the improved amenities and social structure of St. John's. Streets had been widened and stone houses built; Duckworth Street was 40 feet wide and lined with small private apartment houses.[373] J.B. Jukes, a visiting geologist, in 1840 observed that in St. John's "large stone houses, good-sized churches, chapels, and court-houses: shops built of wood and painted white, a tolerably regular street, and a road or two, mark the seat of greater wealth and a more numerous population." Merchants

---

371 CO 194/54, Keats to Bathurst, 18 Dec. 1813.

372 *ENL*, s.v. "Fisheries."

373 ASCD MF89, Phoenix Fire Co., Report on Fire Risks in St. John's, 8 Nov. 1845.

had supplied much of the initiative and some of the money for civic improvements in the 1830s and 1840s—roads, sewers, gas, water supplies, etc. In 1845 the Water Street stores had been lit by gas. The offices of the merchants dominated Water Street; most of the professional middle class resided in the eastern end of the city, and many of the working classes lived in rookeries in the lower part of the town.[374]

• • •

In the first three decades of the century, the growth of trade and the increasing complexity of society were transforming St. John's from a fishery to a modernizing metropolis, able to overcome the fishery crisis of 1816–1826 and become the powerhouse of the economy. In 1841 over a million of quintals of fish were exported, and that figure, or just under, was maintained for several years. In the 1840s the country, in Patrick O'Flaherty's words, began to enter the modern world, symbolized by the entry of the first steamship into the capital in 1842.[375] Observers were also quick to note that consequent upon the material development of the city important social changes were occurring: the gradual division of society into separate social classes, and the explosive growth of mass entertainment. Bonnycastle, analyzing the social structure of St. John's, distinguished four classes: first, the upper class ("which at home would almost without exception be the middle class"), which consisted of the clergy, judges, councillors, and officers of the state, plus the oldest and wealthiest of the merchants. Second, the middle class—the newer merchants, business agents, and the second generation of respectable citizens; professional men, lawyers, and medical men belonged to both these classes according to status. Next came small farmers, small shopkeepers, and fishers. Beneath these were those employed in "hewing wood and drawing water," or as carters, farm servants, or menial workers. Tocque made a similar classification a generation later, when the social

---

374 J.B. Jukes, *Excursions in and about Newfoundland during the Years 1839 and 1840*, 2 vols. (London, 1842), 1:225; E.B. Foran, "St. John's City; Historic Capital of Newfoundland," and M.P. Murphy, "Glimpses of Old St. John's," in *The Book of Newfoundland*, 2:1–27.

375 Prowse, *A History of Newfoundland*, Table 1, 692; O'Flaherty, *Old Newfoundland*, 164–65, 174–79.

situation would not materially have changed. His four classes were principal merchants, high officers of government, and some lawyers and medical men; small merchants, large shopkeepers, secondary officials, and lower-ranking doctors and lawyers; grocers, master mechanics, and schooner-owners; and fishers.[376]

The census of 1845, in which the categories were incomplete, gave the population of St. John's as 20,941. Professional men and "others" numbered 376, planters, fishers, and shoremen 1,617, tradesmen 876, and farmers 378—a rough picture of a society divided into classes not inconsistent with the observations of Bonnycastle and Tocque. The populace recognized and respected these social divisions, evident in a curious custom noted by the folklorist P.K. Devine:

> in St. John's ... shutters were used on all the shop windows. For the death of a man of the highest social standing, all the shutters would be put up: for the next grade, six shutters, then four for a middle-class citizen, two for a nondescript, and one for the lowest social grade.[377]

Sociologists and historians have observed that different social classes tend to spend their leisure in different ways, broadly corresponding to their economic position and educational level. St. John's was no exception. The class division of society governed the manner in which the different social strata reacted to the boom in entertainment—from vaudeville to the circus, from lectures and exhibitions to concerts and charity balls—which crowded the social space of St. John's in the 1840s. It is expedient, therefore, to describe the leisure recreations in social terms.

ENTERTAINMENT FOR THE MASSES

Although many of the ways in which people enjoyed their leisure time were socially specific, some entertainments could be described as popular in that they attracted a mass audience, drawn from more

---

376 Tocque, *Newfoundland*, 86; Bonnycastle, *Newfoundland in 1842*, 2:120–22.

377 Abstract, Census and Return of the Population &c., of Newfoundland, 1845; Devine, *In the Good Old Days!*, 73.

than one social group—in this case, the upper ranks of the fishing producers and associated trades plus the shopkeeper-artisan middle class. What appeared to have the widest appeal were shows based on music and variety, and these elements found expression in the vaudeville troupe and the circus. In the 1830s and 1840s vaudeville was blossoming in England and the US. Touring companies were popular, and Newfoundland appeared on the itinerary of some of the more celebrated troupes. In the spring of 1844 the Hughes family arrived in St. John's. They came direct from Halifax, where they had been rapturously received. The main performers, the Hughes children and two others, who sang songs and played the harp, gave two concerts. They were followed, in the spring of 1845, by the Harmoneum family, from Boston, who gave a concert at the theatre on 9 May, comprising "solos, glees, quartets, melodies and choruses." The audience encored many pieces, and the *Courier* declared that the artists were "the most superior band of singers that has ever visited Newfoundland."[378]

The Harmoneum family gave several other concerts during May. Their major presentation was the oddly named "Grand Ethiopian Opera," the centrepiece of which was "Carolina Slaves upon a Holiday," a play with patently racist stereotypes—Fanny, Pompy, Sambo, and Tony—interspersed with a comic (anti-feminist) recitation, "Miss Jemina Twist, a Disappointed Lover of 45," by Mr. Pike. Praise was not unanimous. The *Patriot*, the editor of which, R.J. Parsons, was a leading member of the Natives' Society, condemned the "Patronizing Strangers," who were "paid and upheld" to the detriment of local talent, but the *Courier* dismissed the *Patriot*'s observations as "illiberal, ungenerous and … inhospitable," and took satisfaction in noting that the family's farewell concert had "a bumper house."[379] In August the *Patriot* elaborated on its criticism of visiting musical troupes, reminding its readers that the theatre was originally built for the exclusive benefit of the poor, which purpose had attracted many non-devotees of the drama; but in recent years it had been put to "base purpose," against the spirit and letter

378 *Ledger*, 27, 30 Aug. 1844; *Courier*, 9, 12 May 1845.
379 Notices in *Ledger*, *Newfoundlander*, and *Courier*, May 1845.

of its original mandate:

> Every *Negro Song Singer*—every *Jim-Along-Josey*—every *Cacoucha and Polka Dancer* desirous of displaying their graces—every strolling player who may come among us on *speculation*—each and all of these amusingly idle characters, are allowed free use of our Amateur Theatre for their own individual benefit by the directors, who seem utterly regardless of the *exclusive object* for which the Building was erected.

Furthermore, the *Patriot* continued, the encouragement of players who made a living by "continued *Harlequinade* and personal exhibition" was particularly objectionable, not to mention the "evil effects" on society of their "lude songs, immoral dances, and witch-like tricks." Horse racing and the Regatta had their benefits, but "nothing on earth good, virtuous, wise, or proper, can be obtained by the encouragement ... of *Harlequinship*!"[380]

Possibly the criticism levelled at the Harmoneum family caused the theatre management to have second thoughts about vaudeville, for in the late summer of 1845 they engaged two sensationalist performers: "The Celebrated Enchantress" Miss Mary St. Clair, who was assisted by W.P. Grimaldi "the French Necromancer," in a programme of novelties, tricks, illusions, metamorphosis, and dances.[381]

Outside the theatre, citizens were regaled with various kinds of exhibitions, displays by travelling magicians, waxworks, and panoramas. The precedent was set in July 1840 when the *Ledger* advertised a "Great and Unprecedented Attraction" at the Mechanics' Hall—a collection of "living curiosities," including an immense anaconda, a giant boa constrictor, kangaroos, Chinese golden and silver pheasants, and "many other rare curiosities." The serpents, the notice pointed out, "are so perfectly docile that the most timid lady may view them with pleasure and safety." The following year, Mr. Dixon, "the celebrated Canadian Wizard and Professor of Natural

380 *Patriot*, 7 Aug. 1845.
381 *Courier*, 4, 8 Aug. 1845.

Magic," performed his "beautiful illusions" with cards and other magic paraphernalia at the Hall. A collection of wax figures from Madame Tussaud's London Museum was on show at Kielty's Long Room in St. John's in August 1845. In September the theatre hosted, "at great expense," Senor Carrera, the celebrated delineator of Ancient Sculptures.[382]

In addition to these attractions, huge paintings, panoramas, and dioramas were exhibited at various locations. They included Rossiter's "magnificent paintings": the Mississippi and Ohio rivers—"the largest painting in the world"; a "monster panorama" of the Hudson River; a "Dioramic Panorama" of Mont Blanc; and the Russian War, "the largest work of art ever exhibited."[383]

A very different type of popular entertainment was the circus. The smell of sawdust, the crack of the ringmaster's whip, the sight and sound of galloping horses, the thrill of acrobatic displays, the raw humour of the clowns, and the blare of the brass band immediately appealed to the senses and transported the audience to a world outside mundane reality. Several renowned international circuses visited St. John's between 1843 and 1847: the North American Circus in 1843, the New York Circus two years later, followed by Bunting's Olympic Circus in 1846. The New York Circus returned in 1847. All offered spectacular displays of horsemanship by both male and female performers.[384]

Although most of the popular diversions were commercial ventures designed to attract by means of bizarre or wonderful features, taken as a whole the offerings gave citizens a window on a world beyond insular preoccupations—glimpses of foreign countries, natural history, various types of art and sculpture—which would have widened the mental horizons of the viewers.

SOCIAL GRACES FOR THE MIDDLE CLASS

One of the more interesting developments in this period was the growth of a middle class—in Newfoundland terms that section of

382 *Ledger*, 2 July 1840, 5 Nov. 1841, 2 Sept. 1845.
383 Notices in *Courier*, *Ledger*, and *Express*, 1844, 1850, 1852, 1853, 1855.
384 Notices in *Courier*, *Ledger*, and *Newfoundlander*, 1843, 1845, 1846, 1847.

society between the workers in the fishery and the ruling elite. According to Bonnycastle, the middle class consisted of newer merchants, merchant's agents, and the lower ranks of professional men, lawyers, and doctors, and also "a growing, most important, and rapidly increasing number of the sons and daughters of those respectable men who have chosen Newfoundland as the country of their children ... a finer, healthier, or better dressed and behaved colonial 'gentry' ... does not exist." Well-to-do artisans also enjoyed middle-class status; from the late 18th century they had built much of the infrastructure of St. John's and colonized numerous auxiliary services.[385]

Many of the middle class were descendants of the immigrants of the late 18th and early 19th centuries, particularly of the arrivals in the period 1811–1815. Immigration from England and Ireland had been increasing from the mid-18th century, but it surged in the second decade of the 19th century. Some of the Irish were escaping persecution following the failure of the 1798 Uprising, but all were attracted to the relatively high wages in the expanding Newfoundland labour market. Between 1811 and 1815, 15,255 immigrants arrived in British fishing ships: 2,010 from England and 13,245 from Ireland. They crossed the Atlantic in these vessels in atrocious conditions—fishing ships were exempt from the regulatory provisions of the 1803 Passenger Act. For a 40 shilling fee each immigrant had 6 feet of space, a chest to sleep on, and meagre rations of herring, potatoes, oatmeal, and eggs. Governor Cochrane likened these vessels to slave ships; overcrowding was rife—the greater number a merchant could put on board the greater his profit.[386] Some more genteel individuals of both nationalities also arrived on the island in this period.

The educational level of the generality of the immigrants can approximately be estimated from contemporary sources in England

---

385 Bonnycastle, *Newfoundland in 1842*, 2:120–21; Cadigan, *Newfoundland and Labrador*, 80.

386 Ryan, *A History of Newfoundland*, 195–95, 224; PP, 1826, IV, Report from the Select Committee Appointed to Inquire into the Expediency of Encouraging Emigration from the United Kingdom, 46; CO 194/74, Cochrane to Goderich, 25 Sept. 1827.

and Ireland. A survey of Devon parishes for the period 1805–1814 shows that adult male literacy (based on the ability to sign marriage registers) stood at 55 per cent, lower than the national average of 65 per cent.[387] In 1841, literacy figures for Waterford, Tipperary, and Wexford were 29 per cent, 49 per cent, and 59 per cent respectively; a generation earlier they would have been much lower, perhaps half those numbers, for in 1818 the percentages of the age group five to 15 years in schooling in these counties were 18 per cent, 22 per cent, and 28 per cent respectively.[388] These figures must be taken as indicators of the state of literacy, but it can be hazarded that at the peak of immigration about half the English and perhaps a quarter of the Irish could be classed as literate by the standards of the time.

The transformation of the descendants of these relatively poor and undereducated immigrants into the moderately well-to-do, sophisticated, and educated middle class of 1835–1855 and beyond is a subject for further research, but its lineaments can be traced in the increasing diversity of economic development, the gradual improvement of trade and commerce that followed the crisis period of 1816–1826, and opportunities for education and lifestyle improvement open to those with increasing incomes. In the first decades of the 19th century, 20 per cent of the households in St. John's could broadly be classed as artisans (mainly craftsmen) and service workers. A number of them were property owners and a few rose to become merchants. The Irish occupied a prominent position, especially in the retail trades.[389]

Decisive evidence for the existence of a middle class in the capital is contained in a petition to Lord Grey, the Colonial Secretary, from sufferers in the fire of 18 June 1846. Describing themselves as "Certain of the Middle Class in St. John's," 360 persons appended

---

387 W.B. Stephens, "Illiteracy in Devon during the Industrial Revolution," *Journal of Educational Administration and History* 8, no. 1 (1976); W.B. Stephens, *Education, Literacy and Society, 1830–70* (Manchester, 1987), 352.
388 Data compiled by Dr. Mary E. Daly, University College Dublin, from Irish censuses and other sources. I am grateful to Dr. Daly for supplying me with these figures.
389 Cadigan, "Artisans in a Merchant Town: St. John's, Newfoundland," *Journal of the Canadian Historical Association* 4 (1993): 96–119.

their signatures.[390] This remarkable document not only establishes the existence of a middle class but it also gives individual occupations, religion, their amount of loss by fire, and the sums received in compensation. Having lost their dwellings, many middle-class citizens were forced to take shelter in makeshift wooden structures and hoped for a loan to replace them with permanent houses. They stated that £50,000 granted for their relief "has been reserved or misappropriated," and prayed that Lord Grey would order assistance "in any … way Your Lordship may Consider most Conducive to the relief of the Sufferers." According to the document, each individual had already received some compensation—a few £150, but most about a third or less of that sum, obviously insufficient for the rebuilding of a dwelling. The social composition of this self-styled middle class was wider than that defined by observers, but broadly similar. Craftsmen and artisans formed the core of the self-assigned middle class: 11 coopers, 11 tailors, eight carpenters, four shoemakers, four blacksmiths, three sailmakers, two bakers, two cooper/tinsmiths, and one shipwright. Retailers were also a large group: 11 shopkeepers, seven innkeepers, three butchers, and a stationer. Apart from these, no fewer than 29 listed themselves as fishers; most of these would almost certainly be planters, as were a handful of others who could be thus assigned. Only half a dozen traders or dealers were listed, but no merchants. Sixteen "house proprietors" made up the bulk of the remaining miscellaneous signatories.

The amount of loss incurred by each individual, as stated in the petition, provides some indication of their property wealth. The stated losses ranged from over £4,000 to about £2,000, mainly suffered by a small number of shopkeepers; virtually all the other claimants submitted figures below £1,000, with a large group around the £600–900 mark, and over 200 individuals below—often well below—£500.

The religious composition of the group can be described with exactitude: 85 per cent of the signatories gave their denomination as

390 CO 194/127, LeMarchant to Grey, 24 Aug. 1847, encl. "The Memorial of Certain of the Middle Class in St. John's Sufferers by the Conflagration of 9th June."

Catholic, a figure higher than the distribution of 75 per cent in the capital's population. The Protestants were mainly Church of England, plus a few Methodists, Presbyterians, and Congregationalists. Again, caution is necessary: the preponderance of Catholics may have resulted from their concentration in the area of the fire, or perhaps because Catholics encouraged each other to sign the petition.

A rough indication of the size of the middle class can be estimated from the number of signatories. Assuming each of these had a minimum of three dependents, 1,086 people were affected by the fire. If this figure represented half the number of the middle class, the total would be 2,200 people; the 1845 census, as shown earlier, gave the number of "planters, fishermen, shoremen and tradesmen" as 2,493. The memorial thus reveals the existence of a fairly large middle group, mainly artisans, shopkeepers, and well-to-do fishing families, of moderate wealth and largely Catholic in religion, a class which had its own aspirations and way of life distinct from the social formations above and below it.

The social outlook of the middle class is less easy to assess. In the early 1840s its members could hardly have escaped the influence of Governor Harvey's cultural revolution, with its encouragement of social harmony, popular patriotism, temperance, informal education, and nativism, sentiments which fostered a Newfoundland consciousness in a community becoming aware of its own identity (see Chapter 13). Moreover, native-born Newfoundlanders were increasingly outnumbering the foreign-born. By the middle 1850s, 24,000 citizens of St. John's, out of a total population of 31,000, had been born in Newfoundland.[391] This was fertile ground for the growth of a nativist sentiment, and as early as 1840 Edward Kielly, Conservative politician and former naval surgeon, had founded a Natives' Society, largely to promote native interests and counter the influence of "strangers" (largely Irish) who had purportedly imported political strife into the island.[392]

During its short life, the Society attempted to improve its public

391 Abstract, Census and Return of the Population, &c., of Newfoundland, 1857.
392 *ENL*, s.v. "Natives' Society, the Newfoundland."

profile and to raise funds for the institution by sponsoring a series of balls, in imitation of those of the upper ranks. That of January 1846 was described by the *Courier* as "most respectably attended, and the display of beauty and fashion ... at least equalled that of former occasions," and dancing was kept up until "bright Chanticleer proclaimed the dawn." Two years previously the event had acquired quasi-official character. Attended by Harvey, a supporter of the nativist cause, and "the elite of the community," the participants enjoyed "the choicest refreshments in great abundance." Before retiring, Harvey presented Richard Barnes, the president of the Natives' Society, with a grant of the land selected as the site of the intended Native Hall.[393] This was subsequently built, but demolished in a gale in November 1846.

The Natives' Society's appeal was largely to the middle class. This was evident in Kielly's speech at the inaugural meeting in September 1840, which embraced what could be called middle-class values. The Society, he declared, aimed at

> advancing and promoting our general interests by co-operating with the peaceable, orderly, respectable, and well-disposed inhabitants of this island, in measures of general usefulness, to be respectful and obedient to the laws of the land, and to manifest on all occasions, our loyalty and attachment to our most gracious Sovereign and the constitution under which we live.

A year later the Society presented an address to Sir John Harvey, assuring him that the native population would be ready to lend "their cooperation in maintenance of British constitutional principles, and to further the cause of good government."[394] Despite attracting both Catholics and Protestants, enjoying official encouragement, and reaching a membership of 544 by 1844, the political influence of the Society was never great, and it had withered by

---

393 *Ledger*, 22 Jan. 1841, 2 Feb. 1844, 18 Jan. 1845, 28 Jan. 1846; *Courier*, 28 Jan. 1846.

394 *Patriot*, 15 Sept. 1840; *Times*, 22 Sept. 1841.

1846. It appeared, however, to have played a part in upholding middle-class standards of social respectability, patriotism, and obedience to the law.

• • •

American sociologist Thorstein Veblen, in *The Theory of the Leisure Class* (1899), analyzed the lifestyle and social ambience of the moneyed elite which, in "its manner of life and its standards of worth," established norms of taste and behaviour followed by every level of society. This was particularly true of expenditure on dress, which "affords an indication of our pecuniary standing to all observers at the first glance." The enduring influence of Veblen's thesis is evident in the historian Eric Hobsbawm's elaboration of the theme in *The Age of Capital* (1975). The middle class of the mid-Victorian period, he states, was experiencing a degree of upward social mobility and felt obliged to assume the appropriate costume. Clothes marked bourgeois men and women as persons of some importance.[395]

An interest in fashionable apparel, stimulated by the example of George "Beau" Brummell in England, eventually appeared in St. John's. H.F. Shortis, recalling life in St. John's in the 1840s and early 1850s, wrote:

> I have witnessed the evolution of dress … I have seen the comfortable and serviceable paisley shawl tightly fitting about the throat and the "puke" bonnet made of warm and serviceable material give place to the modern flimsy and open-breasted dress and lightly textured and fashionable hats, and incidentally have seen a phenomenal increase of consumption in every successive generation.[396]

A sample of newspaper advertisements for the 1840s reveals a

---

395 T. Veblen, *The Theory of the Leisure Class* (London, 1970 edn.), 70, 118–19; E.J. Hobsbawm, *The Age of Capital* (London, 1975), 230.
396 H.F. Shortis, "Random Jottings of By-Gone Days," in *Garrison Town to Commercial City: St. John's, Newfoundland, 1800 to 1900*, ed. R. Rompkey (St. John's, 2012), 73.

thriving trade in clothes and finery for "Ladies and Gentlemen of St. John's and the Outports."[397] At least 25 vendors and shopkeepers in this trade advertised their wares during the decade. Most numerous were milliners: more than a half dozen offered for sale every variety of hat, cap, and bonnet. In June 1845 Mrs. and Miss Lush opened their showrooms to display "a handsome and fashionable supply of millinery," including velvet bonnets, French Blonds, Tuscan Bonnets, and Dress Caps, plus lambswool muffs, laces, and ribbons. A range of headgear was offered to "Ladies of St. John's and the Outports" by Mrs. and Miss Ayre of Gower Street. For the men, Henry Earle, describing himself as "Army and Navy Tailor and General Clothier," supplied black cloth and waterproof Balmoral for overcoats, while John Roden opened a business devoted to renovating gentlemen's clothes. Ladies' and gentlemen's boots and shoes also had their outlets. A growing love of display among the middle class was catered to by several jewellers, at the premises of which watches, bracelets, rings, and other trinkets could be bought, or gold and silverware made to order.

An indication of the desire of the middle orders to acquire records of their status was the presence of professional photographers. In October 1841 Messrs. Valentine and Doane advertised daguerreotype portraiture, "an ART which has attained great celebrity and popularity in almost every city of Europe and America," and was a means of obtaining "accurate LIKENESSES at a comparatively small expense." A few years later George E. Clow, an iterant photographer, prospered as a camera salesman and practitioner of the "beautiful art" of the daguerreotype. That the piano, the middle-class status symbol par excellence, was a feature of a number of homes was evident from the advertisements of two musicians who offered to tune and repair the instrument.

• • •

Apart from the fascination with fashionable attire, a wave of interest in education swept England in the late 18th and early 19th

397 The following, unless otherwise stated, is based on advertisements in the *Public Ledger* from January 1840 to December 1850.

centuries. It was pre-eminently the age of the private, fee-paying academy, the promoters of which offered in particular a range of "accomplishments" to girls of middle-class families.[398] Mr. Bingley, in Jane Austen's *Pride and Prejudice*, delivered a concise description of the accomplishments a young lady should possess—"a thorough knowledge of music, singing, drawing and the modern languages ..." Austen's contemporary Maria Edgeworth outlined the purposes of the achievement of these graces:

> Accomplishments ... are valuable, as being the objects of universal admiration. Some accomplishments have another species of value, as they are tickets to admission to fashionable company. Accomplishments have another, and a higher species of value, as they are supposed to increase a young lady's chances of a prize in the matrimonial lottery.[399]

In St. John's an interest in accomplishments was the other marker, besides fashion, of a middle class growing in self-confidence and wishing to see its children, especially its daughters, ascend the social ladder. The appearance of advertisements in the press for these schools for over a quarter of a century strongly suggests that many of them were well patronized. In the years 1810–1836, that is, before the advent of public elementary education, at least 68 private, fee-paying schools were established in St. John's, teaching over 40 subjects;[400] about 30 academies advertised the teaching of dancing, music, painting, needlework, and French, and six dancing schools were opened. Artistic crafts such as velvet painting, etching on glass, inlaying, transferring, and Japonning, were offered. The educational entrepreneurs also provided a range of commercial subjects for young men aspiring to posts as superior clerks in merchant offices

---

398 M. Hyndman, *Schools and Schooling in England and Wales* (London, 1978), 14ff., 61ff., 234–35; A. Fletcher, "Polite Accomplishments," *History Today* 58, no. 4 (2008): 43–49.
399 Jane Austen, *Pride and Prejudice* (Folio Society edn., London, 1975), 41; M. Edgeworth and R.L. Edgeworth, *Practical Education* (London, 1798), 522.
400 This section, unless otherwise stated, is based on notices in *Gazette*, *Times*, *Ledger*, *Newfoundlander*, and *Patriot* from 1810 to 1836.

and those interested in various professions requiring some skilled training. In 1828 the Rev. F.H. Carrington had noticed two or three "very respectable schools," and many of minor note, for children whose parents were in "sufficiently easy circumstances" to pay for their education.[401] The fees of these and other schools, in fact, ranged from 30 guineas (£31, 10 shillings) per year to £5 or £10 for a course of lessons, which restricted access to the middle ranks. Many of these, however, had an interest beyond conspicuous consumption and selective education, forming an audience for lectures on serious subjects and giving their patronage to classical music.

In the late 1840s and early 1850s visiting savants lectured on diverse subjects. For example, six lectures on phrenology by Mr. Bigney in January 1845, and three lectures on geology by Philip Tocque in December of that year. At the end of the decade R. Alexander lectured on "Biology! Or the Electrical Science of Life," with accompanying "experiments" involving the audience. Three years later Moses Roper, a former American slave, gave accounts of his life under slavery. For those with a taste for botany, William Leahy opened a botanical garden and museum. The garden contained 3,500 plants, many of them in flower. For the price of 1 shilling and threepence, visitors to the Museum could view 20 cases of birds from around the world, a case of Chinese butterflies, and numerous preserved specimens of flora and fauna from different countries. A 28-volume "cyclopeadia" lay open for inspection.[402]

The musical scene was enriched by a series of concerts. In 1851, Krollman, a young German violinist, and his wife gave three well-received concerts, with a return visit in 1852. In April 1850 the *Ledger* announced that weekly concerts were to be held at the Factory, the services of the band of the Royal Newfoundland Companies having been secured. A performance of vocal and instrumental music was held at the Factory, a local hall, on 16 March 1852 and another on 30 March.[403]

It is clear that the foundations were being laid for a more perma-

---

401 SPG C/Can/NFL 2, Carrington to Society, St. John's, 30 July 1828.

402 Notices in *Ledger*, *Newfoundlander*, and *Courier*, 1845, 1848, 1849, 1850, 1853.

403 Notices in *Ledger*, *Courier*, and *Express*, 1850, 1851, 1852.

nent musical culture.[404] This was provided by the St. John's Athenaeum, opened in 1861. Essentially a literary institution on the model of those founded in the US, Canada, and Britain, it held a spring concert at the end of every lecture season, attracting hundreds of people. In 1863 the *Times* noted "the gradual spread of a taste for the study and practice of music among so many of the classes of the community," inaugurating a musical tradition that has continued to the present day.

DIVERSIONS OF THE ELITE

All observers of the period—R.H. Bonnycastle, J.B. Jukes, John Mullally, Lieutenant-Colonel R.B. McCrea, and Philip Tocque—were agreed that there was little social intercourse, trust, or fellow feeling between the elite and the rest of society.[405] In fact, Tocque asserted, "There is no colony belonging to the British Empire where influence and name tend so much to form a caste in society, and where it is more regarded than in St. John's." The higher classes pursued a social and cultural life of their own. In the Christmas season, for instance, the merchant-administrative class shut up shop and devoted themselves to sleighing excursions and a round of dinner parties, evening parties, and dances.[406] Bonnycastle noted that

> their hours of relaxation are usually spent either in dinner parties ... or in evening assemblages at each other's houses, where quadrilles and dancing keep the younger members of society in pleasant occupation, whilst their elders look on, play at cards, or converse upon the topics of the day.

Jukes described a sleighing party in which he participated:

---

404 The following paragraph relies on G.D. Colton, "The Athenaeum Concerts: Music and Society in 19th Century Newfoundland," *Newfoundland Quarterly* (Fall 2003): 27–31.

405 Bonnycastle, *Newfoundland in 1842*, 2:138; Jukes, *Excursions in Newfoundland*, 1:221; R.B. McCrea, *Lost amid the Fogs: Sketches of Life in Newfoundland* (London, 1869), 89; Tocque, *Newfoundland*, 86; Mullally, *Newfoundland*, 47–48.

406 Tocque, *Newfoundland*, 86–87; Jukes, *Excursions in Newfoundland*, 1:221.

> In the sleighing parties every gentlemen took a lady in his sleigh, and away we went, twelve sleighs one after the other, into the country. Grog, wine, &c. were stored under the seats; and picking a nice smooth place, as on a pond, for instance, where it is sheltered from the wind, we cut down some trees, made a great fire, warmed up the soup &c. and picnicked on the snow. Returning to town by dark, we adjourned to the house of some one of the party, and finished off with a quadrille. Dinner-parties were likewise abundant, in very good style and taste.[407]

During the year, the most popular diversion of this class was the charity ball. Tickets were usually priced at 10 shillings for gentlemen and 5 shillings for ladies. (The average weekly wage of minor government servants at this time was 12 shillings.) The balls were held annually, despite the near-famine conditions for fishing families in the 1830s and 1840s.[408] These social occasions were similar to, but distinct from, those of the Benevolent Irish Society, which attracted their own clientele.

In the second week of April 1833 two balls "on a very magnificent and sumptuous scale" were held: the Irish ball for the funds of the OAS, the other for the benefit of the Factory. "A very brilliant and numerous assemblage was congregated on both evenings," reported the *Newfoundlander*, "who entered most heartily and warmly into the gaiety and delightful good feeling and harmony which always characterises such parties in this town …" The exclusive nature of these occasions was evident in a report of a special event for the benefit of the poor in March 1848, held in "the stone buildings" of Messrs. Rennie Stuart and Co. A cross-section of the upper class acted as stewards—high-ranking military officers and lawyers, members of the Council, several merchants, and several local public men.[409]

The balls of the elite were, however, usually held in unsuitable premises, such as the OAS schoolroom or the Factory, and attracted numbers beyond their capacity. The atmosphere, with 300 or 400

407 Bonnycastle, *Newfoundland in 1842*, 2:146; R. Cuff and D. Wilton, eds., *Jukes' Excursions* (rev. edn., St. John's, 1993), 100.
408 CO 199/33, Blue Book 1836; Cadigan, *Hope and Deception*, 164.
409 *Newfoundlander*, 18 Apr. 1833; *Courier*, 23 Feb. 1848.

people present, could be oppressive. In 1841, dancing went on to "a very early hour" in a room "filled to repletion"; the "excessive heat," according to the report, did much damage to the "cosmetic arrangement" of the ladies.[410] The atmosphere was probably similar to that described by the Scottish novelist Tobias Smollett at a British ball:

> a compound of villainous smells, in which the most violent stinks, and the most powerful perfumes, contended for the mastery ... mingled odours, arising from ... hungary-water, spirit of lavender, assafoetida drops, musk, harts-horn, and sal volatile, besides a thousand frowzy steams ...[411]

• • •

Society in St. John's in the 1830s and 1840s was divided along the lines of class, ethnicity, and religion, and entertainment of various kinds tended to follow the demarcations of social class. Although the social-administrative elite kept aloof from the ranks below them, the middle and working classes to a large extent formed the audience for various entertainment and amusements. Arguably, the popular culture of the period tended to foster ties of community and social cohesion among these sections of society.

The range of entertainment was wide, from the productions of the Amateur Theatre—drama, melodrama, vaudeville, and concerts—the sensations of the circus, exhibitions, and lectures both curious and intellectual, and sporting occasions such as horse racing and the Regatta. Most of these events had their origin in the mother country and, suitably adapted, provided the citizens of St. John's with a varied cultural life that had some resemblance to that of Britain, and was hardly equalled by other colonies. This calls into question the view, not unknown in some historical writings, of the capital and its environs as a somewhat primitive outpost. Pertinent here are the observations of immigrants to St. John's who, before they left England in the 1820s, had envisaged Newfoundland as a

---

410 *Ledger*, 29 July 1841, 2 Feb. 1844, 13 Apr. 1855; *Courier*, 28 July 1846; *Times*, 22 Feb. 1851.

411 T. Smollett, *The Expedition of Humphry Clinker* (Penguin Classics edn., 2008), 76.

land of "desolation" and "a place of craggy rocks, and barren houseless land."[412] They would soon have found that the capital was a city which could stand comparison with many others of its size in the British Empire.

412 See Chapter 2.

CHAPTER 9

Sport for All: Horse Racing and the Regatta

> [A]mateur sport, which is the best and soundest thing in England.
> —A. Conan Doyle,
> "The Missing Three-Quarter" (1905)

HORSE RACING

As with other recreations, horse racing in Newfoundland followed the British model. In 1819 the *Mercantile Journal* took pride in the fact that this was so, particularly as it brought all ranks together:

> We are so attached to everything British, and in a particular manner to those amusements, such as horse-racing which collect in one circle all ranks and descriptions of the people; they form an agreeable break in that uniformity of life which is so irksome: on this subject we are almost disposed to adopt the sentiments of Windham. We think, that, the national character considerably depends, and is essentially formed, by its amusements.[413]

Horse racing in England had a long pedigree, dating from at least the 17th century. It grew rapidly in the 18th century consistent with the growth of towns, which were able to support and supply race tracks on their periphery. By the early 19th century the leisure activities of the gentry and middle classes had migrated from areas where they might mix with the working classes toward admission-charging private spaces—zoos, pleasure gardens, circulating libraries, art galleries, and museums—which effectively excluded the lower orders. Horse racing, however, at least until the enclosed race courses of the

---

413 *Mercantile Journal*, 1 July 1819.

later 19th century, was one of the few arenas where the social classes could mingle. Early races in England, usually run between two horses, were known as matches, and run for wagers placed by the owners and their friends.[414]

The first races in Newfoundland followed a similar pattern—run as matches on Circular Road. "[T]he best of three heats for 100 guineas between the mare Lady Betty Piper and Mad Moll Trip" was an early race, followed by a contest between Nicholas Phelan's Bright Angel and Bennett Routledge's Phoenix for 50 guineas (£52, 10 shillings). Dr. Carson and Dr. Kielly (later political opponents) entered horses for a race on 21 August 1818. An advertised meeting of "St. John's Races" took place on 8 September 1818. It was well-organized, with a committee, a treasurer and secretary, a clerk of the course, and stewards, most of whom were officers of the Army and Navy. Two sweepstakes were on the card, the first of 2½ miles, the second 1¼ miles, with "catch weights to be run by gentlemen only." Several by-matches were also held. Five horses, with riders in colours, were entered for the first race, three for the second. The owners were mainly service officers, some of whom rode their own horses.[415] Similar meetings were held on 1 and 10 October, with several sweepstakes, run under specific regulations. The horses were entered by several service officers, with appropriate colours. By 1819 the races appeared to be an established event. In July 1819 "the gentlemen amateur admirers of horse racing" dined together at the Crown and Anchor Tavern, shortly after a match between Flower and Black Bess, at Best's Farm, a contest which caused "quite a bustle" in the town.[416]

During the 1820s horse racing apparently grew in popularity; on 14 August 1833, an advertisement in the *Times* requested gentlemen who were interested in promoting field sports by the formation of a Turf Club to meet at Perkins' Hotel at 8 p.m. The first race following the establishment of the club was held on 19 September;

---

414 J. Flanders, *Consuming Passions: Leisure and Pleasure in Victorian Britain* (London, 2001), 421, 424.

415 H.M. Mosdell, *When Was That?* (St. John's, 1974), 151; O'Neill, *Oldest City*, 257; *Mercantile Journal*, 28 Aug. 1818.

416 *Mercantile Journal*, 24 Sept., 1 Oct. 1818; 1, 18 July 1819.

four horses started for the St. John's plate and the prize of $80 was won by Rufus. The weather, however, was inclement; and the well-dressed "beaux and belles" who were watching were drenched with rain, "to the great disparagement of their gay habiliments."[417]

Judging by press coverage, the flowering of horse racing took place in the 1840s. At the end of September 1844, the so-called St. John's Races were run at Mount Pearl, and despite the distance from the capital and the inclement weather, "a great number of spectators," the *Ledger* reported, "assembled on both days to witness these popular amusements." Three races were run—the St. John's Stakes ($60), the Tradesmen's Cup ($40), and a third race for hacks. The owners were mostly merchants—Messrs. Douglas, Grieve, Bennett, among others.[418]

A well-organized meeting was held on 12 and 13 August 1845, in Mount Pearl, "agreeably to the rules of the St. John's Turf Club." An enlarged program listed eight separate races: the St. John's purse (entrance fee $10) netted the winner $200, and the tradesman's purse $150. The stewards were nearly all prominent merchants of various political and religious allegiances. The conditions under which the races were run were set out in detailed and stringent instructions as to registration, membership of the Turf Club, entrance fees, and race times. Only the officers and stewards of the Club were allowed on the course, and dogs found on the course during races were to be shot. Horse racing led to a growth of trade in horses. In August 1843 James Clift, acting as auctioneer, offered to "gentlemen wishing to purchase TWO SUPERIOR HORSES for the approaching races ... [a] very handsome BLOOD HORSE, only 5 years old [and] a superior CANADIAN HORSE, 17 hands—5 years old."[419]

A meeting on 17 August 1845 was attended by the governor and the visiting prince Henry of the Netherlands with his suite, who were conducted to the stand-house and entertained by the band of the Royal Newfoundland Companies. Perhaps the presence of the prince attracted spectators for, according to a report, "[a]t an early hour,

---

417 *Times*, 14 Aug. 1833; *Ledger*, 20 Sept. 1833.

418 *Ledger*, 27 Sept. 1844.

419 *Newfoundlander*, 7 Aug. 1845; *Ledger*, 18 Aug. 1843.

equestrians and pedestrians, carriages, jaunting cars and various other descriptions of vehicles thronged the road leading to the Course."[420]

The regulations of the St. John's Turf Club had been promulgated on 14 July 1845, and again England provided the model. The Jockey Club had been founded in 1752 and found a home in the inland town of Newmarket, where the "Newmarket Rules" were published, and widely distributed in the *Racing Calendar*, which began publication in 1773. The St. John's Turf Club regulations consisted of 24 paragraphs, covering every aspect of the organization of races. The stewards were given sole charge of the organization of races and the examination of horses; particular attention was paid to the duties and obligations of members, who were accepted by ballot and paid an entrance fee of one guinea (£1, 1 shilling) and a further guinea as annual subscription. These charges, added to the cost of owning, training, and entering horses, limited the membership to an exclusive club for the middle and upper ranks of society. Non-members paying an annual fee of £2 could, however, enter a horse on the same terms as members.[421]

Races were also run at Harbour Grace on the Cochrane Course. On 9 and 10 September 1845, the programme included a ladies' purse of $24, two races for beaten horses in other contests, a pony race, and one for cart horses. The last caused much amusement as four of the five entrants bolted into the woods, supposedly for berry picking. After the races a match was held between two horses, Don and Sarsfield, for $30. After the latter had bolted, Don was brought in by "honest Tom Webb," who was hailed at the winning post as "the man of the people." The whole show was less well-organized than the St. John's races, the purses lower, and the atmosphere light-hearted, with amateur equestrian gymnasts entertaining the throng. "A vast concourse of spectators of the humbler grades" watched the proceedings. Members and guests included local merchants, service officers, officials, and local notables who, at the end of the second day, retired to the stewards' tent for "an excellent cold dinner" with

420 *Gazette*, 18 Aug. 1845.

421 Flanders, *Consuming Passions*, 425, 426; *Newfoundlander*, 14 July 1845.

port and champagne.[422] The organization of horse racing was exclusive, the province of merchants, the upper ranks of the professional classes, and politicians. For the populace, however, it was primarily a spectator sport, and with access to the arena, if not the actual track, apparently unrestricted, large numbers of ordinary citizens took advantage of this to enjoy a day at the races.

THE REGATTA

Newfoundland can justly claim to host the oldest continuous sporting event in North America: the annual Regatta on Quidi Vidi Lake. Born of the fishery—the earliest entrants were gigs, skiffs, and whaleboats—it established itself as a Newfoundland institution and is, in fact, the only form of popular entertainment that has survived unchanged from the early 19th century to the present day.

The date of the first Regatta has long been a matter of dispute. A sailing match took place in St. John's harbour in 1818, and Jack Fitzgerald, the historian of the Regatta, has found evidence of other sailing or rowing matches in the harbour before that date. But he maintains that the first recorded mention of a Regatta on Quidi Vidi Lake took place in 1826, although according to the wording of newspaper reports it appeared that some races had taken place there in previous years.[423]

The first recorded account of a Regatta at Quidi Vidi took place on 14 and 15 August 1826. It was preceded by a meeting of "the Amateurs of BOAT RACING" on 4 August at the Commercial Room, attended by nine supporters, apparently mostly merchants. On the first day four classes of boats were to take part:

1st class: 6-oared whaleboats and gigs.
2nd class: 4-oared gigs (not exceeding 21 feet).
3rd class: 4-oared whale boats (not exceeding 21 feet).
4th class: 4-oared boats of any description.

422 *Newfoundlander*, 22 Sept. 1845.
423 J. Fitzgerald, *A Day at the Races* (St. John's, 2003), 91, 92–94; *Mercantile Journal*, 24 Sept. 1818.

On the second day three classes of boats and yachts were to compete in the harbour:

1st class: Fishing skiffs all dimensions and rig
2nd class: Pleasure Boats and Yachts, 1st size
3rd class: Ditto ditto ditto, 2nd size

Two committees were constituted, one to make arrangements, the other to draw up rules and regulations.[424]

On the day of the race many booths were erected on the southwest bank of the lake, and tents placed at convenient situations, plus a marquee for the governor. The first race was won by a boat steered by T.H. Brooking. The other three races were strongly contested. On the second day half a dozen boats took part in the first race in the harbour, covering a distance of 7 miles for a purse of $40. The second and third races were contested for prizes of $25 and $20. The bets, it was reported, "ran high," and as on the previous day "money was freely borrowed and lent." The boats were mainly those used in the fishery and the crews classed as "professionals" (those used to hard labour) and "amateurs" (clerks, professional people, merchants, etc.).[425] The whole event bespoke a society in which a certain standard of wealth and sophistication was emerging.

The second Quidi Vidi Regatta took place on 21 August 1827. Notwithstanding the lowering weather, at an early hour the approach to the lake was a scene of "unusual bustle and gaiety from the numberless gigs, wagons and carts … filled with happy passengers, who were jogging, with joyous expectancy, to the scene of amusement." But before the races started, the clouds (according to a reporter waxing lyrical) "were dispelled by the magic influence of the blaze of beauty, elegance, and fashion which graced the borders of this beautiful sheet of water." The first race was won by a six-oared whaleboat owned by W. and H. Thomas, the second by a boat belonging to Mr. Moore.[426] The event was already attracting num-

---

424 *Mercantile Journal*, 10 Aug. 1826; *Ledger*, 17 Aug. 1826.
425 *Mercantile Journal*, 17 Aug. 1826; Fitzgerald, *A Day at the Races*, 92.
426 *Newfoundlander*, 22 Aug. 1827.

bers of the citizenry, attired in their best clothes for a day's outing.

Regattas were held annually for the next few years, with the usual format of rowing matches at Quidi Vidi and sailing events in the harbour. On 17 August 1828 a meeting of subscribers, mostly merchants, was held in the Commercial Room to draw up regulations on the basis of previous patterns and to allot prizes, which ran from $36 to $5. The owners of the boats in the three races of the event were largely merchants, government officials, and naval officers. The governor was present and dined with some "distinguished individuals"; at an adjoining tent "several of the gentlemen of the town" dined together. The spectators were "of all ranks and description," but many of the fashionable females stayed away, apparently because of "the inattention with which they had been treated for the last three or four years." At the end of the usual races 70 subscribers and friends enjoyed "an excellent picnic repast," at which several "loyal and appropriate toasts" were drunk.[427]

The usual preparations were made by the subscribers for the following year's Regatta, to be held in early September 1829. The attendance was larger than ever, with people arriving from "town and country." In the first race, two gigs (one built in Halifax) owned by the regular participants Brooking and Thomas ran foul of each other, and a decision was referred to three umpires, "in consequence of the number of bets pending." Mr. G. Winter steered the winner of the second and third races.[428]

There is no record of a Regatta in 1830, nor in the years 1832 to 1837. The 1838 event, which took place in September, was notable for the presence of the governor and chief justice and naval and military officers, who partook of "a sumptuous *déjeuner à la fourchette*," to the sound of the band of the Royal Veteran Companies. The races, between whaleboats and gigs, aroused a great deal of interest, particularly the amateur race. The event was, however, not as peaceful as on previous occasions; a report stated that "as is usual in this community, those who had not got an invitation to the entertainment ... set to work to abuse those who were more fortunate."

---

427 *Newfoundlander*, 21, 22 Aug. 1828; *Ledger*, 28 Aug. 1828.
428 *Newfoundlander*, 3, 17 Sept. 1829.

Another not very creditable episode occurred at the 1840 Regatta. This event attracted 4,000 spectators, who witnessed a dispute between a Halifax boat crew and local fishers. Later that evening some persons, in an excess of chauvinism, cut the Halifax tent to ribbons, beat holes in the hull of the boat, and stole the oars.[429]

The incident led to a spate of boat building by St. John's craftsmen in an effort to overcome the challenge from Nova Scotia. The local boats were built by Messrs Loveys, Ould and Kearney, one of Kearney's being described as "a fine one as you'd see on the lakes of Killarney." Loveys's boats, the *Ripple* and *Lucy Long*, disputed several races with the *Lalla Rookh* of Halifax, generally being victorious in the main race, "clearly proving," observed the *Ledger*, "that we are not to be outdone in boat-building by the architects of our sister colony."[430]

The Regatta continued to be held annually during the early 1840s, under strict rules which included an entrance fee in shillings, though the prizes were in dollars. The 1844 Regatta "came off with great éclat" reported the *Ledger*, the brilliant weather attracting "great crowds" to a two-day event. The competition between Halifax and St. John's boats, particularly the *Lalla Rookh* and the *Lucy Long*, aroused the usual interest, each taking prizes. On the second day a special race for the five best boats on the lake—"bets being taken to a large amount"—resulted in the *Lucy Long*'s beating the *Lalla Rookh*, as it did in the last race, the sweepstakes.[431] The *Lucy Long* was again victorious the following year, enhancing its reputation as "the swiftest boat we have amongst us," and attesting to Loveys's "own scientific skill and ingenuity of construction." These and later boats were essentially racing shells.[432]

This survey of the races in the early days of the Regatta can conclude with an account of the special Regatta organized in the

---

429 Fitzgerald, *A Day at the Races*, 97; *Ledger*, 23 Sept. 1838, 21 Aug. 1840; *Times*, 26 Aug. 1840.

430 *Times*, 14 Aug. 1844; *Ledger*, 13 Aug. 1841, 20 Aug. 1844, 8 Aug. 1845; *Newfoundlander*, 11 Aug. 1845.

431 *Ledger*, 12 Aug. 1842, 20 Aug. 1844; *Newfoundlander*, 19 Aug. 1843.

432 *Ledger*, 8 Aug. 1845; *Newfoundlander*, 11 Aug. 1845; Fitzgerald, *A Day at the Races*, 82.

harbour on 19 August 1845 in honour of Prince Henry. Merchants were prominent on the managing committee of the harbour event; following a sailing match, three rowing races were held—for six-oared whaleboats, four-oared punts, and four-oared jolly boats. Prince Henry gave an additional prize to the winners of the first race, and invited the governor and council to witness the races from the deck of his frigate.[433] No Regattas were held at Quidi Vidi in the years 1846 to 1850.

• • •

If the Quidi Vidi Regatta was essentially a sporting event based on competitive rowing races, it was also a working-class holiday, a festive occasion which afforded the populace an opportunity to dress in their best, mingle with others, and, for some, to cast off the restraints of the workaday world. At the 1826 Regatta there was a great deal of merrymaking, with parties held in tents to the sound of "lots of fiddles and tin whistles." Three years later, at the end of the races, a picnic party adjourned to Coaker's Farm and spent the evening in "the greatest harmony and conviviality"; it was becoming the custom for people to attend the Regatta "dressed in their gayest attire," and for the social elite—the governor, military and naval officers, and administrators—to dine in tents on the rising ground at the north of the lake, and for the band of the Royal Veteran Companies to provide them with music.[434] The paternalistic nature of the event was summed up by the *Ledger* in 1854:

> It is all very right, proper, and desirable, that the labouring classes should have occasional opportunities of recreating themselves, and of receiving the countenance and the encouragement of "the upper crust" in all such healthful and recreative amusements as they may choose to select, provided that they be restricted to the proper limits which temperance, sobriety, and therefore of good behaviour always enjoin.

433 *Newfoundlander*, 19 Aug. 1845; *Times*, 20 Aug. 1845.
434 *Newfoundlander*, c. 7 Aug. 1826, c. 11 Sept. 1829; *Times*, 30 Oct. 1838, citing *Ledger* (n.d.); *Times*, 3 Oct. 1838.

In other words, the labouring classes were entitled to the holiday occasion provided they behaved themselves. But even from the guarded reports in the press it was clear from the beginning that numbers of the populace exceeded the "proper limits." In 1838 the *Ledger* had complained that, at the August Regatta, "some of the proceedings … were exceedingly discreditable," and at the October event the aforementioned entertainment for the social elite aroused resentment among a section of the crowd. In 1840 the *Ledger* was, however, pleased to report that there was "much less of disorder and riotous conduct than have been witnessed for many years."[435]

Much of the riotous conduct could be attributed to drink. Fitzgerald, in a chapter in *A Day at the Races*, significantly titled "The Liquor History of the Regatta," stated that, from the early years, liquor and rowdiness were endemic, indeed on occasion a serious threat to the event's existence. As we have seen in other chapters liquor, mainly rum, was plentifully supplied by the British authorities in the early and middle 19th century. In one year in the 1820s, Fitzgerald states, 220,000 bottles of rum were consumed by a Newfoundland population of approximately 20,000. The Bunch of Grapes, a public house on the north side of the lake, was a convenient source of liquor for the Regatta, but many spectators brought their own. Men used the occasion to go on drinking binges that might last a week. This sort of behaviour aroused opposition from businessmen (whose workers became absentees), housewives (who suffered neglect), and temperance organizations, and pressure from these and other groups forced cancellation of the Regatta on several occasions, notably from 1860 to 1870, when it was feared that disorder there might ignite similar outbreaks in the city during the turbulent political situation of the 1860s.[436]

During the first half of the 19th century, the citizens of St. John's below the middle class lived in a society economically controlled by merchants, without social welfare (except that delivered by charity), low and irregular remuneration, and no trade unions to protect

---

435 *Ledger*, 23 Aug. 1838, 21 Aug. 1840, 1 Aug. 1854; *Times*, 3 Oct. 1838.
436 Fitzgerald, *A Day at the Races*, 146–49.

their interests. Although there was plenty of entertainment on offer—from theatre to concerts, from exhibitions to horse races—the Regatta was the only non-commercial event open to all, where no rules or regulations restricted behaviour. It was the one occasion on which thousands of the labouring poor could congregate in the open air and shake off the restraints of working life. Most of the entertainment was commercial in that participation was by ticket price, but horse racing and the Regatta were freely open to spectators, and the citizens flocked to them in their thousands—4,000 people attended the 1840 Regatta.[437] The event was the one genuine indigenous recreation, and highly regarded from the 1820s to the present day.

437 *Times*, 26 Aug. 1840.

CHAPTER 10

*Sir John Harvey, J.V. Nugent, and the Inspectorship Controversy in the 1840s**

> But you, Luka Lukich, as Inspector of Schools, really must take those teachers of yours in hand.
>
> —Mayor to Inspector of Schools, in N. Gogol, *The Government Inspector*

In April 1843 the city of St. John's was buzzing with the rumour that the governor of Newfoundland, Sir John Harvey, intended to appoint John Valentine Nugent, a Liberal-Catholic member of the House of Assembly, to the post of Inspector of Schools. Opponents and supporters of Nugent reacted immediately. The Conservative-Protestant *Public Ledger* fervently hoped that Harvey would not "so utterly ... confound and astonish the public" as to bestow the Inspectorship on an "itinerant political agitator ... the last man in the colony upon whom the office should be bestowed." The rival Liberal-Catholic newspaper, the *Patriot*, predictably welcomed the news, asserting that no one in the colony was better qualified or more competent to undertake the duties of inspector than Nugent.[438] Harvey's intended action awoke slumbering antagonisms and for the following three years dissension over the inspectorship flared intermittently, often heated, occasionally acrimonious and, like many educational controversies of the period, concerned less with pedagogy than with the role of the denominations in school governance. Furthermore, the whole dispute, though ostensibly about education, threw a revealing light on the tensions within a so-

---

* This chapter was first published in *Newfoundland Studies* 11, no. 2 (1995), and is reprinted with permission. The text has been edited only for style consistency.

438 *Ledger*, 14 Apr. 1843; *Patriot*, 19 Apr. 1843.

ciety struggling to find social stability and a political identity within a colonial context.

The intensity of the passions aroused by the inspectorate issue can best be understood against the background of the political struggles of the 1830s, when the Liberal-Catholic majority of the House of Assembly, in pursuit of democratic rights and privileges, had unceasingly harried the Conservative-Protestant Council over a range of issues, including the supply vote, revenue bills, the election of officers, the administration of justice, the construction of roads, the development of agriculture, and the structure of the educational system. The Liberal-Catholics had the support of the great majority of Catholic fishing families and artisans, and a sizeable number of their Protestant brethren. The Conservative-Protestants, on the other hand, largely represented the merchant-administrative ruling elite, dubbed a "mercantocracy" by a British observer, Sir Richard Bonnycastle.

Merchants took the lead in presenting to the Imperial Parliament and the Colonial Office a highly coloured version of the admittedly tempestuous political scene—uproars at election times, popular demonstrations against the administration (often quelled by the military), and the rumbustious activities of Catholic priests in support of Liberal politicians. Harvey's predecessor, Sir Henry Prescott, likened the conflicts to a war, and the *Public Ledger* accused the Liberals of severing the union between employer and employed. The situation, in fact, had many of the elements of a class struggle, which might have threatened the status quo in the colony. The British government, led to belive that Newfoundland was in a near-insurrectionary state, took swift action: the Constitution was suspended in 1841, a Select Committee on Newfoundland set up in the same year and the Newfoundland Act passed in 1842, which modified the franchise and inaugurated an Amalgamated Assembly of appointed and elected members, thus effectively reducing the political influence of the Liberal-Catholics.[439]

In September 1841 Sir John Harvey had been appointed governor, charged with the mission of bringing harmony to the troubled

439 See Chapter 4.

colony. Harvey had arrived in Newfoundland with a reputation as a reconciler of warring factions in the North American colonies. Though of humble origin, he had made a brilliant career in the army by a combination of bravery in many expeditions in various parts of the world, assiduous attention to duty and a talent for administration. A colonel at 38, Harvey became Inspector-General of Police in Leinster in 1828, governor of Prince Edward Island eight years later, and governor of New Brunswick in 1837. Despite occasional errors of judgment, his policies in these years were distinguished by a combination of firmness, conciliation, and judicious support for reform in the spheres of the law, education, communications, agriculture, and social welfare, strategies which he was to employ to some effect in Newfoundland. However, as a member and supporter of the Church of England, with Evangelical sympathies, Harvey found little favour with "Old Dissent." The Congregationalists, in particular, were to attack his educational policies.[440]

Harvey soon discovered, below the surface of political life, simmering resentments which the establishment of the Amalgamated Assembly had barely been able to conceal. Not the least of these divisive issues was the education question. The factional feuds over non-denominational schools (which lasted from 1836, the date of the first education act, until 1843) were still fresh in the memory of the participants. From the beginning, militant Protestants, abetted by the Conservative newspapers the *Public Ledger* and the *Times*, had attacked the non-denominational system of public elementary education established by the act of 1836 as too favourable to Roman Catholic interests. Protestants had sponsored defiance of regulations by school boards, resignations of members, parent strikes, and vituperative campaigns in press and pulpit, which had resulted in the near collapse of the system. The Amalgamated Assembly, with weakened Catholic interest, gave Protestants an opportunity to press home their advantage, and Richard Barnes, the member for Trinity, successfully presented a bill in 1843 which divided the education grant between Protestants and Roman Catholics, thus inaugurating a denominational system. The Liberal-Catholic mem-

440 *DCB*, s.v. "Harvey, Sir John."

bers of the Assembly, heavily outnumbered, reluctantly acquiesced in the vote, John Valentine Nugent ruefully conceding that separate education was better than no education at all.

A clause establishing the post of inspector of schools had been tacked on to the 1843 Education Bill by Bryan Robinson, the member for Fortune Bay, apparently against the wishes of Barnes.[441] Robinson, an Irishman from Dublin, but a prominent member of the Church of England, had emigrated to Newfoundland in 1828 at the age of 20, practised law, and in 1843 was making his name as a rising young barrister. His clause (which became Section 19 of the act) enjoined the inspector to make an annual visit to all schools established or supported under the act and to report to the governor their state, the character and description of the teachers, and the proficiency of the scholars. The appointment was to take effect at the end of 12 months at a salary of £300[442]—roughly 14 times that of the average for all teachers.

Robinson's action had not been anticipated, but as a member of the Executive Council it was possible that he had received a hint from the governor, with whom he had close financial ties. Robinson later admitted that the matter had been "suggested to him," but he could scarcely have had Nugent in mind when he proposed the clause. Indeed the *Patriot* alleged that Robinson had created the office for one of his political cronies.[443] Whatever the origin or intent of the clause, its inclusion in the bill was a maladroit move. However estimable in principle, the appointment of a single inspector, added to a bill expressly designed to split the educational system into two parts on religious lines, would have posed a problem in a society considerably more homogeneous than that of Newfoundland in the mid-1840s. The appointment of Nugent merely exacerbated the situation created by Section 19.

Robinson later justified the clause on the grounds that the principle of inspection was "almost indispensable" as a measure of surveillance over an educational expenditure then running at £5,200

---

441 *Weekly Herald*, 11 June 1845.

442 6 Vic., cap. 6, An Act for the Encouragement of Education in this Colony (22 May 1843), sect. xix.

443 Assembly 15 Mar., *Ledger*, 19 Mar. 1844; *Patriot*, 29 Mar. 1844.

per annum. The post, he suggested, should go to "a man of very superior ability" and "a very high order of talents," and he even proposed bringing in a person from Britain if there were no suitable candidate in Newfoundland.[444] Robinson's arguments in favour of the appointment would suggest that he proposed school inspection in order that central control might be strengthened by the investigation of the extent to which local units were carrying out the aims of the administration which financed them. It is unlikely, however, that his action sprang from any deep interest in education or the working of school systems. More probably, both he and Harvey were influenced, in a general way, by the movement for the inspection of schools (and many other institutions) then sweeping the English-speaking world. Harvey, at least, could scarcely have been unaware of that classic document on Canadian governance, the Durham Report. In 1839 Arthur Buller, the educational observer attached to the mission, had observed that "the vitality of every system of education must essentially reside … in the provisions for inspection and supervision," adding that no educational scheme could prosper unless it was matched and regulated by "an honest and active inspectorate."[445]

• • •

In most circumstances, the inclusion of an inspectorship clause in an education bill would have given rise only to the mildest comment. In fact, the first reaction of the Liberal-Catholic *Newfoundlander* was to declare that though the post was "essentially important," much would depend on the character of the person appointed. The *Patriot* initially derided the clause as a "useless appendage" to the bill, a waste of money and a post created merely for a friend of Robinson.[446] Furthermore, so great was the uproar when Nugent's name was mooted that few noticed the presence of three applicants for the post of inspector: John M. Brine, 35 years old and a member of the Church of England; Robert Rodgers, a Scot, who sub-

444 Assembly 20 Apr., *Newfoundlander*, 30 Apr. 1846.
445 C.P. Lucas, ed., *Lord Durham's Report on the Affairs of British North America*, 3 vols. (Oxford, 1912), 3:283–88.
446 *Newfoundlander*, 30 Mar. 1843; *Patriot*, 29 Mar. 1843.

mitted memorials and testimonials with his application, and who claimed he was put out of business as a schoolteacher by the success of Bishop Feild's school; and an unnamed Roman Catholic teacher with 23 years experience who was supported by both Protestants and Catholics.[447] It was only when Nugent's appointment was mooted that political and religious passions were stirred, the *Patriot* and *Newfoundlander* came out strongly in support and the Conservative-Protestant *Public Ledger* and *Times* launched into vociferous opposition.

Nugent's appointment, as was recognized in the press at the time, was part of Harvey's policy of conciliation and harmony, which involved, among other things, giving a limited number of public positions to leading Catholics. The elevation of Laurence O'Brien and Patrick Morris, both prominent Liberal-Catholic politicians, to the Executive Council, had aroused little comment, partly because they had the reputation of being more moderate than Nugent, but mainly because their duties did not directly impinge upon interdenominational relationships. As the *Harbour Grace Herald* bluntly phrased it, Harvey exercised "a conciliatory system of policy, preserving the peace of the country by meeting the prejudices of the different sections of the community, and stopping the mouths of the most noisy of them by throwing down an occasional bone."[448]

In fact, as O'Brien later revealed in the Assembly, the Catholic church had taken Harvey's policy to heart and pressed the appointment of Nugent upon him. O'Brien, an Irishman from Waterford County, had been in Newfoundland over 35 years, building up a business as a general merchant and participating in politics as a Liberal reformer. As a member of both the Amalgamated Assembly and the Legislative Council, he led a deputation to the governor (presumably in early April 1843) on behalf of the Catholic bishop, Michael Anthony Fleming, who had recommended the appointment of Nugent. Harvey, according to O'Brien, had not committed himself at the meeting, but it is clear that he later acquiesced.[449]

447 The Rooms Provincial Archives Division, GN 2/2, May, Sept. 1844.
448 *Herald*, cited in *Ledger*, 26 July 1844.
449 Assembly 15 Mar., *Ledger*, 19 Mar. 1844.

After the flurry of concern in the *Public Ledger* in April, the issue lay quiescent for the remainder of 1843, the actual appointment not being due until May of the following year. Harvey, however, having shown his hand, had time to reflect on the consequences: the alternative of continuing with the appointment and having to face a crisis that would threaten his policy of harmony, or of making some other arrangements, which might contravene the provisions of the 1843 Education Act.

In November 1843, Harvey wrote a lengthy letter to Lord Stanley, the British Colonial Secretary, describing what he felt were harmonious educational relations between Catholic and Protestant following the 1843 Education Act. Obviously unwilling to disturb this state of affairs, Harvey reneged on his decision of April and declared his intention to recommend a provision for a second inspector in order to relieve the government of the difficulty, if not the impossibility, of finding one acceptable to both parties. Harvey did not make it clear whether or not he had in mind two inspectors serving in the same year or in alternate years, but subsequent events showed that he meant that the latter course should be adopted. He justified this step, in his speech to the General Assembly in January 1844, on the grounds that it was "in entire accordance with the principle" upon which the act was based—a reading which could hardly be supported by a strict analysis of Section 19. He duly informed Stanley that this section would have to undergo revision during the current session of the Assembly.[450]

Harvey, having made his decision, lost little time in acting upon it; he instructed Joseph Noad, the Surveyor-General, whom he had nominated to both the Amalgamated Assembly and the Legislative Council, to introduce a bill to provide for two inspectors, one Protestant and one Catholic, to take effect in 12 months.[451] The debate on the bill was acerbic, and from Harvey's point of view disappointing. Robinson, caught in the position of advocating one inspector in 1843, and feeling constrained to support the provision of two

---

450 CO 194/17 Harvey to Stanley, 30 Nov. 1843; CO 194/120, Harvey to Stanley, 31 Jan. 1844; JGA 1844, 10 Jan. 1844.
451 Assembly 1 Feb., *Ledger*, 2 Feb. 1844.

in 1844, took refuge in the curious argument that as the original appointment had to wait 12 months before becoming operative, he was not violating his principles when he endorsed the present bill which, like the act of 1843, also had to wait a year before coming into effect. The governor, he felt, had "perhaps" seen the anomaly of the appointment of only one inspector for two sets of schools, and now submitted a correction of it. The main opposition to the bill came from Richard Barnes, the member for Trinity, who declared he was against the appointment of two inspectors—the duties could be performed by one man of moral honesty, without reference to his religious feelings. He felt, however, that even one inspector was impractical, unnecessary, and costly. Inspection of schools could be left to board members themselves, some of whom carried out semi-annual inspections by two of their own members. John Kent, the leading Liberal-Catholic spokesman in the Assembly, considered the bill to be unnecessary, and O'Brien thought its object was to defeat Nugent's appointment. In the event a motion by Barnes to kill the bill was passed.[452]

The confusion and conflicting reactions surrounding the whole issue were evident when Thomas Glen, a Congregationalist Scot and the Conservative member for Ferryland, on the day following the introduction of Noad's bill brought forward another bill to suspend Section 19 of the act for three years. In presenting his measure Glen came out against inspectorships per se, on the now familiar ground that they were a useless waste of public money for a duty that could well be performed by the clergy on the boards. Kent protested that the bill was "wholly influenced by party feelings," and attempted to kill it, but failed; all the Protestants except Noad then voted for a second reading. Parsons, the foremost Protestant Liberal, though he supported the bill, asserted that "party spirit" was as strong as it ever was, and that if any person but Nugent had been named as inspector the appointment would have been adhered to.[453]

The Conservatives denied party motives behind the bill, Glen stating that there had been every reason to believe that Rodgers

452 Assembly 1 Feb., 15 Mar., *Ledger*, 2 Feb., 19 Mar. 1844.
453 JGA 1844, 16 Mar. 1844.

would be appointed. The arguments were familiar and repetitive. Only Nugent, feeling he could not remain silent, spoke about education as such. He had, he declared, no idea of the appointment when he supported Clause 19 the previous year. The system was an experiment which might be altered, and an inspector was necessary to determine this. Somewhat surprisingly, Nugent suggested that the Austrian system, in which education, he alleged, was forced on the people, might be necessary in Newfoundland. In the end Glen withdrew the bill on 24 April, "in consequence of the advanced period of the session,"[454] giving an effective, if temporary, check to the introduction of school inspection in Newfoundland, at a time when it was developing rapidly in other countries.

• • •

School inspection was an important element in the regulation of compulsory education for the masses, which developed virtually on a world scale in the first half of the 19th century. In Britain, the Industrial Revolution of the late 18th and early 19th centuries, accompanied by a vast increase in population, the mushrooming of great industrial cities, and the rise of a working class employed in the factory production of commodities, presented new and complex problems of governance, quite different from the paternal relations of the pre-industrial era. New forms of social power were needed, not only coercive, but also moral-regulatory. Education, in the basic form of instruction in the 3Rs and religious morality, was the most expedient means to this end, and monitorial schooling—in which child monitors supplemented the work of adult teachers—spread rapidly from the beginning of the century, concerned with inculcating in the mass of the population moral attitudes concerning their place in the social order.

Systematic state intervention in schooling began in Britain in 1839, with the establishment of the Committee of Council of Education, an arm of the executive government. Under its able secretary, James Kay-Shuttleworth, a former Poor Law inspector, the Council quickly introduced a set of bureaucratic regulations which

---

454 Assembly 2 Feb., 15 Mar., 24 Apr., *Ledger* 6 Feb., 19 Mar., 3 May 1844.

enjoined schools to hold regular public examinations, keep attendance registers, and submit to regular inspection by a corps of specially selected inspectors, usually "gentlemen" of high social and intellectual standing. Inspection of this kind had long been known on the continent of Europe and in Ireland.[455]

Inspection, a key mechanism of state regulation, was part of a new style of governance which involved the solving of practical problems by the collection of data. Information on local educational conditions became the necessary condition for the implementation of government policy. By means of guidance and assistance to teachers and the overseeing of examinations, inspectors were able to ensure uniformity of curriculum and teaching method, thus marginalizing alternatives. Above all, however, inspection had a moral-regulatory function. Kay-Shuttleworth issued a questionnaire (containing 140 questions) to be administered by inspectors; apart from searching inquiries into every aspect of school life, 13 questions were aimed at ascertaining the state of "religious and moral discipline," which in his view should regulate "the thoughts and habits of the children." In 1853 he felt able to claim that the labours of his inspectorate had promoted such a degree of "political repose" among the English poor as to save the country from revolution.[456]

School inspection was thus seen by its promoters to have both moral and political, as well as pedagogical, functions. It had evolved less out of mere technical necessity arising from the expansion of a school system than as a response to socio-political imperatives inseparable from the construction of a rational industrial-capitalist state, based upon, in the words of Home Secretary Russell in 1836, "system, method, science, economy, regularity and discipline."[457]

British colonies had not reached the level of economic and social development, nor achieved the same expansion of education-

---

455 R.J.W. Selleck, *James Kay-Shuttleworth: Journey of an Outsider* (London, 1944).
456 F.M.S. Paterson, "Measures of Schooling: Registers, Standards and the Construction of the Subject," *Journal of Historical Sociology* 1, no. 3 (1988): 278–300; Nancy Ball, *Her Majesty's Inspectorate 1839–1849* (London, 1963), 67, 243–51; J. Kay-Shuttleworth, *Public Education* (London, 1853), 87–88.
457 Cited in Selleck, *James Kay-Shuttleworth*, 143.

al institutions as the mother country; nevertheless, in some of the so-called white settler colonies the beginnings of mass schooling were under way, accompanied by attempts at a system of inspection. Bruce Curtis's study of school inspection in Canada West, *True Government by Choice Men?*, depicts a burgeoning colony facing the problem of bringing schools in isolated local communities, lacking both a dominant class of proprietors and municipal institutions, into contact with the central administration. The need to generate forms of consciousness, habits, and outlooks suitable to representative government stimulated the creation, in the 1840s and 1850s, of a corps of school inspectors based on English and Irish models. "Choice men" of some intellectual and social standing, they were charged with much the same duties—the collection of data on local educational conditions, the implementation of central directives, and moral-regulatory governance of the rising generation, which functions, Curtis argues, were fundamental to the process of state formation.

The situation in Newfoundland had more in common with that of Canada West than England or Ireland. Outside St. John's, the capital, with its concentration of political, administrative, and legal authority, the numerous small fishing outports were isolated by the virtual absence of communications and lacked local or municipal government structures. The pool of "respectable" men of substance in small outports was usually no larger than the local merchant or his agent, a minister or priest, and the customs official. Even in St. John's, the civil and judicial establishment in the mid-1840s was small, numbering no more than 82, or 0.1 per cent of the island's population of 96,000.[458]

By the mid-1840s St. John's had become the core area of the country, an *entrepôt* for the whole island and the focus of its political, commercial, and administrative life. Most financial transactions were concentrated there, merchants and traders forming 17 per cent of recorded occupations. In fact, the social and economic inequalities between the capital and the outports, exemplified by

458 Colony of Newfoundland: Blue Book 1844, 72ff.; Abstract, Census and Return of the Population of Newfoundland, 1845.

the exploitation of the latter by the St. John's merchants, amounted to a species of "internal colonialism," the dominance by the core of the periphery. School inspection, whether or not fully articulated by Harvey, Robinson, and others, could only strengthen this situation, by subjecting the localities to inquiry and regulation, gathering standardized information on local conditions and defining a mechanism for the operation of central policy.

Harvey, undoubtedly feeling that school inspection was an essential element of his whole policy, was determined, despite the setback in the Legislature, to press ahead with his plan for two inspectors. "I am led to the conclusion that I have no other escape," he explained to Lord Stanley, the Colonial Secretary, "than to select two Inspectors who shall perform the duties and receive the assigned salary on alternate years ..." To make provision for only one would be to deny the benefit of inspection to one or other of the two denominations, for it could be assumed that each would close the doors of its schools to an inspector of the rival religion. He had no option but to appoint Nugent, Harvey continued, as he was backed by Bishop Fleming and all the Catholic members of the Assembly; with regard to the Protestant inspector he would consult the Anglican bishop, and the confirmation of the appointments he would leave to the Colonial Secretary.[459]

Stanley was unlikely to welcome this turn of events; not only was he the progenitor of the Irish National System of education (which was both non-denominational and had a functioning inspectorate) but he had only reluctantly agreed to sanction the 1843 Education Act, which he felt was a hurried affair, beset with doubtful clauses. In fact, in his reply to Harvey he did not conceal his displeasure. The proposal was "manifestly a most inconvenient arrangement," he wrote, and one he would be unwilling to sanction; he advised Harvey to make a further appeal to the Legislature, but in the meantime to see both bishops and make a "satisfactory temporary arrangement," despite possible opposition. If the opposition were chiefly from one side, he suggested, he would be inclined to appoint the first inspector from the opposition. No school receiv-

459 CO 194/120, Harvey to Stanley, 2 June 1844.

ing government aid, he concluded, could close its doors against any inspector.[460]

Harvey was in a difficult position. On the one hand he had somehow to satisfy the two opposing politico-religious groups in Newfoundland; on the other he was being pressured by the British Colonial Secretary to take a course of action different from what he felt was the best solution of the problem. "I certainly feel indisposed to sanction the plan you have mentioned of appointing, for alternate years, an inspector entertaining different religious opinions," reiterated Stanley on 19 July, and suggested, to obviate the possibility of one class of schools being left uninspected for a year, that Harvey nominate joint inspectors, dividing the salary between them. He felt strongly enough about the issue to write to Harvey again on 27 August, urging him to reread the despatch of 19 July. His advice came too late. Harvey, deciding to pursue his own plans, had already written to Stanley on 13 July, informing him that he had secured an assurance from the Church of England bishop that he had no objection to his schools being inspected by an official of any religious persuasion, and enclosing a copy of the minutes appointing Nugent as inspector.[461]

• • •

What manner of man was to receive the post of first inspector of schools? John Valentine Nugent, dubbed "the O'Connell of Newfoundland" by the Conservatives, was an Irishman from Waterford, 48 years old in 1844. He had come to Newfoundland 11 years earlier, under the patronage of Bishop Fleming, having been forced to leave Ireland, according to his political opponents, because of his "violence in politics." He was well-educated, with a classical background and some training in law, and had opened a classical school in St. John's soon after his arrival. He plunged into politics, however, and as we have seen, became one of the leaders of the Liberal-Catholics, though not a member of the "family compact" gathered around

460 CO 194/120, Harvey to Stanley, 2 June 1844, attached note by Stanley.
461 CO 195/20, CO 194/120, correspondence Stanley-Harvey, July/Aug. 1844.

Bishop Fleming. "A party man … educated in the school of Irish politics," a contemporary journalist observed, "moderation is seldom a characteristic of his conduct." He was one of the foremost popular orators in (and outside) the stormy Assembly of 1837–1841, and in 1842 was elected to the General Assembly as a member for St. John's, following the *cause célèbre* of his arrest during the campaign for non-payment of libel damages. In the early 1840s he became the editor successively of the *Vindicator* and *Indicator*, both Liberal-Catholic journals. Though a colourful political figure, with a somewhat haughty mien, he was an amiable and conscientious man in private life.[462]

None questioned his ability, or his fitness to undertake what the *Ledger* termed "the quiet and respectable duty of supervising … schools"; the whole objection of the paper was that this supervision should be undertaken by an "itinerant political agitator." Nugent was undoubtedly a radical, an Irish Nationalist, and a repealer of the O'Connell school; shortly after the formal arrangement of his appointment he spoke at a Repeal meeting in St. John's which proposed an address to "O'Connell and his Associate Martyrs," and launched a petition demanding "a local Legislature for Ireland." It was for this type of behaviour that his detractors opposed his appointment, rather than (they claimed) for his religion. His supporters naturally took a different line, praising Nugent for defending Catholicism from insult, its ministers from outrage, and its followers from exclusion from office.[463]

The first intimation of his appointment that Nugent received was a letter from James Crowdy, the Newfoundland Colonial Secretary, dated 10 June 1844. "Re the appointment of Catholic and Protestant Inspectors in alternate years under the Education Act …," the letter began, "His Excellency has been pleased on the recommendation of the Right Reverend Dr. Fleming to select you as the Catholic Inspector." The actual appointment, Crowdy continued, would take place on the arrival of Dr. Edward Feild, the new Church of England

462 *Times*, 24 July 1844; *DCB*, s.v. "Nugent, John Valentine"; "Observer," *Newfoundlander*, 8 Aug. 1844.
463 *Ledger*, 14 Apr., 9 July 1844; *Indicator*, 6, 27 July 1844.

bishop, whom the governor wished to consult regarding the selection of the Protestant inspector.[464]

A month later Nugent, who had made all his arrangements for departure, including "a vessel fully prepared," was surprised to find that a formal announcement of his appointment had not appeared in the official *Gazette*—despite the fact that Feild had arrived several days earlier—and urged Crowdy to expedite the matter. On 16 July, Governor Harvey, in a notice in the *Gazette*, formally appointed Nugent as "Inspector of Schools throughout the Island of Newfoundland … by virtue of the power and authority invested in me by an Act of the Legislature." So far, so constitutional. But two appended letters from Crowdy, the Colonial Secretary, addressed to Nugent, certainly did not fall within the letter of the 1843 act. The first reminded Nugent that at the end of his year of office he would be succeeded by "a Protestant gentleman," and that he was to inspect only Roman Catholic schools, except where Protestant boards might invite him; the second was a copy of a circular to be sent to Protestant boards, intimating that "As His Excellency is sensible to the objections that may be felt to the Inspection of Protestant Schools by a Roman Catholic Inspector, he has limited Mr. Nugent's term of office to one year …" Copies of Crowdy's letters were sent simultaneously to Nugent himself; the second letter, however, contained the name of one Bertram Jones, who was to be the Protestant inspector.[465]

In attempting yet another stratagem, this time to placate the Protestants, Harvey had landed himself in further trouble. These highly unusual arrangements gave rise to a storm of controversy in the press and among the public. During the summer of 1844, the issue "engrossed much of the conversation of the day," noted the *Ledger*,[466] and the *Patriot* felt that at no point during the past year had political feelings run so high as at the present moment.

464 The Rooms Provincial Archives Division, GN 2/1, Crowdy to Nugent, 10 June 1844.
465 The Rooms Provincial Archives Division GN 2/2, Nugent to Crowdy, 9 July 1844, and GN 2/1, Nugent, two letters dated 15 July 1844; *Gazette*, 16 July 1844.
466 *Ledger*, 30 July 1844.

"Are St. John's pupils wearing Repeal Buttons?" inquired a Protestant schoolmaster from Conception Bay. Protestant urchins should carry banners inscribed "No Popery—No Surrender," riposted a Catholic. In June the *Patriot* had attacked Harvey's restrictive qualification as "a most extraordinary proceeding," asserting that the governor had no more power to make such an arrangement than the *Patriot* had; to have two inspectors "on the plea of having one of them a Protestant," at an expense of £1,000, would be "a wanton and criminal waste of the public money, and as such should be strongly denounced." A month later the *Patriot* returned to the attack, alleging that Harvey was attempting to appease the Protestants by cutting the situation into two slices, politely tendering one to the anti-Catholic party, and rather reluctantly throwing the other in the opposite direction.[467]

All sections of the press were agreed that Harvey had landed himself in a constitutionally untenable position. The *Ledger* found "no little amusement" in Harvey's attempt to "back out of the 'fix' in which he had found himself," and pooh-poohed the injunction not to inspect Protestant schools except by invitation as so much verbiage, for the act enjoined the inspector to visit all schools. The same paper further maintained that Harvey had acted illegally by assuming the legislative as well as the executive functions of government; if it proved difficult or impossible to provide an inspector "without distinction or reservation, then the clause of the Act was a dead letter until the next meeting of the Legislature." The *Newfoundlander* derided Harvey's action as an exercise of "despotic authority." The *Times* urged direct action, pressing parents and guardians to send in petitions to the Executive if they disagreed with Harvey's proceeding. The Liberal-Catholic press linked the issue to the broader constitutional changes of the recent past. "The small proportion of constitutional material retained in the Amalgamated Legislature is practically growing beautifully less," observed the *Newfoundlander*. The *Patriot* felt that the reform of the Assembly had destroyed the power of the victorious Radicals and infused new life into the Con-

467 Editorials and correspondence in *Patriot* and *Ledger*, June, July, and Aug. 1844.

servative faction, who would never have rallied but for "the kind assistance of the 'Amalgamated' system."[468]

At the beginning of August the *Ledger* made a last desperate attempt to keep the anti-Catholic pot boiling. It printed a letter which alleged that Harvey was aware, or ought to have been aware, that Clause 19 had been added to the bill with the specific object of "securing the superintendence of a Protestant Inspector over the expenditure of public monies entrusted to priestly hands"; the Roman Catholic inspectorship was thus objectionable to Protestants, not from intolerance or bigotry, but because it frustrated the object the legislature had in view. The *Patriot* thought the allegation might be correct, and if so the act had the ultimate design of "insulting, calumniating, and degrading" the Catholic priesthood and people. But if Robinson were not guilty of the ploy—and the *Patriot* could not conceive he had such an intention—then the writer was "a wretch" to utter or conceive the statement. This kind of abuse from the "Orange Press," the paper grimly forecast a week later, would result in opposition that would sweep the "Orange party" from the Assembly.[469]

Some three weeks before this incident, a more well-argued but equally partisan criticism of Harvey and Nugent had been made by Richard Barnes. Using the *nom de plume* "Cato," he wrote four letters, printed in the *Public Ledger* by the editor Henry Winton, a fellow Congregationalist, who shared Barnes's political sentiments. A native Newfoundlander, born in St. John's of a family long established in the shipping business, Barnes, though retaining a measure of independence, had some claim to be considered the foremost ideologist of what today we might term the "radical right." First elected to the Assembly in 1837 (and again in 1842) for the Protestant stronghold of Trinity, Barnes soon became, in the words of the *Patriot*, "one of the most rabid opponents of the Liberal party." In the late 1830s and early 1840s he played a prominent role in the cultural and political life of the colony, notably as treasurer and later

468 Editorials in *Ledger*, *Newfoundlander*, *Times*, and *Patriot*, July and Aug. 1844.

469 "A Catholic," letter to the editor, *Ledger*, 6 Aug. 1844; *Patriot*, 14, 21 Aug. 1844.

president of the Natives' Society, and as the leader of an unsuccessful attempt to abolish the Amalgamated Assembly and redraw political boundaries, a ploy which the Liberals criticized as an attempt to reduce Catholic legislative representation. Barnes's main claim to fame, however, lay in his piloting of the 1843 education bill through the Assembly, crowned by a long speech which revealed a remarkable knowledge of contemporary educational trends.

The first letter of the series in the *Ledger* was published on 19 July, the day on which Barnes, as secretary of the relatively Liberal St. John's School Board, had written to Crowdy informing him that the board would take a neutral stance on the inspectorship issue, neither inviting nor excluding any inspector the governor might appoint.[470] Barnes himself, however, took a strongly pro-Protestant stance, melodramatically critical of Harvey—"Her Majesty's Protestant Representative"—whose government, he alleged, was "sinking into ruin," and whose patronage policy would drive the people to embrace republicanism. That Nugent should not inspect Protestant boards unless invited, Barnes termed "one of the grossest insults ever offered to the Protestants of this country," tantamount to accusing them of "bigotry and intolerance." By thus throwing the responsibility for the rejection of Nugent upon the Protestant boards, Harvey would "keep himself clear of the odium which he supposes will attach to it." The Protestant boards, Barnes predicted, would, on reference to the act, find they had no power to reject Nugent, who was therefore *de jure* and *de facto* the inspector of Protestant schools—despite his "base career" of anti-Protestant agitation and general unfitness for the post.

Notwithstanding his reiterated abuse of Nugent ("a violent political wrangler," "this rabid impugner of Protestantism," etc.), Barnes had sufficient political acumen to situate the issue in the context of political changes of the recent past and Harvey's policy of conciliation. The political strife of the previous decade, he argued, had caused the people to long for peace; the introduction of

470 The Rooms Provincial Archives Division, GN 2/2, Barnes to Crowdy, 19 July 1844. The following paragraphs are a summary of the letter, signed "Cato," *Ledger*, 19, 26, 30 July and 2 Aug. 1844.

the Amalgamated Legislature had killed their political senses to the extent that they had sunk into an "unwise indifference" and reduced the parties to "shattered elements." Harvey, perceiving that some members of these parties now sought personal aggrandizement, sympathized with them and "administered to their necessities." The appointment of Nugent was thus "a link in that chain upon which his whole policy has been suspended."

But Barnes, a nativist and populist to the core, put his faith in the great bulk of the country's "essential inhabitants" rather than in governors or the contending political coteries; the populace, he forecast, would soon display their dissatisfaction with current politics in "the tangibility of action" and sweep from the legislature and the government "moral imbecility, quasi-political pandering, and executive tergiversation." It was not to be, of course. The apocalyptic predictions of both Barnes and the Liberal-Catholics lay more in the realm of political rhetoric than in the realities of practical politics. Harvey was too experienced to be shaken by these outpourings, and he emerged from the controversies relatively unscathed; his policies, until he left Newfoundland in 1846, continued to receive a measure of public support, though the fires of sectarianism were not effectively quenched.

• • •

"Well, a fortnight has passed," wrote the *Indicator* at the end of July, "and the expected *feu de désespoir* has been poured out by the rabid hacks of Faction. Peal after peal has passed over the poor devoted head of Mr. Nugent … and yet, really, we find the poor fellow alive!"[471] Alive indeed, and making final preparations for his travels.[472] He left St. John's on 6 August 1844 and sailed for Fortune Bay; bad weather forced him into several harbours en route, delaying his arrival until 24 August. Landing at Harbour Breton, be was immediately faced with a *contretemps.* He found the members of the Protestant board scattered and unable to meet, and its

471 *Indicator*, 27 July 1844.
472 The following paragraphs summarize JGA 1844–1845, Appendix, First Report of the Inspection of Schools in Newfoundland, 154–92.

few available members unaware of his appointment. On calling at the school, kept on the premises of Newman's, the local merchant house, he was immediately prevented from entering by the teacher, Mrs. Trude, wife of the storekeeper; she stated she would allow him to enter only by sanction of the board or the local members, both of whom declined to act. Nugent had no option but to leave the school unexamined.

Whether or not his reception at Harbour Breton had been due to anti-Catholic bias or pedantic insistence on the letter of the law is an open question, but Nugent found, contrary to the predictions of his opponents, few similar difficulties with Protestant schools in other places. Following journeys through the districts of Burin, Placentia, and St. Mary's, he returned to St. John's from Trepassey in the last week of October. After a fortnight's vacation, he sailed for Twillingate on 3 November, returning to the capital, after some hazardous winter journeys by sea and land, on 21 December 1844. His report was submitted to James Crowdy, the Colonial Secretary, on 17 February 1845.

At a rough count, Nugent had visited 44 schools, 22 in each of the main southern and northern districts, about a third of those currently in operation. He had been prevented from inspecting more by bad weather, the closure of the school, or the absence of the teacher. He had found most schools in poor condition; many classes, in fact, were held in tilts, shacks, lofts, or rooms in houses. In general, however, the inhabitants of the settlements had built, or were willing to build, a schoolhouse. Teachers were conscientious but often unqualified for the task, and all were underpaid, the annual salaries usually hovering around the £15–20 range. Most schools taught reading and writing, a few adding arithmetic. Attendance was usually about from one-half to two-thirds of the enrolment, though in every district there were almost as many children without access to schooling as those on the books.

Except for the principal schools of the Newfoundland School Society, there was no uniform system, declared Nugent; he felt this was hardly surprising in view of the low teachers' salaries consequent upon the "extreme inadequacy" of the education grant. The situation could only be improved, he argued, by the establishment of a Normal School in St. John's and he urged the Imperial Parliament to assist the colony in the matter of education. Nugent's reports on individual communities were concerned as much with the lack of roads as with schooling. Time and again he found that hundreds of children were being kept from the benefits of education by the absence of any form of land communication. On this issue also he felt an appeal to Britain for aid was an urgent necessity.

On the whole, Nugent had carried out a difficult assignment in a conscientious, if limited, manner. Although he had gathered a certain amount of useful material on local educational conditions, he could scarcely claim to have examined the achievements or capabilities of the young scholars, nor inspired the teachers with the latest pedagogical knowledge. He had, however, pioneered the link between centre and periphery. But how far would the legislature take to heart the tremendous difficulties involved in the construction of a viable school system, and accept the probable cost of providing the necessary infrastructure?

These questions were certainly not addressed by the press or by public opinion—insofar as the latter was represented by correspondents in both Liberal and Conservative newspapers—when Nugent's report was released in the spring of 1845.[473] Comment was almost universally hostile, both to the report and to the institution of inspectorship itself. "Unnecessary," "a sinecure," "an unpardonable waste of public money," "an indirect insult to members of Boards," complained an incensed "Iota" to the *Ledger*. The *Weekly Herald*, describing the inspection as a "ridiculous failure," argued that it was needed only where there was dereliction of duty, in which case no board would invite inspection, later adding that £500 had been expended on "a pleasant summer excursion" in which the inspector had done nothing at all. In Trinity a public meeting was to be held to pass resolutions condemnatory of the office and send a petition to the legislature to expunge Clause 19 from the act. Correspondents also alleged that accounts of certain schools in the report

473 The following paragraphs are based on editorials, correspondence, and reports of Assembly debates in *Herald*, *Patriot*, *Ledger*, *Times*, and *Newfoundlander*, 1845–1846; JGA 1846, Appendix, Report upon the Inspection of Schools in Newfoundland, by Bertram Jones, Esq. (Dec. 1845, Mar. 1846), 117–61.

were misleading or that many schools were not inspected at all. After this flurry of public interest the situation was virtually quiescent for nearly a year, during which time Nugent's successor, Bertram Jones, a Protestant and an Oxford graduate, proceeded on a second tour of inspection. His report, delivered to government in March 1846, was in many ways a more thorough and professional production than that of Nugent, though laying similar stress on the undeveloped state of the school system, the deficiencies of the schoolhouses and the teachers, and the physical obstacles hindering progress.

Almost simultaneously with the presentation of Jones's report, the mercurial John Kent took steps to put an end to inspection altogether. In the Assembly on 16 March he announced his intention of bringing forward a bill to repeal the inspectorship clause of the 1843 Education Act. His motive was unexpected and idiosyncratic; on perusing the 1846 census he claimed to have found that a great number of female schools had male teachers who, he felt, were "not the proper persons to communicate information to the minds of the future mothers of this country." To remedy "this evil" he would give notice to repeal that part of the act which provided for school inspection.

This was an argument to "puzzle all the logicians who ever lived," wrote a correspondent in the *Ledger*, and the *Times* felt it was "somewhat singular that the very men whose lungs, on a former occasion, shook again with their declarations in favour of the appointment, are now raising their voices to undo what they have already done." Undeterred by criticism, Kent persisted with his intention, though changing his argument when he presented his bill in the Assembly a week later. Inspection of schools had been shown to be useless and its inutility universally admitted, he asserted, and fearing a resumption of strife on the appointment of the next inspector—who would be a Catholic—he brought forward the bill "to silence all cavil."

Jones immediately protested that Kent was doing him an injustice by implying that his work had been useless, particularly as it had yet to be printed and placed before the House.[474] In subsequent weeks Jones's report did receive some criticism, much on the lines of that which had greeted Nugent's work—that the whole operation was a waste of money, and that the text contained many inaccuracies.

The debates on Kent's bill during April showed that the proposal, on this occasion, did not divide the House on strict party or religious lines. Nugent argued that the inspectorship was a useful office, recognized and found of service in every country and of great advantage to Newfoundland. James Simms, the Protestant Attorney-General, also supported the concept of inspection, announcing that he had been converted by Jones's report. Robinson, the author of Clause 19, expressed "great unwillingness" to vote for the abolition of the inspectorship, feeling that if £5,200 was to be expended on education, then surveillance of schools was necessary and "almost indispensable," as the vast amount of information in the two reports demonstrated; his only inducement to vote for the bill was that the expenses of inspection would be added to the general educational grant. Inspection, he hoped, might be resumed after a few years—a sentiment echoed by Barnes, who supported the bill but desired another round of inspections before the termination of the Education Act.

The presentation and circulation of the two reports—in April the *Times* began serializing that of Jones in its pages—stimulated some members of the Assembly to deliver comments on the state of the schools, a somewhat rare occurrence on these occasions. Kent, impressed by Jones's report, felt more than ever convinced of the importance of education; the report may have inspired him to suggest that priests would take it on themselves to improve Catholic schools, as these were in a worse state than those of the Protestants. J.L. Prendergast, a Liberal-Catholic from Conception Bay who often took an independent line, went further, and after reading extracts from the reports of Protestant and Catholic school boards in St. John's and Conception Bay, asserted that boards in general

474 The following paragraphs are based on *Times*, 4, 22 Apr. 1846, and subsequent issues; *Herald*, 8 Apr. 1846; Assembly 14, 17, 20 Apr., *Newfoundlander*, 20, 30 Apr. 1846; *Ledger*, 22 May 1846.

were entirely inadequate in the discharge of their duties. They misapplied their funds and were indifferent to the interests of schools, which lacked books and stationery, were filthy and disorderly, and had insufficient accommodation for pupils. At the end of the debate, Prendergast opposed Kent and tried to have the bill "read this day six months"—the normal mode of killing a bill—but was unsuccessful; the bill was passed, and the inspection of schools thus terminated, not to be resumed for 12 years.

• • •

The inspection controversy in Newfoundland raises the question of the level of a country's socio-economic development necessary to sustain a viable educational system. The minimum conditions could include a level of national revenue sufficient to provide schools for at least a majority of the population, for an infrastructure of communications and ancillary services, for an adequate programme for teacher education, and for an intellectual elite capable of stimulating interest in education and promoting pedagogical innovation.

Few, if any, of these conditions, it is arguable, were met in the Newfoundland of the mid-1840s. The economic picture was one of modest increase accompanied by large fluctuations; export values dropped by 20.3 per cent in the mid-1840s, and the surplus of revenue over expenditure in 1846 was a mere $13,013. Revenue was largely derived from customs dues, which fluctuated between 75 and 95 per cent of total government income in the late 1840s,[475] an unstable basis for economic planning, or for making up the deficiencies in the number of schools, ancillary services, and road communications. Moreover, few politicians or public men were interested in, or had more than a passing knowledge of, educational trends in other countries. In the Assembly debates, the capabilities and achievements of pupils, the role of teachers and the state of the curriculum received virtually no attention.

---

475 P. McCann, *Schooling in a Fishing Society: Education and Economic Conditions in Newfoundland and Labrador 1836–1986* (St. John's, 1994), 33; McCann, *Schooling in a Fishing Society: Companion Volume*, Tables 1.38, 1.39, 1.42.

A system of school inspection, under such conditions, was always open to the frequently made criticism that it was a luxury the country could not afford, and that the comparatively large inspectors' salaries could be better spent on more urgent projects. When inspection was first mooted, these points had been quickly made. A writer in the *Times* queried the value of paid inspectors. A *Ledger* correspondent contrasted the position of legislators who talked of appointing inspectors at £500 per year and the "utter destitution of the poor"; many schoolmasters were so poor, he added, that they were permitted to fish for six weeks in the spring. Another correspondent from Trinity urged the legislators "who think nothing of spending days, weeks, and months in legislating on College School Inspectors, etc., etc.," to turn their attention to the seal and cod fisheries, which were facing ruin and destruction.[476]

Furthermore, the concept of inspection had not arisen after careful discussion and examination of its functions and possibilities, but had been added as an afterthought to a bill designed for a different purpose; the concept of inspection, in fact, had been appropriated from systems with a different level of social and economic development. All colonies borrow from the mother country, more often than not modifying what is taken for their own uses, but Newfoundland's adoption of school inspection in the 1840s can be seen as premature, an action in advance of its time, before the system of public schooling or the degree of receptivity of politicians and populace was sufficiently advanced to accept it. Inspection, in contradistinction to the situation in Canada West, thus played little or no role in the process of state formation.

The rock upon which plain sailing to inspection foundered was, however, what Harvey termed the "state of society" in the colony, the division of the populace into two antagonistic camps—Protestants (largely Conservative in politics) and Catholics (overwhelmingly Liberal), each with its own school system.[477] Robinson, and to some extent Harvey, misjudged the mood of the country. Catholics and Liberals were still smarting from the effects of the 1843 act,

476 Correspondence in *Ledger*, Jan. and Feb. 1844.
477 CO 194/117, Harvey to Stanley, 26 May 1843.

which they considered, not without reason, to be "nefarious," "divisive," and filled with "the elements of future strife." The Protestants, on the other hand, considered themselves to be in the ascendant, having been instrumental in demolishing the non-denominational school system, pushing through the 1843 act and, moreover, achieving a majority in the Assembly under the 1842 Newfoundland Act. The unfortunate conjuncture of Protestant triumphalism and Harvey's otherwise praiseworthy policy of conciliation, involving the promotion of Catholics to public positions, was bound to lead to conflict. Ironically, this transformed the two men with some claim to be educationists, Richard Barnes and John Valentine Nugent—who in other circumstances might have co-operated in spearheading modernization of the system—into antagonists in a politico-religious battle.

After Kent's bill was passed, the issue of inspection faded from public notice; more important events supervened—not least the Great Fire in St. John's in June 1846—and the chief protagonists left the scene. In August 1845 Nugent had been appointed Junior Master of the newly founded (and non-denominational) St. John's Academy. Richard Barnes died in September 1846, tragically early at 41 years of age. The previous month Harvey had left Newfoundland to take up the governorship of Nova Scotia. In his address on the closing of the legislature in April, he concluded his labours with a characteristically emollient epitaph on Newfoundland's short-lived brush with inspection, commending the Assembly for initiating the inspection of schools "by competent persons, whose Reports will form the basis of future improvement."[478]

---

478 *Gazette Extraordinary*, 28 Apr. 1846, citing Harvey's address.

CHAPTER 11

St. John's Academy 1845–1850: A Battle Won and Lost

> [E]very office of honour or enrolment [is] filled by aliens. What, I freely ask, is the cause of a situation so unusual, so degrading, so humiliating? I answer freely, that ... the principal reason is, the want of the means of educating our native youth ... let us carefully provide the means of training up our tender youth—that they may grow up citizens, useful to the state and honourable to themselves ... I shall move that a Select Committee be appointed to frame and bring in a bill for establishing an Academy in the town of St. John's.
>
> —Dr. William Carson, in the House of Assembly, 19 January 1836

In September 1827 Bishop John Inglis of Nova Scotia, whose see included Newfoundland, wrote to Governor Cochrane on the subject of education. Inglis had first-hand acquaintance with Newfoundland, having toured the island in that year, and written up his experiences in a pamphlet entitled *An Account of the State of the Schools in the Island of Newfoundland*. Inglis drew Cochrane's attention to "the obvious want of some classical school ... in St. John's" and felt that it was "quite deplorable" that many children of the most respectable inhabitants should be sent to England for their education, "or what is still more to be lamented, to the United States of America." He added that so many persons would have an interest in supporting such an establishment that the government contribution might be as low as £200 per year. Cochrane did not reply immediately, but when he took up the question three years later, he informed the Colonial Secretary that he agreed with the bishop's suggestion, but could not at the time recommend financial support. In early 1833

Cochrane impressed upon the Colonial Office the urgency of providing a seminary for the "higher classes"; they sent their children for education to other countries, he stated, "at the risk of returning with feelings estranged from the land of their birth, and with prejudices which may never be wholly removed."[479]

The governor felt that this was an important social question, for on 3 January 1833, in his first address to the newly elected House of Assembly under representative government, he had referred to the need for a seminary for the education of the higher classes and felt persuaded that "this important subject will in due time receive from you that attention it is so well entitled to." His suggestion was not taken up by the House, and the issue lay dormant for another two years. Then in 1835 the veteran leader of the Reform movement, Dr. Carson, decided it was time to act. He had been urging the development of education since the early part of the century, and in July 1835 he announced that he would lend his efforts to the establishment of a classical academy, "with the view of preparing and fitting our native youth for filling the highest and most responsible offices in the state."[480] Emboldened by the statement of Governor Prescott, Cochrane's successor, at the opening of the Assembly of 1836, that "a public seminary for the higher branches of learning and useful and elegant accomplishments would do honour to our society," Carson, on 18 January, successfully moved for a select committee to prepare a bill for the establishment of an academy for the town of St. John's. Carson's long, eloquent, and emotional speech was, however, less a case for a classical academy than plea for social enlightenment through education. His educational ideas were firmly rooted in 18th-century enlightenment principles, with their emphasis on happiness, reason, and nature, and were perhaps in advance of the thinking of most of his contemporaries. The great object of man, he declared, was happiness. It was in the province of

479 CO 194/74, Cochrane to Goderich, 26 Sept. 1827, encl. Inglis to Cochrane, 10 Sept. 1827; CO 194/80, Cochrane to Murray, 11 Mar. 1830; CO 194/85, Memoranda on the Judicature of Newfoundland and on Other Subjects Connected with That Colony (n.d. [early 1833]).

480 JHA 1833, 3 Jan. 1835, Address to the Assembly; Carson, letter to the editor, *Patriot*, 21 July 1835.

the legislator, he continued, to point the way, and to restrain by wise laws the evil propensities of man, to divert him from crime and lead him to virtue. Education was the means by which useful and virtuous objects could be promoted and the individual led to happiness.

Carson then argued that Newfoundland had been retarded in its progress "to happiness, to civilization, to its due rank as a state" for want of the means of educating the native population. The interests of the people had been sacrificed to those of a small minority of seasonal adventurers, and governments and worshippers of mammon had actually cherished the ignorance of the people, for ignorance, Carson maintained, was the best shield of the despot. Eventually, however, a "patriot King" and his wise councillors had granted Newfoundland "the freest and best constitution in the world"; some "dark spots" existed, he acknowledged, but these arose from the administration, not the constitution. One was undoubtedly the fact that every office of honour or emolument in the colony was filled by an alien—a humiliating fact which demonstrated the urgency of founding an academy and "calling from the shades the spirits of our native youth."[481]

Carson's speech was a mixture of Enlightenment principles, political radicalism, and local patriotism. However, it cut little ice with Peter Brown, a Liberal-Catholic who, with a propensity for standing up for the common man of Conception Bay, vigorously opposed spending any of the revenues on such a project. He characterized the proposed academy as a measure which would benefit only St. John's, while the outports lacked schools and other amenities. "As long as I shall have the honour of having a seat in the House," he announced, "I will oppose every measure that will have for its object an unfair distribution of the Revenues of the Colony." However, despite Brown's opposition, Carson's motion was carried without a division and a representative committee set up to draft a bill; the members were Carson himself, Newman Hoyles, Robert Carter (both Protestants), and the Catholics John Kent and Patrick Kough.[482]

The promise of a bill for an academy excited newspaper com-

481 JHA 1836, 7 Jan. 1836, Address to the Assembly; *Patriot*, 19 Jan. 1836.
482 Ibid.

ment, which generally favoured a mercantile education. The Conservative *Ledger* opposed the immediate adoption of the bill, believing elementary schools should have priority, and advocated an academy which would give the mercantile youth "a practical, mercantile, and withal a polite education," including a knowledge of living languages, rather than "soaring into the higher branches of Greek and Hebrew Literature." A correspondent in the same paper considered the establishment of a classical academy to be premature, and advocated instead a number of public schools teaching the basic subjects to tradesmen. Another correspondent in the *Conception Bay Mercury* felt that an academy should be situated in Harbour Grace, away from "the diseases … noises, bustle … and vices" of the capital. The *Star and Conception Bay Journal* favoured grammar schools in populous outports as a preliminary step.[483]

When the bill went to the committee stage on 6 February, Brown moved to have the committee sit again, "this day six months," that is, to throw out the bill. The vote was tied, but the bill was saved by the casting vote of the Speaker, T.R. Bennett, a Protestant. On 10 February the bill was passed and sent to the Legislative Council. The Council received the bill, discussed it in committee, made some amendments, and requested a conference with the Assembly, to which the latter agreed. The Council put forward four objections to the Assembly's bill: the brevity of period of office of the directors and trustees; the exclusion of clergymen and religious teachers as masters, which precluded graduates from British universities; the small amount allotted to expenses as compared to salaries; and the shortness—"five years"—of the duration of the act.[484]

During the remainder of February, March, and early April, there ensued a round of debates, conferences, and reports in the Assembly and the Council, none of which settled the differences between the two bodies. When Carson moved for a free conference on 2 April, Brown replied with an amendment to kill the bill; with the support of a number of outport members, he was successful, and the bill was

483 *Ledger*, 2, 9 Feb. 1836, citing "Philomath," letter to the editor, *Mercury* (n.d.); *Star*, 10 Feb. 1836.
484 JHA 1836, 6, 10 Feb. 1836; JLC 1836, 3 Mar. 1836.

lost.[485] Thus ended the first phase of the movement for an academy. Although the debates on the bill were neither consistently nor fully reported, it is clear that the Reformers wanted a secular institution situated in St. John's and staffed by three well-paid masters.

The Reform party continued to press for an academy during the turbulent years of the late 1830s and early 1840s, when the Assembly and Council were at war on nearly all issues of religion, education, and governance.[486] Bills for an interdenominational academy were introduced in the Assembly every year from 1837 to 1841. In 1837 the Assembly failed to proceed with its bill after the Council had made unacceptable amendments; the following year the bill, again amended by the Council, failed to get beyond the first reading in the Assembly, almost certainly because of the urgency of more important matters; in 1839 the bill was crowded out of the Assembly's program after six weeks of debate; a year later the Assembly passed a bill and sent it to Council, where it died at the committee stage. In 1841, the Protestants organized public opposition to the bill, and the Council unceremoniously threw it out.[487]

During these debates, Brown continued his opposition to the academy. If money were to be granted for education, he had insisted in 1837, it should be for the poor to learn to read and write, not for "educating the rich in unknown tongues of learned languages"; to waste public money on classical education while the poor remained in ignorance was like a man "shipping a master and crew before he had the keel of the vessel laid down." In 1839 he had spoken against a proposal, emanating from the Council, to include several members of the administration among the academy's directors on the grounds that public office was no qualification for a directorship. Brown's interventions had little effect on the supporters of the bill, who derided his views; in H.A. Emerson's words, they were "all froth and no argument."[488]

---

485 JLC 1836, 28, 30 Mar. 1836; JHA 1836, 3, 5, 9, 28, 30 Mar., 2 Apr. 1836.
486 See Chapter 4.
487 JHA 16 Aug., 7, 8, 12, 28 Sept. 1838; 3, 6, 9, 27 June, 11, 16, 17 July 1839; 13, 16, 18, 20 Mar. 1840; 21, 26, 27 Jan., 1 Feb. 1841; JLC 5, 8 Sept. 1837; 25, 28 Sept. 1838; 8, 10, 13, 21 Apr. 1840; 5, 9, 19 Feb. 1841.
488 *Patriot*, 9 Sept. 1837, 20 July 1839.

• • •

The constitutional changes of 1841–1842—the suspension of the constitution, the passing of the Newfoundland Act, and the resultant appointment of an Amalgamated Assembly—formed the framework for a renewal of the conflict over the structure of an academy for St. John's. The debates in this period thus took place in an Assembly, engineered by the British government, of 15 elected members and 10 nominated members, but which contained only 10 Liberal-Catholics, a significant reduction of their majority position in the previous Assembly. The amalgamation upset the balance of parties and introduced new members to the House and, as Nugent pointed out, members of the Council, who had formerly rejected academy bills, were now part of the Assembly, and thus directly answerable to elected members.[489]

In this atmosphere Protestants attempted a new strategy. Instead of opposing the Reformers' position, they introduced a bill for the establishment of two academies, one Protestant, the other Catholic. This was brought before the Assembly on 6 February 1843 by Bryan Robinson, the Conservative member for Fortune Bay. The essentials of the bill: the academies would be financed from "unappropriated funds" in the hands of the Colonial Treasurer, and the sum allocated would be administered by nominated boards of seven directors; Protestant directors would be chosen on the basis of the numerical strengths of the Church of England and other Protestant denominations, with the bishop of Newfoundland a permanent member; the Catholic directors were to be chosen at the discretion of the church; the directors of the respective colleges would appoint as senior professor a graduate of Oxford, Cambridge, or Trinity College Dublin, together with junior professors or assistants, and have full power to prescribe the curriculum; none of the teachers could be a clergyman or hold public office.[490]

Opposition to the proposal immediately came from Methodists and other Dissenters, who opted for a single interdenominational

489 Gunn, *Political History*, 195–96; Assembly 18 Feb. 1843, *Times*, 1 Mar. 1843.

490 "Bill for the Establishment of Two Colleges in Newfoundland," *Ledger*, 14 Feb. 1843.

college; the prospect of the domination of the Church of England in a Protestant college was at the root of Dissenting unease, and they expressed their case in meetings and petitions. The Catholics also opposed the bill, despite the fact, as the *Ledger* remarked, that they had "so large a sugar-plum thrown to them." The *Patriot* unexpectedly took the side of the Dissenters. Finding the idea of two colleges preposterous "in our present state of semi-barbarism," the newspaper viewed Robinson's bill in much the same light as the Dissenters—"a most insidious attempt to enable the Church by law to place her *ascendant* foot upon the necks of the people of Newfoundland"—but it also considered the Dissenters would have done better to have demanded a third college for themselves, as the example of Nova Scotia had demonstrated. Bishop Fleming also sent in a petition against the bill. He objected to it on four grounds: there was no provision for the appointment of Catholics as directors of their college; no mention was made of the fact that the Catholic bishop was the Superior of every Roman Catholic college; the bill ignored the rights of the bishop regarding the nature of his powers of suspension of directors; and the privilege of electing the professors and principal of the college should be subject to the approval of the Roman Catholic bishop. Nugent and Kent also criticized the bill but did not oppose it outright.[491]

Robinson's bill was poorly drafted—he admitted that he had not entered fully into detail, stating he would be willing to make alterations in the text if necessary. He apparently failed, at first, to recognize the increased power of the Methodists and, together with other Dissenters, their willingness to take up the mantle of resistance to the Church of England. But eventually he acknowledged the strength of the opposition; on 28 March, in the course of the debate on the Harbour Grace Grammar School Bill, he announced that he had abandoned the Two Colleges Bill.[492]

With the defeat of the Two Colleges Bill, the way was open for

---

491 *Ledger*, 17, 21 Feb., 21 Mar. 1843; *Newfoundlander*, 16 Feb. 1843; JGA 1843, 18 Feb., 18 Mar. 1843; Assembly 18 Feb., *Times*, 1 Mar. 1843; *Patriot*, 22 Feb. 1843; Assembly 15 Mar., *Ledger*, 28 Mar. 1843; M.F. Howley, *Ecclesiastical History of Newfoundland* (Boston, 1888), 231.
492 *Ledger*, 10 Feb.; Assembly 28 Mar., *Newfoundlander*, 30 Mar. 1843.

the Reformers to bring in another bill to establish an academy. On 1 February 1844 John Kent introduced "A Bill to Provide for the Establishment of an Academy in St. John's." It appropriated £3,500 for the erection of a building and furniture, £300 and £250 per year for the salaries respectively of a senior and junior professor; the masters were to be appointed by a board of directors chosen by the Executive; no minister of religion with a pastoral charge would be eligible for a professorship, and no religious instruction was to be imparted.[493]

In piloting the bill through the Assembly, Kent stressed the social importance of providing for the education of "the higher classes," and though he took a conciliatory attitude toward supporters of religious instruction, he felt that, to obviate differences of opinion and restrict proselytism, religious instruction should be totally excluded. Bryan Robinson argued that this was placing education on too narrow a foundation but, sensing the prevailing mood, declared he would not offer a "factious opposition" to the measure. Other potential opponents of the bill—Attorney General James Simms, Richard Barnes, and J.F. Bennett took a similar position. The bill was read a second time and committed.[494]

Though the *Newfoundlander* called the bill "a wise deference to public opinion," leading members of the Church of England and the Evangelicals were opposed to the measure. At a public meeting on 8 April Rev. T.C.H. Bridge and Rev. Charles Blackman voiced their fears that it would lead to social convulsion and Catholic supremacy. A petition was sent to the legislature, followed by a letter on similar lines from Bridge to Harvey. A last minute attempt by Robinson to delay or kill the bill failed, and it was passed by the Assembly.[495]

The act, which became law on 29 April, differed only in detail from the bill presented by Kent: £3,000, rather than £3,500, would be granted for the erection and establishment of the academy; the directors would number nine rather than 10; the governor rather than the directors would appoint the senior and junior masters; the

---

493 JGA 1844, 1 Feb. 1844; *Gazette*, 6 Feb. 1844.

494 Assembly 30 Mar., *Newfoundlander*, 4 Apr. 1844; Assembly 30 Mar., *Ledger*, 2 Apr., Assembly 30 Mar., *Times*, 17 Apr. 1844.

495 *Newfoundlander*, 11 Apr. 1844; Assembly 24 Apr., *Times* 15 May 1844; JGA 1844, 13 Apr. 1844; CO 194/120, Bridge to Harvey, 26 Apr. 1844.

six-year period of the act was omitted in favour of the enactment resting upon Her Majesty's pleasure; the bill's words "that religious instruction shall not form one of the branches of learning to be taught in the said Academy" were omitted.[496]

This last omission was the decision of Governor Harvey; he felt unable to sanction a clause excluding religion, and persuaded Kent to omit it. Harvey also added the clause suspending the bill until the Royal Assent was given.[497] On the face of it the measure was remarkable for establishing a secular educational institution in a community with strong religious allegiances and a history of denominational conflict, but to some extent it was a product of peculiar circumstances which were not likely to be repeated.

Harvey explained his position regarding the act to Stanley, the Colonial Secretary, representing himself as an experienced administrator, better able to deal with the difficulties inherent in colonial educational schemes than ecclesiastics, especially in a religiously divided community. He would not recommend rejection of a measure calculated to do much good; to render colonial education establishments "too exclusive in their character" could, in his experience, have injurious consequences. Stanley was convinced. Although he felt the proposed academy to be "far from satisfactory," in view of the social and ecclesiastical state of Newfoundland and the "evils" arising from want of general education, he transmitted the order confirming the act.[498] On 17 December 1844 the *Royal Gazette* printed the order of the Privy Council giving the Royal Assent to the act.

• • •

Two months after the Academy Act became law, a formidable opponent of interdenominational education arrived in Newfoundland in the person of Edward Feild, the new Church of England bishop. When Feild stepped ashore in St. John's on 4 July 1844, he had been greeted by a military Guard of Honour of the Royal New-

---

496 7 Vic., cap. 3, An Act to Provide for the Establishment of an Academy at St. John's (29 Apr. 1844).

497 CO 194/120, Harvey to Stanley, 6 July 1844.

498 CO 194/120, Harvey to Stanley, 20 July 1844; CO 195/20, Stanley to Harvey, 16 Nov. 1844.

foundland Companies and an assembly of Anglican clergy and laymen. "I made my best bow," he wrote in his diary, "and that, I fear, a bad one, for I felt in a very strange and uncomfortable situation. There were, of course, many spectators. I just thanked them for their kind and dutiful attention, and walking to the head of the wharf found Lady Harvey's carriage waiting to convey me to Government House."[499] That the arrival of a bishop of the Church of England should be celebrated with such pomp was indicative of the importance felt in governing circles of the role of the Anglican religion as a bulwark of the social order.

Feild brought to Newfoundland a new and very different set of beliefs from the Evangelical credo of his predecessor Aubrey Spencer, namely the High Church principles of the Tractarians of the Oxford Movement. Anthony Trollope, the novelist and essayist, in his *Clergymen of the Church of England* (1866) describes how "the old, rich, bewigged bishops" had been largely superseded by the modern bishop who was "a working man, and … selected in order that he may work"; the new breed were energized by the Oxford Movement, which made "episcopal idleness impossible."[500]

Feild fitted this stereotype in every respect. His belief in the doctrines of the Tractarians, in the words of the author of a recent study, "lay at the core of his being."[501] Some years after his arrival a visiting clergyman spent an evening at the bishop's residence. "[T]he conversation," the visitor recalled, "was about Oxford and Keble, English parsonages and Christian art. A few poems were read from Keble's *Christian Year*, and commented on by the Bishop, who is a personal friend and admirer of the poet." The Oxford Movement which had influenced Feild was founded in Oxford University in the early 1830s by a group of divines, which included John Keble, J.H. Newman, and R.B. Pusey, as a reaction to the tumultuous social conditions of the early 1830s—the advance of liberalism and militant

---

499 Rompkey, *Diary of Bishop Edward Feild*, 31; see Chapter 1.

500 A. Trollope, *Clergymen of the Church of England* (Leicester University Press reprint, 1974), 23–26.

501 S. Sanderson, "How High Was He? The Religious Thought and Activity of Edward Feild, Second Church of England Bishop of Newfoundland (1844–1876)" (MA thesis, Memorial University, 2007), 16.

Protestantism in Britain and revolutionary upheavals in Europe. Hobsbawm has described Tractarianism as "[the] flight from the horrors of liberalism into a truly godly and organic past" by a number of sensitive young men of the upper classes.[502] The movement spread its message via the issue of numerous tracts (hence the nickname "Tractarian") and Feild would have been familiar with these.

Tractarians saw the church as a divinely appointed order instituted by Christ and the apostles, by which God was revealed to men and grace was imparted through the sacraments of baptism and eucharist. Those who administered this communion were seen to be in direct line from the apostles, and all subsequent manifestations were viewed in the light of the undivided Catholic church of antiquity. The doctrines of the Protestant Reformation, and the 39 Articles, had to be interpreted in a manner which revealed the church as the Catholic church in England. The sacramental principle was emphasized in prayer, worship, confession, and retreat, and salvation was effected by submission to the authority of the church.[503]

Feild's exclusive beliefs, allied to his interest in education—he had been an inspector for the National Society of Education in England—led him to busy himself with ecclesiastical and educational affairs. Within two weeks of his arrival, supported by Bridge, a convert to Tractarianism, he was writing to Lord Stanley, the Colonial Secretary, about his objections to the Academy Act. Feild opposed the governor's power to appoint the directors on the grounds that it gave officialdom an unprecedented degree of control over the whole system. More seriously, he felt that giving the directors effective authority to control the curriculum could open the way for a faction of them to advance "their own true faith" which "our laws and institutions" might not recognize.[504]

---

502 Rev. L.L. Noble, *After Icebergs with a Painter: A Summer Voyage to Labrador and around Newfoundland* (London, 1861), 74; G.K. Clark, *Churchmen and the Condition of England 1832–1885* (London, 1973), 54–55, 82–84; E.J. Hobsbawm, *The Age of Revolution 1789–1848* (London, 1962), 281.
503 E. Jay, *The Evangelical and Oxford Movements* (Cambridge, 1983), 7–13.
504 F. Jones, "Edward Feild, Inspector of Schools, 1840–1," *Journal of Educational Administration and History* 9, no. 2 (July 1977); CO 194/120, Bridge to Feild, 17 July 1844, and Feild to Stanley, 19 July 1844.

Feild followed up this declaration by delivering a deliberate blow to the viability of St. John's Academy. On 14 August 1844, he announced that "The St. John's Collegiate School" would open shortly for the education of boys of "the upper classes," giving education in the classics and mathematics, in order to prepare pupils for the universities and for any professional or commercial pursuit. The headmaster would be an Oxford graduate. On 6 September 1844 St. John's Collegiate School opened, established by Feild under his personal direction and superintendence and intended for children of members of the Anglican church. It had been "desired and projected before," Feild wrote later; according to Governor Harvey, the "wealthy and comfortable" Anglicans in St. John's had long contemplated importing a well-qualified teacher from England to supervise the instruction of their children in the higher branches of education.[505]

The curriculum of the Collegiate School included (besides "those things which a Christian ought to know and believe to his soul's health") modern languages, Greek and Latin classics, arithmetic, mathematics, and "the usual subjects of a Gentleman's education." The scriptural instruction would be given by a person in holy orders, and pupils had to attend daily prayers in the church. The fees, £20 per year (with modern languages extra), were payable quarterly, and books were provided at a moderate charge. "It is hoped," stated the prospectus, "that it may never be necessary hereafter to send children from the island for the benefit of a religious and useful education." "I hope by this means," he had informed E. Hawkins, secretary of the Society for the Propagation of the Gospel, "to prevent the establishment or mitigate the evils of a public Academy upon liberal principles ..." Feild declined the offer of a directorship of St. John's Academy. The "single aim of repudiating religious instruction," he explained, made it impossible for him "to lend it aid or countenance"; it also had other defects which would

505 SPG C/CAN/NFL 6, leaflet headed "Bishop's Court, 14 Aug. 1844"; [E. Feild], *A Charge Delivered to the Clergy of the Diocese of Newfoundland, by the Bishop* (Bermuda, 1847), 38; CO 194/120, Harvey to Stanley, 20 July 1844.

render its success "problematical and precarious."[506]

Feild supported the application of Charles Durnford Newman, a graduate of Wadham College, Oxford, for senior master of the academy, with a glowing reference as to his character and scholarship; Newman had arrived in Newfoundland to teach in Feild's Collegiate School, and was thus Feild's protégé. With the bishop's backing, Newman was appointed to the post of senior master ahead of J.V. Nugent, who became second master.[507] Feild had thus placed his man in the key post in the institution to which he was opposed, a position which was to become crucial when the religious issue arose.

The opening of the academy was inordinately delayed. The Privy Council in London, to which the act was referred, did not decide it would receive Her Majesty's "special confirmation" until 6 November 1844, six months after the act was passed in the General Assembly. Further delays ensued, not least the problem of finding suitable premises, and the institution did not open until 29 September 1845, at Castle Rennie, in premises belonging to John Dunscomb, a former Member of the General Assembly. The general course of instruction embraced the Greek and Latin classics, French, mathematics, navigation, bookkeeping, and "the usual branches of an English Education"; Spanish and other modern languages except French would be considered as extras and charged accordingly. The fee would be £8 per year payable in half-yearly instalments in advance. Books and stationery would be supplied at reasonable rates. The academy was open to pupils from the age of eight years upwards, on examination. The hours of attendance were from 9:30 a.m. in winter and from 9 a.m. to 3 p.m. in summer, with a break from 1 p.m. to 1:30 p.m.[508]

On 24 June 1845, three months before the academy opened, the

---

506 CO 194/120, Feild to Stanley, 4 Sept. 1844, encl. "Rules and Regulations of the St. John's Collegiate School" (n.d.); SPG C/CAN/NFL 7, Feild to Hawkins, 19 July 1844; [Feild], *A Charge Delivered to the Clergy*, 38.

507 The Rooms Provincial Archives Division, GN 2/2, Newman to Colonial Secretary, 12 June 1845; Feild to Colonial Secretary, 17 June 1845; *Gazette*, 19 Aug. 1845.

508 JHA 1845, Appendix, Greville to Harvey, Nov. 1844; *Gazette*, 17 Dec. 1844, 16 Sept. 1845; *Patriot*, 17 Sept. 1845.

Gazette had announced the names of the nine directors which Governor Harvey had appointed: Chief Justice Thomas Norton; James Crowdy, Colonial Secretary and Speaker of the House; William Thomas, MGA, an Evangelical merchant; Patrick Morris, Colonial Treasurer; Thomas Bennett, MGA, merchant and brother of the Conservative Charles Fox Bennett; T.B. Job, MGA (1846) Congregationalist merchant; John Kent, MGA, Liberal-Catholic and pilot of the act; John Rochfort, MD, physician and community activist; and John Stuart, MGA, a merchant. They were hardly a representative selection of the community, and few had been concerned with education. The governor's "irresponsible favourites"[509]—office holders or nominated members of the General Assembly—numbered eight out of the nine members; Liberal-Catholics, and those who had championed an academy from the beginning, had to be content with one representative.

This imbalance caused less concern than the fact that none of the members were natives of Newfoundland, which led to a nativist uproar which lasted throughout the summer, cutting across religious and political divisions. Editorials and letters (the latter usually signed "A Native") crowded the pages of the *Patriot*, the *Newfoundlander*, the *Weekly Herald*, and the *Ledger*, giving vent to what the *Newfoundlander* termed a feeling of "general indignation" among the native population. The *Gazette* and *Times*, however, supported Harvey, with the *Courier* neutral. Although the *Newfoundlander* professed itself satisfied with a "fair proportion" of native officials, the *Patriot* declared that natives had an "indisputable right" to a preference before all others regarding official appointments. Nativists pressed their case at a public meeting attended by Parsons and other prominent adherents of the cause. Harvey, however, denied partiality, maintaining that if there were two equally qualified candidates for office, his feeling would be to give preference to a native.[510]

---

509 Biographical details from *ENL* and *DCB*; *Patriot*, 2 July 1845.

510 *Newfoundlander*, 7 July 1845; *Gazette*, 8, 15 July 1845; *Times*, 16, 19 July 1845; *Courier*, 21, 28 July, 8 Aug. 1845; *Patriot*, 16 July 1845; The Rooms Provincial Archives Division, GN 2/1, Memorandum of Sir John Harvey, 19 July 1845.

The appointment of Harcourt Mooney as secretary of the academy at a salary of £150 per year—"some hungry cormorant from another soil," as the *Patriot* termed him—aroused both nativist and class passions. Public opinion was further inflamed when it became known, at the end of August 1845, that the fees for the academy—still to be opened—were to be set at £8 per year. Catholic opinion in particular reacted angrily to what they saw as class discrimination. The *Indicator* hoped that the institution would be open to all, including "the shopkeeper and the industrious mechanic," but the directors had opted for "an exclusive establishment for the benefit of a few would-be Aristocrats." We do not blame the directors, the paper continued; "[they] were appointed to work an Act to which the majority of them had proved hostile"; the real culprit was Harvey: "on His Excellency alone the onus lies," for he knew that the majority of the Council was against the academy and would eventually attempt to make it an "exclusive establishment." When the Council had been brought face to face with the Assembly (in the General Assembly), wrote a perceptive correspondent in the *Patriot* in July, they passed the bill they had rejected so often; after that the only alternative they had left was to destroy its usefulness.[511]

These developments on the part of those less enthusiastic than the Reformers about the success of the academy did not argue well for its future. To make matters worse, less than six months after its opening in September 1845 the academy found itself in financial difficulties. In March 1846 the directors petitioned the House for a sum equal to the interest on the non-expended loan of £3,000 (the initial cost); receipts had not covered the rent of the building and other expenses, and the directors wished to employ a third master to superintend the English department.[512]

The first report of the directors was also issued on 12 March 1846 according to the Journal of the General Assembly, but was not printed in the Appendix; the General Assembly debate on the same date, however, covers its substance. Those directors present—Kent,

511 See newspaper press, 30 June–5 Aug. 1845; *Patriot*, 2, 9 July 1845; *Ledger*, 11 July 1845; *Indicator*, 20 Sept. 1845. Cf. also *Patriot*, 12, 19 Nov. 1845; "A Native Youth," letter to the editor, *Patriot*, 16 July 1845.
512 JGA 1846, 12 Mar. 1846, petition of Thomas Norton.

Morris, and Thomas—defended the document. Bryan Robinson and Richard Barnes were its main critics, attacking the high fees charged and deploring the lack of information on the number of pupils, the monies received or spent, and any information on the character or progress of the institution. The directors pleaded that the institution was still in its early stages, that suitable accommodation had been hard to find, and that the fees were set at £8 per year in order to prevent injury to private schools.[513]

Life in the capital was interrupted by the Great Fire of June 1846 and its aftermath, which lasted well into 1847. This was probably one of the reasons for the delay in the publication of the next report of the directors, which was dated 15 January 1849, but covered the years 1847 and 1848. It revealed that by the beginning of 1847 the academy had become "considerably in debt" and faced a decreasing income. Thomas Talbot, who had been taken on as third master in the middle of 1846 at a salary of £100 per year, was dismissed, and the secretary's salary cut by half, and steps were being taken to find accommodation other than Castle Rennie, which was costing £100 per year. Furthermore, the directors declared that there was a general impression that the academy had failed to accomplish the objects for which it was established and had disappointed public expectations of its general utility; the number of pupils had never exceeded 26 at any one time. They attributed the relative weakness of the institution to three circumstances: the inconvenient situation of the building at Castle Rennie, which was scheduled to be relinquished in favour of cheaper temporary accommodation; the annual fee of £8, now reduced to £5; and the classical and higher scientific curriculum, which had been modified in favour of an "extensive mercantile education" based on modern languages, history, and practical science. The most disquieting aspect of the report was, however, the disclosure that enrolment was falling—from 26 to 16—and that the financial situation was weak; £58 was owed in fees, £135 worth of books remained unsold, and the balance at the end of the year was a mere £4.[514]

---

513 JGA 1846, 12 Mar. 1846; Assembly 12 Mar., *Times*, 21 Mar. 1846.
514 JHA 1848–1849 Appendix, Report of the Board of Directors of the St. John's Academy for the Year 1848 (5 Jan. 1849).

Newspaper comment was mixed. The *Times* took the most extreme stance, alleging that the academy was "a job" from the beginning, with some members of the Assembly voting for it for the sake of popularity or expediency. The paper called for the Academy Act to be repealed rather than amended, on the grounds that the institution had failed in its object and was now a public burden. It also raised for the first time the religious issue, alleging that the exclusion of religious teaching was one of the principal grounds of opposition; once the advocates of "worldly education" had won the day, the paper concluded, "the right-minded parts of the community could only evince their displeasure by withholding patronage."[515]

The *Newfoundlander*, though agreeing that the academy had serious defects—the building was too distant and the fees too high—urged remodelling rather than abolition in order to meet the requirements of the people, especially the middle classes. The Methodist-orientated *Courier* was in basic agreement; children of masters, mates, clerks, shopkeepers, and superior tradesmen deserved a sound education in literature and science at a moderate cost. If the act were repealed, the paper prophesied, the inevitable outcome would be three academies, which would be more expensive and less efficient.[516]

In November 1848 a long-awaited general election was called, and the political landscape was modified. The Legislative Council and the House of Assembly were restored and the Liberals returned nine membe rs, though Nugent lost his seat, probably because of his public office. In January 1849, in the newly convened Assembly, Shea and Hoyles moved for a Select Committee to inquire into the working of the act. Both argued that the intentions of the legislature had not been realized, professed to find themselves at a loss as to where the fault lay, and urged the importance of higher education for the colony, Hoyles pointing out that an education abroad was not only expensive but tended to denationalize the youth. However, John Delaney, the Liberal member for Placentia St. Mary's, successfully

515 *Times*, 10, 17, 24, 28 June, 1 July 1848.

516 *Newfoundlander*, 15, 22 June 1848; *Courier*, 17, 20, 22, 27, 29 June, 13 July 1848.

moved that the inquiry be postponed until the next directors' report was received.[517]

• • •

The year 1850 had opened with the publication on 31 January of what was to be the last report of the directors—of which the Conservatives Thomas Bennett and Hugh Hoyles were now members. The report began, curiously, with letters from Newman and Nugent.[518] Unsurprisingly, Newman began his missive with the oft-repeated statement that the inhabitants of St. John's "have evidently no confidence in the system of education there pursued," professed himself unsurprised at its "failure," and hoped that his suggestions for reform based on "general principles" would be taken up by the legislature. The most obvious objection to the academy was the absence of all religious instruction. Children ought to be taught good habits and right principles, that is, the application of Christian doctrines "to the actions and business of everyday life," which was impossible in the present academy. Discipline, moreover, should be based on an appeal to a boy's religious principles, emanating from a person whose religion the boy respected. The only way forward for the academy, Newman pronounced, was "entire separation," and the establishment of three schools—Roman Catholic, Church of England, and "Protestants of other denominations." He would give up £100 of his salary to help fund a master for the third school, relying on fees to top up his salary, with the management of the school in his own hands.

Nugent began his letter by stating that an education for the middle class, leading to professional positions, was unavailable in Newfoundland; work in a counting house or in command of a trading vessel was the most such parents could obtain for their children. Reformers in the Assembly had sought to correct this state of things by passing bills for an academy in six successive sessions, none of which became law until the Academy Bill was passed in the Amal-

---

517 Gunn, *Political History*, 107–109, 116–17; Assembly 18 Jan., *Newfoundlander*, 25 Jan. 1849.

518 JHA 1850, App., Report of the Directors of St. John's Academy (31 January 1850), on which the following is based.

gamated Assembly. Children of mechanics and of people in middle life had most distinguished themselves at the academy, which was sufficient evidence that it was fulfilling its objective, despite all difficulties. However, he proposed a compromise on the religious issue: an academy under the control and management of the masters, with religious instruction imparted by three chaplains.

The report of the directors which followed was short. It began by stating that the anticipation of a rapid improvement in the academy's state and condition had not been realized. Neither the move to a more central position in the town nor the decrease in fees had resulted in an increased attendance. An examination of the pupils in the summer of 1849, in the presence of Governor LeMarchant and local notabilities,[519] had satisfied the directors as to the competence of the masters, but the directors felt that the division of powers, with the teachers responsible to the government and the directors merely guiding the masters, was productive of the worst consequences. Following Newman, they emphasized that the most serious cause of the lack of success of the academy was the "entire absence … of all religious teaching"; the confidence of the public would never be obtained without it. Newman's suggestion of three schools in the same building, plus a new principle of instruction, would restore the public's faith in the institution; without these changes, the directors concluded, the academy "ought no longer to be continued a burden upon the funds of the Colony …"

Hugh Hoyles, the intrepid exponent of the Conservative position on education, leapt in to give the *coup de grâce*. In the Assembly on 19 March he proposed that the academy be reorganized, with three masters representing Roman Catholics, Episcopalians, and Wesleyans, with salaries of £200, £200, and £150 respectively. Opposition, not unexpectedly, came from the Liberal benches, mainly in the persons of J.L. Prendergast and R.J. Parsons, whose talent for invective ("malignant movement," "unmitigated baseness," "foul design," etc.) tended to obscure their party's policy; they accused Hoyles of a factional plot against the academy involving the unseating of Nugent as second master. Opposition was carried on outside

519 *Post*, 7 July 1849.

the Assembly at a meeting in the Market House, convened by 52 citizens aiming to petition the legislature to repeal the Academy Act; it was broken up by what were apparently pro-Nugent forces.[520]

The debate in the Assembly was resumed a week later. It ended with the Liberal John Delaney successfully moving that both masters be heard at the bar of the House[521]—an unprecedented measure significant, perhaps, of the Assembly's impatience with the continuing discussion. When Newman and Nugent appeared before the House on 2 April, the former commenced his speech by emphasizing his conception of an academy—an institution to give youth of the higher and middle class "the education of gentlemen," thus fitting them for the learned professions. He once again placed the academy's failure on the absence of religious teaching; religion, he maintained, would be the principle to which the pupils could relate every action of their lives. He reiterated his proposal for three academies—Church of England, Roman Catholic, and other Protestants. Nugent, as might be expected, took a diametrically opposite view, strongly supporting the continuation of one academy, mainly on the grounds that the education of the middle classes would stimulate a general intellectual advance. He denied that the academy had failed, though he conceded that it had not succeeded as well it might have done, partly because it had been attacked by the press from the beginning. Attendance was not the issue—Feild's school had only 14 pupils, whereas the academy had 17. The appointment of masters by the Executive had no effect on the school, and he maintained that there was no difference of opinion between them. The academy, he concluded, had whetted the appetite for education among the middle classes; it was "fulfilling its destiny," and the legislature was bound to support it.[522]

Two conceptions of an academy were thus placed before members of the Assembly: on the one hand, a tripartite denominational institution devoted to the preparation of the higher classes for the professions; on the other, a single secular academy for the middle

520 Assembly 18, 19 Mar., *Post*, 19, 21 Mar. 1850; *Post*, 20 Mar. 1850; *Courier*, 23 Mar. 1850.
521 Assembly 27 Mar., *Post*, 1 Apr. 1850.
522 Assembly 2 Apr., *Post*, 3 Apr. 1850.

classes which would stimulate a general intellectual advance. This was the position when Hoyles (called "the leader in remodelling St. John's Academy") introduced a second proposal on 2 April. He began by dismissing as "trivial" the reasons for the failure of the academy given by Newman, Nugent, and others—residence disputes, the amount of fees, difficulties with fuel, the situation of the building—but made much of complaints, "frequently made to the Directors," about the number of holidays given to the children and the numerous absences of the masters—both allegations hotly denied as "utterly false" by Nugent in a letter to the *Patriot*.[523] Hoyles then turned to what he considered the most important issue—"the propriety of dividing the school"—which was the crux of the position of the Feild-Newman-Hoyles axis.

His resolution followed his previous one—the tripartite division of the Academy—with one important difference: the substitution of "other Protestants" for Methodists, which had been part of his proposal of 19 March. Specifically, he proposed that the directors should appoint three or more masters, one Roman Catholic at £250 per year, one Church of England at £200 per year, and a master or masters of "one or more of any other Protestant denominations with salaries in the whole of £150." Until a suitable building was established the masters would provide school rooms at their own expense, retaining the fees themselves.[524]

The suggestion of a school for "other Protestants" rather than for Methodists was an astute move, holding out to the whole body of Dissenters the prospect of their own institution, rather than confining it to the largest group. That his calculation was sound was demonstrated two weeks later, when the Methodists, Congregationalists, Presbyterians, and the Scottish churches, in a joint petition, agreed to the formation of a combined school.[525]

On 4 April the House resolved itself into a committee and, on

---

523 J. Condon to Hoyles, *Post*, 19 Mar. 1850; Assembly 2 Apr., *Post*, 4 Apr. 1850; Nugent, letter to the editor, *Patriot*, 6 Apr. 1850.

524 Assembly 2 Apr., *Post*, 3 Apr. 1850.

525 JHA 1850, 17 Apr. 1850, The Petition of the Undersigned Presbyterians of the Established Church of Scotland, Wesleyans, Congregationalists, and Presbyterians of the Free Church of Scotland.

the motion of Hoyles, resolved:

> That it is the opinion of this Committee that the appointment of masters should be vested in the Directors; that three or more masters should be appointed as follows:—one Roman Catholic with a salary of £250; one of the Church of England with a salary of £200; one or more of any other Protestant denomination at salaries in the whole of £150; that until a building for such purposes may be erected by the colony, the said masters shall, at their own expense, provide school-rooms and the necessary contingencies for their respective Schools; and that they shall be permitted to retain for their own use all fees which they may respectively receive, except such amounts as may be necessary to defray the contingencies of the Board of Directors.[526]

G.H. Emerson, the member for Twillingate and Fogo, though he approved of the directors' appointing the masters, opposed the resolution on the grounds that no public money should be devoted to different religious sects. Prendergast dismissed the resolution as "one of those crude attempts at legislation … of which they had several examples from the hon. member for Fortune Bay." Shea, however, aligning himself with the opposition, declared there was "an absolute necessity" for a division of the academy into three parts; though not meeting his own arrangement, it was the best under the present circumstances. The resolution was adopted; the Colonial Treasurer, Hoyles, Job, Shea, and Winser voting for it, with Prendergast against—only five members in favour out of a House of 15. It was hardly a representative vote, but it revealed that some members of the opposition, presumably influenced by the statements of Newman, Hoyles, and the directors, were beginning to think in terms of a tripartite institution. Hoyles then gave notice that he would bring in a bill to amend the act for the establishment of an academy in St. John's. On 5 April he duly brought in his bill, to be read a second time the following day. Job (Congregationalist, Trinity Bay), though

526 JHA 1850, 4 Apr. 1850; Assembly 4 Apr., *Post*, 5 Apr. 1850.

in favour of one academy, believed that the issue had become "either a repeal of the act or a division of the institution." The bill was actually read on 15 April. A motion by Prendergast to kill it was defeated, and it was set to be committed on the 16th. The Council agreed.[527]

The House did not, however, go into committee until the 17th, when Hoyles explained that he saw no alternative but either to leave the institution as it was, "a useless burden on the revenues of the colony," or to add another £100 to the expenditure for its maintenance, which was not possible. Therefore, he felt, that the only means of improving the academy was division into three sections. If this were done, however, he would not be a party to reducing the salary of either master, and as he would certainly not consent to the institution remaining as it was, he would put an end to the academy altogether, by moving an amendment to repeal the act under which it was established. Hoyles's "amendment" thus became a proposal to abolish the academy. It was met with a wall of opposition. Hanrahan (Liberal-Catholic, Conception Bay), Parsons, Job, Prendergast, Emerson, and Shea, though they expressed themselves differently, were all adamantly against Hoyles's position.[528] If some members of the Assembly had been in favour of division, they had now changed their minds and a greater number now wanted to keep the academy in being.

In the face of this obduracy, Hoyles withdrew his motion and, feeling he was on surer ground, moved that five-member boards of directors for each of the schools be appointed. The opposition inexplicably capitulated, the motion was carried, and the bill passed. It became law on 30 April 1850. The act appointed three five-member boards of directors—Roman Catholic, Church of England, and General Protestant—who were empowered to appoint masters—one each to the Catholic and Anglican boards and "one or more" to the General Protestant, the posts of present masters being vacated. The masters were to provide suitable rooms for their own schools at their own expense until a suitable building for the Academy be

527 Assembly 4 Apr., *Post*, 8 Apr. 1850; Assembly 5 Apr., *Post*, 8 Apr. 1850; Assembly 15 Apr., *Post*, 19 Apr. 1850; Council 19 Apr., *Post*, 20 Apr. 1850.
528 Assembly 17 Apr., *Post*, 23 Apr. 1850.

erected, and were to receive the fees of their respective schools, from which they might also employ assistants. Their salaries were £200 for the Church of England master, £250 for the Catholic master, and £150 for those of the General Protestants.[529]

Thus the battle for a single interdenominational academy was lost. The *coup de grâce* had been delivered by Hugh Hoyles who, building on the efforts of Newman and his mentor Feild, conducted his campaign with the skill of a seasoned politician. He had refused to be drawn into a lengthy debate on "trivial" reasons for the "failure" of the academy, and concentrated on the division of the institution on a sectarian religious basis. He had taken care to win over the Dissenting interest with the offer of an academy of their own. Finally he outflanked any renewed opposition by threatening to abolish the academy altogether, which made division into three schools appear a lesser evil. It is difficult to pinpoint the reasons for the support given by the Liberals and Reformers for Hoyles's plan. Admittedly the debates took place at the end of the session when they had to jostle for attention with those on the reduction of the grant for elementary education. J.G. Falle (Protestant, Burin) charged some members with "no small degree of inconsistency" in that they had opposed the principle of separation regarding elementary education, but now advocated it for the academy. Ambrose Shea, whose stance on education had been somewhat indeterminate, argued that support for division was the only one that could be adopted under the circumstances—there was no other alternative left them, and "the present arrangement was necessarily forced upon us as the only one to which recourse could be had under existing difficulties."[530]

In wider perspective, the project had weaknesses from the beginning. It began under the shadow of Feild's Collegiate School; the appointed board of directors consisted of members who were, to say the least, lukewarm to the project, and who failed to carry out their duties with any enthusiasm; furthermore, the hostile propaganda of Newman, and Hoyles's stratagems in the Assembly, did not

529 13 Vic., cap. 5, An Act to Provide for the Establishment of an Academy in St. John's (30 Apr. 1850).
530 Assembly 17 Apr., *Post*, 23 Apr. 1850.

meet with the opposition that might have been expected from the Reformers and Liberals who had founded the academy. The turning point proved to be the resolution for three academies of 4 April, when Hoyles manoeuvred a handful of opponents into voting for division. After that, it was exceedingly difficult for the academy's supporters to uphold the concept of a single interdenominational institution.

The Roman Catholic academy, with J.V. Nugent as principal, opened on 13 May 1850 at his residence, Eton Buildings, Monkstown. The curriculum, divided into four parts, consisted of the basic subjects, mathematics with application to land and marine surveying, commercial subjects, and Greek, Latin, French, and Spanish. The fees ranged from £1.10 to £2.10 for each of two terms. The directors—John Kent, John Rochford, MD, Lawrence O'Brien, and Philip Little, were headed by Bishop Mullock.[531]

C.D. Newman was the headmaster of the Church of England academy, which opened on 22 July 1850 in the building of the Collegiate School. The directors included the Rev. Bridge and Hugh Hoyles. It was advertised as preparing boys for "the Learned Professions or for Commercial pursuits." Divided into lower and upper schools, the curriculum and fees were much the same as those in Nugent's academy. The General Protestant academy, with Adam Scott as master, was advertised to open on 1 October 1851, and an advertisement for a centrally situated house "suitable for the purpose of the Academy" was appended to the notice. The directors were prominent Dissenters.[532]

By March 1852 the three academies were in full operation, and the number of pupils in each was published. The Roman Catholic academy had 36 pupils, including two Protestants; the General Protestant had 24, consisting of 11 Church of England, eight Presbyterians, three Methodists, and two Congregationalists; the Church of England numbered 18 pupils, including one Congregationalist and two Methodists.[533] In this way denominationalism entered higher education in St. John's.

531 *Patriot*, 18 May 1850; *Gazette*, 7 May 1850.
532 *Post*, 30 May 1850; *Gazette*, 7 May 1850; *Patriot*, 6 Sept. 1851.
533 JLC 1852, Appendix No. 32.

CHAPTER 12

Bishop Feild, Hugh Hoyles, and the 1852 Division of the Protestant Education Grant

> The chief and special object of requiring for the Church its just portion of the legislative grant is, that the poor children of the Church may be instructed, among other things, in the religious belief of their parents, without let or hindrance ... the Church of England does consider her special doctrines and articles of faith of sufficient importance to be inculcated in her schools ...
>
> —Bishop Edward Feild, Remarks on the Subdivision of the Legislative Grant (1852)

> I can see no reason why children of all denominations may not be instructed to read and write, and receive the rudiments of a good education in the same school, without either endangering their faith or morals.—Any system which divides the different Protestant denominations must have a vicious tendency in a moral point of view; it must foster sectarian differences and cherish invidious distinctions; if these bad feelings are instilled in childhood, they must materially influence the conduct of men in the after life.
>
> —G.H. Emerson, Address to the Electors of Fogo, 23 August 1852

It is a proposition generally acknowledged by historians that education in Newfoundland, after the passing of the 1843 Education Act, was, until 1874, structured on the division of the education grant between Protestant and Catholics. Almost hidden from history has been the breaching of the provisions of the 1843 Education Act by a further act in 1852 which encroached on the hitherto inviolable preserves of denominational education.[534] This act divided the Protestant Education Grant between schools of the Church of England and other Protestant churches in the districts of St. John's and Conception Bay, the two most populous districts of the island, containing 65,000 people or 52 per cent of the total population.[535] This highly unusual proceeding took place in an Assembly dominated by anti-division Liberals. The act remained on the statute book for one year. Perhaps more important than the passing of the act is the light thrown on the workings of the Council and Assembly in the last years of responsible government and the machinations, both political and ecclesiastical, which led to the result.

The chronicle of these events begins in 1850, the year in which the 1843 act, which had divided the education grant more or less equally between Protestant and Catholics, was due to expire. In that year Bishop Feild who, three years earlier in a charge to his clergy, had reiterated his view that the Church of England deserved its own grant-aided schools, began what Frederick Jones, his biographer, called an "assault" on the educational settlement of 1843.[536] On 19 January 1850 Feild chaired a meeting at the Theological Institution in St. John's. Prominent Anglicans—T.F.H. Bridge, James Clift, Charles Fox Bennett, C.D. Newman—were present, and Bridge, who by this time had forsaken his Evangelical principles to become Feild's right-hand man, moved a resolution which encapsulated the fundamentals of the Anglican case for the whole of the campaign:

> That it is consistent with the principle already recognised by the Legislature, and essential to the due promotion of Education in this Colony, that a proportionate part of any grant for the support of Education according to Population, be awarded for the maintenance of schools to be placed under

---

534 Rowe mentions it in *The Development of Education in Newfoundland*, 84–86, but does not investigate further. John Greene refers to it in passing, but does not comment on the significance (*Between Damnation and Starvation*, 239).

535 Figures derived from Gunn, *Political History*, 205.

536 *A Charge Delivered to the Clergy of the Diocese of Newfoundland, 1847* (Bermuda, 1847), 38; Jones, "Bishop Feild," 114.

the direction of the Bishop, Clergy and other members of the Church of England only.

A petition on the lines of Bridge's resolution, signed by Feild and 500 others, was forwarded to the Council and Assembly.[537]

It was now up to Hugh Hoyles to fire the opening shots in the Assembly. He was well-fitted to assume the mantle of a crusader for subdivision. A handsome man of 36, he was the son of Newman Hoyles, merchant and former Colonial Treasurer. Educated at Pictou Academy in Nova Scotia and called to the Bar in 1837, he returned to Newfoundland to set up a legal practice and was elected as a Conservative for Fortune Bay in 1848. Described by his biographer as "a crusted Tory" and "a trenchant debater and profound parliamentarian,"[538] he was willing patiently to raise the same issue year after year and speak for hours if necessary. As Feild's most effective disciple in the early 1850s, he was the leading figure in the subdivision battle in the Assembly.

Governor Harvey had opened the session of 1850 on 27 January with an Address, which included an appeal for an improved system of education. He informed the members that their "financial condition will not … admit of any increase … to the present grant"; nevertheless, he felt that a more efficient system of instruction was urgently required and he hoped for a measure to this effect.[539]

Hoyles opened the debate on 4 February 1850 by moving for the establishment of a select committee on education to consider the whole subject. Its first item, he stated, should be the size of the education grant. He compared the 1 shilling and fourpence per head which Newfoundland spent on education with the 6 shillings spent in Prussia; Newfoundland's expenditure was inadequate for the maintenance of efficient schools and, despite Harvey's caveat, he proposed the grant should be increased to £7,500. He claimed that it was "very generally" desired that the Protestant grant should be

537 *Times*, 23 Jan. 1850; JHA 1850, App., Petition of Edward Newfoundland et al.

538 A. Morine, *Sir Hugh Hoyles* (St. John's, n.d.); *DCB*, s.v. "Hoyles, Sir Hugh William."

539 JHA 1850, 27 Jan. 1850, Governor's Address to the Assembly.

divided, and that it would not lead to antagonisms but rather to the effectual supervision of schools. He added that he would increase efficiency by establishing an inspectorate and a central board to supervise local boards and administer qualifying examinations for teachers. It was a practical, pro-education speech, designed to garner wide support. But he made clear that he was "strongly inclined" to support subdivision of the education grant.

There was some Liberal opposition to parts of the speech. Prendergast (Liberal, Conception Bay) and Shea (Liberal, Placentia St. Mary's) were against division of the grant, Hanrahan (Liberal, Conception Bay) opposed a central board, and Parsons (Liberal, St. John's) thought the main issue was not education but the poverty of the people and opposed an inspectorship and an increase of the grant. The proposal that a select committee be appointed to bring in a bill for the encouragement of education was, however, carried.[540]

So Hoyles received the mandate for his select committee, with himself as chairman; several of the other members—Shea, Prendergast (both Liberals and Catholics), and Job (a Congregationalist) were opposed to division. Although Hoyles, in moving for the select committee, had stated that the amount of the education grant was "the first consideration," the report of the committee submitted to the House—a mere paragraph—contained no mention of finance but surprisingly, in view of the composition of the committee, asserted the principle of subdivision. The majority of the committee, however, the report emphasized, did not mean to express any opinion in favour of such a principle, nor to recommend its adoption to the House; they took their position in fairness to those who desired a separation to allow them an opportunity to put their case before the House. This outcome was a tribute to Hoyles's "generalship," according to Falle, the Protestant member for Burin.[541]

On 12 February 1850 Hoyles threw down the gauntlet and presented "A Bill for the Encouragement of Education in this Island." The key sections were section 1, which read that the grant for edu-

540 Assembly 4 Feb., *Post*, 5, 6 Feb. 1850.

541 JHA 1850, 12 Feb. 1850, Report from Select Committee on Education; Assembly 12 Feb., *Post*, 14 Feb. 1850.

cation should proportionately be distributed in support of "Schools appropriated to the instruction of Children of Members of the Church of England, other Protestant Churches, and of the Roman Catholic Church respectively," and section 19, which gave the governor power to appoint a central board of five "fit and proper persons" with wide supervisory powers over district boards.[542] These sections, especially that concerning the division of the grant, represented important changes in the structure of the education system as formulated in the 1843 Education Act.

The introduction of the bill aroused a great deal of public interest. "Each of the various denominations," observed the *Courier*, "wrote and argued, petitioned and agitated, upon every possible phase of its probable tendency, and the press has teemed with excellent writing and sound argument on the subject." Public opinion, insofar as it was reflected in newspaper editorials and correspondence, and speeches in the Assembly, was less interested in changes in denominational structure than in the effect of the unstable state of the economy on schools and teachers. The *Ledger* stated that the main obstacle to an acceptable education measure was the prevailing poverty, especially that of teachers, and correspondents in the *Post*, the *Ledger*, and the *Herald* generally agreed as to the effect of precarious state of the colony's financial situation on the progress of education, and opposed any proliferation of schools. They were also critical of what they took to be the attempt of Feild and Hoyles to consolidate the power of the Anglican hierarchy. The arguments of these and other correspondents were indicative of the "angry discussion throughout the island" which, the *Herald* stated, the bill had aroused. The paper opposed the formation of "a central junto" of "five fit and proper persons" which it feared would superintend religious instruction of the children.[543]

Ambrose Shea, concerned at the "obscure" financial situation in

542 JHA 1850, 12 Feb. 1850; *Patriot*, 1 Feb. 1851, "A Bill for the Encouragement of Education." The text of the 1850 bill was identical to that which Hoyles presented in 1851.

543 *Courier*, 27 Feb. 1850; "W.F.," letter to the editor, *Ledger*, 8 Feb. 1850; T. Glen, letter to the editor, *Post*, 9 Feb. 1850; *Ledger*, 15 Feb. 1850; "Mentor," letters to the editor, *Ledger*, 19, 26 Feb., 1 Mar. 1850; *Herald*, 27 Feb. 1850.

the colony (which Hoyles's select committee had failed to address) successfully moved for another select committee, consisting of Shea, Hoyles, Falle, and Winser, the member for Ferryland. It sat for three weeks and reported on 8 March. Its remit was to inquire into "such reductions and modifications of the public expenditure as circumstances might appear to demand." The committee revealed that at the end of the year there would be an excess of expenditure over receipts of £6,285 and a public debt of £104,000. It further decided that public improvement should continue on moderate lines, financed by a 10 per cent tax on all official incomes and the cancellation of a number of votes. By these means a reduction of £3,674 in public expenditure would be achieved.[544]

The general picture was hardly an invitation to serious changes in the educational structure, and when Prendergast gave the *coup de grâce* to Hoyles's bill and successfully introduced a short bill of his own to continue the 1843 Education Act, Hoyles was left to complain that his bill had been rejected because there was no money in the Treasury.[545]

In the 1851 session Hoyles was confronted with an uncompromising opponent and skilled strategist in the person of the Liberal leader Philip Little. Born in Prince Edward Island of Irish parentage, Little relocated to St. John's in 1844 to practise law. He was elected to the Assembly in 1850, with the backing of Bishop Mullock, and quickly became the leader of the Liberal party, inspiring it to pursue the holy grail of responsible government. The campaign proceeded in tandem with the drive to maintain the educational status quo of 1843. Little took advantage of the situation to enlist the support of the increasingly numerous and influential Methodists (who had no representatives in the Assembly) for responsible government by endorsing their educational objectives. The Methodists had concluded that subdivision was against their interests in that it would lead to

544 Assembly 18 Feb., *Post*, 19 Feb. 1850; JHA 1850, 8 Mar. 1850, Report of the Financial Committee.

545 *Patriot*, 16 Mar. 1850, "A Bill to Continue and Amend an Act …"; Assembly 26 Feb., *Post*, 27 Feb. 1850; Assembly 15 Mar., 20 Apr. 1850, 16 Mar., 7 May 1850.

numerous "petty and rival schools."[546]

Hoyles was undaunted; "the Hector of High Churchism"[547] introduced another education bill in the 1851 session on 27 January. Speaking as usual with the ease of a practised advocate or, as one critic observed, with all the coolness, adroitness, and skill of one accustomed to making the best of a bad case, on 10 February he moved the second reading of the bill, which, he pointed out, was precisely the same as that of the previous year. He declared "the principle was education, not division" and asserted that division had been admitted in the previous session but postponed for financial difficulties. Protestants, he affirmed, now claimed similar rights to those possessed by the Catholics. He revealed that because of an improvement in the revenue he had the consent of the governor to propose an increase in the education grant of £7,000 or more. Ambrose Shea, who had at this time deserted the Liberals on the education issue, seconded the motion. Opposition came from G.H. Emerson, the member for Twillingate and Fogo (who had joined the anti-Hoyles forces), denying that a pledge for subdivision had been given in the previous session. Further criticism came from Job, Prendergast, Falle, and Parsons, the last insisting that there were no differences between the various Protestant denominations. A motion to kill the bill was lost on a division and it went to a second reading.[548]

The debates on the second reading and at the committee stage of the bill were lengthy and repetitious, with hardly anything new presented. Hoyles's arguments can be summed up as follows: the principle of the bill had been conceded by the legislature in the existing division of the grant between Protestants and Roman Catholics; subdivision would cause no damage to existing schools, which would be placed in no worse position than they were at present; it would be "unreasonable, unfair, and unjust" to resist the measure. The introduction of an education bill and the subsequent debates

---

546 *DCB*, s.v. "Little, Phillip Francis"; UCA WY 100, Minutes of the Special District Meeting held in Carbonear commencing on Wednesday, 14 Aug. 1850.

547 So described by "Calator," letter to the editor, *Courier*, 19 Feb. 1851.

548 JHA 1851, 27 Jan. 1851; "Observer," letter to the editor, *Ledger*, 7 Feb. 1851; Assembly 10 Feb., *Post*, 11, 12 Feb. 1851.

generated a more than ordinary degree of public interest. As in the previous year, Hoyles's bill of 1851 was discussed and argued about in the press. "If public opinion in Newfoundland sometimes slumbers," wrote a correspondent in the *Courier*, "when it does awake there is no mistake about it." Hoyles, however, could scarcely been pleased at the general trend of opinion. Of the eight newspapers in St. John's and Conception Bay (excluding the official *Gazette*), only the *Times* supported Hoyles's bill. But even the *Times* recognized that, according to the tone of public feeling, there was "strong opposition" to the measure, and the *Courier* felt it was not "generally approved." "A most determined feeling is getting up out-of-doors in opposition to this measure," declared the Carbonear *Herald*.[549]

Opposition, in newspaper editorials and correspondents' letters, crystallized around three aspects of the bill: the religious dissension which subdivision of the Protestant grant would allegedly bring about, the economic difficulties inherent in multiplying the number of schools, and the dangers of centralizing educational power and decision-making in the capital.[550] But these stirrings of popular opinion had little effect on the policies of the pro-division camp, and both parties continued to hold on to their positions during the first months of 1851. It was not until May that any significant progress was made, when debates centred on the issue of central boards. Hoyles favoured a central Protestant board, while the Catholics suggested the inclusion of a Catholic board. Arguments for and against the adoption of boards, largely on party and religious lines, went to and fro to little purpose. In the end, Hoyles put forward a formal resolution for a Protestant central board, but his motion was lost on the casting vote of the chairman, R. Rankin, a Protestant merchant from Conception Bay. Then, on a motion of Little, a Roman Catholic board was adopted. The measure, essentially Hoyles's bill with subdivision deleted and a Catholic central board added, was passed and sent to Council.[551]

---

549 Assembly 17, 18 Feb., *Post*, 18, 19, 20 Feb. 1851; "Calator," letter to the editor, *Courier*, 5 Feb. 1851; *Times*, 1, 5 Feb. 1851; *Herald*, 5 Feb. 1851.
550 Editorials and correspondence in *Courier*, *Herald*, and *Ledger*, 1–15 Feb. 1851.
551 Assembly 30 Apr., *Post*, 12, 13, 14 May 1851.

Between 9 and 29 May the Council met seven times to consider the bill. The leading Conservative on the Council, the wealthy industrialist Charles Fox Bennett, a charismatic figure with a flowing beard, initially proposed three boards for the Church of England, Roman Catholics, and "other Protestants," but finally moved for a Protestant board with full powers. Several members were doubtful and urged caution. After much discussion and change of views, the House settled for an amendment by James Crowdy the Colonial Secretary—two central boards, Protestant and Roman Catholic, each with powers to distribute the grant for the establishment and support of schools. The Roman Catholic bishop was not to be chairman of his board on the ground that the Protestant bishop was not chairman of the Protestant board.[552] This apparently innocuous clause aroused the ire of Bishop Mullock, who flatly asserted that by the canonical law of the Catholic church the bishop was an authority superior to the state in matters concerning Catholic schools and boards, and threatened if he were not made chairman of the board he would bring the education of the Catholic community to "a dead stop." The Council restored his position as chairman.[553]

On 29 May both Assembly and Council, after further animated discussion, finally adopted a bill which became law two days later. The act was something of a hybrid, the result of the clashing forces of denominationalism, centralization, and local autonomy. It provided for two central boards and a grant of £7,500; a Roman Catholic central board (including the bishop "for the time being") was to receive £1,169 and a central Protestant board £1,231. Each board was to apply the monies for "the establishment and support" of their schools as required. The act was to continue for one year. "This is we presume all that can be done, under existing circumstances, in the present session," the *Ledger* concluded.[554]

Bishop Feild's "assault" on the principles of the 1843 act, in the

---

552 Council 9–29 May, *Post*, May–June 1851; *Courier*, 17, 24 May 1851.

553 J.T. Mullock, Petition to the Legislative Council, printed in *Patriot*, 31 May 1851; debates in Council, 18, 19 May, *Post*, 29–31 May 1851.

554 Debates in Assembly and Council, Apr.–May, *Post*, May–July 1851; 14 Vic., cap. 3, An Act for the Encouragement of Education (31 May 1851); *Ledger*, 23 May 1851.

sessions of 1850 and 1851, had hardly been a success. Moreover, he faced opposition to subdivision from some Anglican congregations—at St. Paul's, Harbour Grace, and St. Thomas's in St. John's. But Feild was not unduly worried by setbacks. In May, replying to an address from St. John's Cathedral, he avowed: "I shall be prepared to take all proper steps to obtain for members of our Communion the same liberty and privileges which the Roman Catholics have … obtained for their Church."[555]

• • •

At the beginning of the session of 1852, Feild issued a detailed exposition of his position on the subdivision question, which reminded the legislature that his views were unchanged and that he would be very much a protagonist in the ensuing conflict. Feild's manifesto, dated 12 February 1852, was entitled "Remarks on the Subdivision of the Legislative Grant for … Education." A closely printed pamphlet three pages long, it set out the definitive case for his policy—in short, "the justice and expediency" of dividing the Protestant education grant between the Church of England and other Protestants, and for the establishment of two central boards for the management of their schools. A key aspect of his argument was that a division of the grant having been made between Protestants and Roman Catholics, a further division of the sum allotted to Protestants would be just and expedient—especially in relation to poor children. Of the three possible types of religious instruction—exclusion of religion altogether, with the Bible used a reading book; general religious instruction, with reading from the Bible without special doctrines; and instruction in "the distinctive principles and doctrines of their church"—the third had been adopted for the Roman Catholics and should be extended to the Church of England. To refuse to do so would perpetrate an injustice. Feild, however, disavowed and disclaimed any tendency of the Church of England either to stir up religious discord or proselytize other Protestants, but he concluded with the uncompromising statement that "[n]o Bishop of the Church of England ought to rest satisfied till he can

555 *Courier*, 5 Mar., 14 May 1851; Jones, "Bishop Feild," 119.

place the religious instruction … [of] the children of his own flock and communion, under the direction of the Clergy and other members of that Church only."[556]

Shortly before Feild had issued his pamphlet, Hoyles had once again brought the issue of subdivision before the Assembly in the form of another education bill. He could count on few supporters—Feild's educational policy had split the Anglican Conservatives, leaving only a few willing to follow Hoyles. The Methodists, who regarded Feild's practices of confession, baptism, communion, daily prayer, adornment of the altar, etc., as little better than Catholic ritual, and who saw subdivision as making it impossible for them to maintain sufficient schools in their desired localities,[557] had, as seen earlier, moved into the orbit of the Liberals and anti-division Anglicans.

When Hoyles spoke to his bill, he declared, somewhat unnecessarily, that it embodied the principle of division ("the identical old proposal," sneered the *Courier*) to which he hoped the members would at last agree. The bill was an elaborate document of 27 sections. Most of them dealt with the usual financial and organizational matters found in any education bill, but it included provision for grants to the Newfoundland School Society and the Methodists, and training for teachers in independent schools of their denomination. The curriculum in all schools was to be a meagre ration of the 3Rs and religion, plus "industrial employment." The act was to be in force for six years. The key sections were numbers 1 and 20, which would distribute the educational grant between the schools of the Church of England, other Protestant Churches, and the Roman Catholics, under the aegis of three denominational central boards.[558]

In the debate on section 1 of Hoyles's bill (embodying subdivision) Peter Winser, the Liberal-Catholic member for Ferryland

556 SPG, D Sers 9A, "Remarks on the Subdivision of the Legislative Grant for the Encouragement of Education in This Colony, by Edward Feild, D.D. Bishop of Newfoundland" (24 Feb. 1852).
557 Jones, "Bishop Feild," 107, 153, 170–71; Sanderson, "How High Was He?," 45; JHA 1852, 17 Feb. 1852, Petition of J.B. Botterell.
558 *Courier*, 21 Feb. 1852; Assembly 26 Feb., *Express*, 17, 27 Feb. 1852.

(in the *Patriot*'s words), "was trepanned by the acute mover of the measure" to vote in favour, on the promise of modifications in the application of subdivision. The section, "to the astonishment of everyone," was carried by one vote in a thin House. The *Times* was satisfied, but the *Courier* stated (correctly in the event) "we think it impossible that this glorious majority of one can stand."[559]

In a continuation of the committee stage Little, in an effort to put an end to the debate, moved that the present act be continued for 12 months longer. Hoyles said he would not vote. Little's motion was carried and the bill sent to Council. The *Courier* optimistically announced that the education question was "finally disposed of."[560] It reckoned without the opposition of the Council.

In the month between the end of April and the end of May the Council and the Assembly fought a battle on the issue. The Council, led as usual by Charles Fox Bennett—"the one fiery spirit on this question," in the *Courier*'s view—was more clear-sighted and determined than in 1851 and took its stand on the basis of Hoyles's bill. The Assembly adamantly kept to its opposition to subdivision. Inspired by Philip Little, it proposed conference after conference with the Council, all of which ended in deadlock.[561]

Despite Bennett's eloquence, the Council was far from unanimous on the issue, with three members in opposition and another three doubtful, but Bennett was always able to get majority backing. It was one of the doubters, James Crowdy, the Colonial Secretary, who opened a rift in the Council's policy. On 19 May he suggested that as there were differences of opinion in the Council on the subdivision question, and some practical inconvenience would result in extending it to the whole island, it would be better to limit subdivision to the Central District and Conception Bay, and next year, if it worked well, there would be little difficulty in extending it throughout the country. Strangely, there was no comment from other members, and Crowdy's proposal was not voted on.[562]

---

559 *Patriot*, 15 Mar. 1852; *Times*, 13 Mar. 1852; *Courier*, 17 Mar. 1852.

560 Reports of Assembly debates, 23, 26 Mar., *Express* 24, 27 Mar. 1852; *Courier*, 24 Mar. 1852.

561 *Courier*, 21 Apr. 1852; *Express*, 27 Apr.–25 May 1852.

562 Council 19 May, *Express*, 25 May 1852.

On 27 May, Job brought in a bill to continue the existing Education Act. Unlike the drawn-out process of previous sessions, the proceedings were hurried along at railroad speed. The bill went through all the readings and the committee stage, and was engrossed and passed in one sitting. Hoyles, astonished and disgusted, declared he would withdraw from the House. During the debates, the unpredictable Prendergast, asserting that neither the Council nor the Assembly would give way, followed the example of Crowdy, and proposed a compromise—that the question should be transferred to a central Protestant board of nine members, authorized to fund separate Protestant schools between Church of England and other Protestants. Prendergast was a man of independent views, and though he hardly deserved John Kent's reproach that he was "a man of crotchets," who was sure to advance his own views in defiance of everyone else,[563] he had a reputation for opposing the Liberal party line.

Whether or not members of the Assembly felt that on this occasion the mercurial Prendergast had taken his opposition to Liberal policy too far, or whether their overriding concern was to maintain their anti-division intact, is not clear. Whatever the case, Prendergast's proposal was put to the vote, and lost. The speaker, John Kent, had, however, somewhat surprisingly given his opinion that some sort of compromise was necessary. In the event, Job's bill was passed and sent to Council on 27 May.[564]

The Council was in no hurry and did not arrive at a third reading until 9 June. During the debates Bennett characteristically complained that, if it had not been for the interference of the Roman Catholics and the alliance between them and the Methodists for the purpose of depriving the members of the Church of England of the privileges enjoyed by the Catholics, the question would have been long set at rest. The Council's amendments to the Assembly's bill once again took the form of a full-scale draft of an act, reiterating a tripartite division of the grant by three boards with appropriate powers. When presented to the Assembly, the draft was inevitably

563 Assembly 19 Mar., 27 May, *Express*, 23 Mar., 2, 3 June 1852.
564 Assembly 27 May, *Express*, 3 June 1852.

rejected.[565]

Once again the two bodies had reached an impasse. The member who broke the deadlock was none other than the persistent Prendergast, who on 10 June transformed his compromise proposal of 27 May into a full-blown bill, containing the key clause that the Protestant education grant be divided between the Church of England and other Protestants in St. John's and Conception Bay.[566] Against all expectations, Prendergast's bill was accepted by the Assembly.

Why this sudden reversal of policy? Possibly the members were influenced by John Kent's earlier suggestion on the need for compromise. More likely they felt it prudent, on the eve of the closure of the session, to end the deadlock with the Council and to place some sort of an education bill on the statute book before it was too late.

During the debates on the bill, Prendergast's transgression was welcomed by Hoyles on the grounds that it augured well for his own cause, which he asserted, would ultimately prevail. The anti-division members, on the other hand, were faced with a difficult situation. Several—Job, Hanrahan, Winser, and Parsons—gritted their teeth and voted for it out of expediency; Little and Emerson, however, declared themselves opposed to any form of compromise on subdivision. The final debate on the bill had occupied the whole of the session of 11 June, and did not pass its third reading until 10 p.m. The proceedings would have been over much earlier had not Hoyles spoken for an astonishing eight hours—from 2 p.m. to 10 p.m.—in a last-ditch effort to expound and defend his policy. The final words were delivered by Little: "under the present system of government, strange things will continue to be perpetrated." On 14 June, the last day of the session, the Council unexpectedly passed the bill.[567]

Press comment was largely muted. The *Courier* remarked that Prendergast's bill was not in accordance with the wishes of his own constituency and contrary to the views of the Episcopalians of St. John's, adding that the subdividers "have gained a triumph … but

---

565 Council 9 June, *Express*, 22 June 1852; JHA, 9 June 1852; Assembly 9 June, *Express*, 12 June 1852.

566 Assembly 10 June, *Express*, 15 June 1852.

567 Assembly 11, 14 June, Council 14 June, *Express*, 15, 17, 19, 22 June 1852.

it is an inglorious one, and we wish them joy of it." The *Newfoundlander* merely reported that the Assembly had partially yielded their position on the education grant. It was left to the *Patriot* to declare that the legislature had consented to allowing "the Ascendant Party to exercise their tyranny in the St. John's District and in Conception Bay."[568]

Prendergast's first action after the passing of the bill was to issue a statement defending his action in a letter dated 22 June and published in the *Herald* on 23 June and in the *Express* on 1 July. He began by outlining the history of the debates on the three bills. When the second bill was returned from the Council with their amendments, he perceived the possibility of their being adopted "by the party which had all along opposed them." Accordingly he obtained Job's permission to introduce a bill containing "in some measure" the Council's principles—conceding to the Council the principle of subdivision in areas where its disadvantages "would be felt with the least inconvenience." The alternative, he believed, would have been to have lost the bill and to have brought education to a standstill, depriving schools of the Newfoundland School Society, the Wesleyans, and the Catholics of the act's provision of financial support, and the consequent loss of teachers.

This appeared to be the last word on the matter. But on 3 July the *Courier* refuted Prendergast's statement, and went on to make an extraordinary revelation. The member for Conception Bay, the paper asserted, was not the begetter of the Education Act, but the instrument of "a power which does its work secretly." On the last day of the session the Council's intention has been to reject the Assembly's bill, but was prevented from doing so by "an intimation from a High Dignitary [Bishop Feild]" who would accept Prendergast's bill as "an installment of justice."[569] Thus it appeared that an aberrant manoeuvre by a member of the Assembly was kept alive by a pillar of the church, who was willing to regard partial subdivision as an instalment of his own policy. The *Courier* (edited by the

568 *Courier*, 19 June 1852; *Newfoundlander*, 14 June 1852; *Patriot*, 14 June 1852.
569 *Courier*, 13 July 1852.

Methodist Joseph Woods), which kept a close watch on the business of the legislature, later added:

> the Bill was the joint concoction of Executive and Ecclesiastical interference, and it is to such an unseemly combination that the country is indebted for a measure as odious, unjust, and oppressive, as ever disgraced our local statute book.[570]

The paper gave no source for its assertion regarding Feild, but it was not denied and, in view of the bishop's penchant for intervention in legislative affairs, was a likely scenario.

Prendergast paid the price of what a correspondent in the *Courier* termed his "treachery,"[571] by losing his seat in the Assembly. Initially he had considered that his best course was to "withdraw into private life," and he did not put his name to the list of candidates for the coming general election. He was dissuaded from taking this step by an address from a group of some 60 worthies of Harbour Grace headed by the leading merchants John Munn and Thomas Ridley, which stressed his contribution to the welfare of the outports, whereupon the *Courier* warned him that unless he was "explicit and satisfactory" in preventing the re-enactment of the partial subdivision measure (which he promised to do), he would go down to defeat in the election, "the influence of the magnates of Harbour Grace notwithstanding." In the event Prendergast did go down to defeat, coming at the bottom of the poll in Conception Bay with only 770 votes out of over 5,000 cast. His career was not over, however; he subsequently continued in public life until his late 80s.[572]

The act of June 1852 provided for two central boards of education, Protestant and Catholic, but the key clause was the 12th:

> XII.—And be it enacted, that it shall be lawful for the Gov-

---

570 *Courier*, 13 Oct. 1852.

571 "B.R.," letter to the editor, *Courier*, 13 Oct. 1852. The editor reminded the writer that Prendergast had been imposed upon by a power "which did its work secretly."

572 *Herald*, 20 Oct. 1852; *Courier*, 27 Oct. 1852; *Express*, 20 Nov. 1852; *Newfoundlander*, 22 Nov. 1852; *DCB*, s.v. "Prendergast, James Luke."

> ernor and Council, on the recommendation of the major part of the member of the Central Protestant Board, to authorise and permit the said Board to divide and separate the Protestant Board Schools now or hereafter to be established within the limits of the Electoral Districts of St. John's and Conception Bay, among the Members of the Church of England and other Protestant Churches: Provided, that such Division shall not take place where the Salary of any Teacher employed in any locality within the said respective Districts will by such change be reduced to an amount under Thirty Pounds Sterling, anything in this Act to the contrary notwithstanding.[573]

The measure was an unprecedented attempt to reorganize the structure of the educational system on partial subdivision lines. It was left to the two central boards to carry out the changes in practice. The Catholic central board submitted its resolutions to the Colonial Secretary on 16 July. Its schools were to continue under provisions of previous acts; the resolutions were concerned with housekeeping—attendance records, the amount of fees, the subscriptions (where possible) of parents, all to be overseen by the clergy. The members of the Protestant central board, unlike the Catholics, submitted a lengthy account of its intentions on 5 July, concluding with an unfavourable commentary on the state of education in the colony. The board had been constituted in June 1852 and brought together a heterogeneous collection of Protestant notables: Archdeacon Bridge (chairman), Hugh Hoyles, Henry Thomas, G.J. Hayward, E. Harvey, Charles Simms ("the Chairman of the Wesleyan Mission"), Nicholas Stabb, and R.H. Job.[574]

The report stated that the board administered 77 schools in 21 districts, with an enrolment of 2,630 pupils at a cost of 2 shil-

573 5 Vic., cap. 2, An Act for the Encouragement of Education (14 June 1852).

574 The Rooms Provincial Archives Division, GN 2/2, Roche to Crowdy, 16 July 1852, encl. Resolutions of the Catholic Central Board of Education; JLC 1855, Appendix, Report of the Protestant Central Board of Education for the Years 1852–1853; *Gazette*, 22 June 1852.

lings and eightpence for each. Pupil numbers accounted for only 53 per cent of Protestants of school age—"a very low average" in the board's opinion. After informing the schools to continue "without change or direction" until further notice, the board declared that its regulations would provide a framework for the introduction of one uniform system of teaching and discipline.

Schools were, however, divided into four categories: those attended by Church of England and Wesleyan children, in which the Authorized Version of the Bible "without note or comment" was to be read by all children twice daily, with added instruction by respective denominational ministers once a week—a throwback to the pre-1843 system; in schools attended chiefly by Church of England children, the catechism and formularies of the church were to be taught under the direction of local clergy; in schools attended chiefly by Wesleyan Methodists, their own catechism would be taught; "The Like Rule and Proviso" was to apply to the schools and children of other denominations of Christians. The curriculum of all schools was to include the 3Rs, and "when required" grammar, geography, history, and navigation. Books used in all schools were to be those supplied by the Christian Knowledge Society and those authorized by the national church in Ireland. Payments, graded according to the child's status in school, had to be made quarterly in advance.

• • •

In the general election of late 1852 the Liberals won a majority, with nine seats. The main planks of their platform had been propaganda for responsible government and opposition to subdivision of the Protestant education grant. Once in office they lost no time in overthrowing the provisions of the 1852 Education Act, introducing a bill which was a virtual transcript of Barnes's act of 1843. Both Catholics and Methodists members asserted that the policy of partial subdivision was abandoned and that the existing system of Catholic-Protestant division was there to stay. Hoyles, completely isolated, admitted defeat; he could not carry a subdivision measure and would not press it. His opinions; however, were unchanged; subdivision would come and he would await it. The bill was passed without division on 25 April and sent to the Council.[575]

During the Council debates, Feild once again intervened in the legislative process. On 25 May he sent an address to the Council, via his supporter Charles Fox Bennett, which reminded that body that lest his silence should be taken for a change of heart, his views on the "justice and expediency" of the Church of England educating poor children in their own schools, for which a division of the grant was requisite, had not changed. Nevertheless the Council appeared to be willing to compromise. After many speeches and a conference, Bennett agreed to pass the bill if the principle of subdivision was affirmed in the future, and on this note the Council capitulated. The Assembly then passed the bill as it stood. The act appropriated £7,880 for the support of schools—£3,646 for Protestants, £3,304 for Catholics, with some grants to individual schools, the Newfoundland School Society and the Methodists, plus £200 for the institution of Protestant masters. Inhabitants were to contribute an amount equal to the grant. Central boards were abolished.[576]

Apart from adding an item to Prendergast's biography—the *DCB* merely notes he was "defeated" in 1852—the education controversy of 1850–1853 appeared on the surface to be a relatively minor issue; it was, however, an important development in Feild's crusade to split the Protestant education grant. Feild would not have intervened in the legislative process as he did unless he felt that the issue was relevant to keeping his aims alive. Hoyles felt that "they let the wedge in, but … they did not drive it home";[577] but Feild had realized that Prendergast's opportunist wedge could be interpreted as a forerunner of his ultimate purpose.

Feild's activities, from his public meeting in 1850, his well-timed pamphlet in 1852, his encouragement of petitions (in April 1852

---

575 Gunn, *Political History*, 128–29; *Newfoundlander*, 20 Aug. 1852; JHA 1853, 10 Mar. 1853; Assembly 13, 14, 20, 25 Apr., *Express*, 7 May 1853; *Express* (and supplement) 7, 14, 19 May 1853.

576 Council, 6, 9, 25, 26 May, *Post*, *Express*, 17–31 May 1853; JLC 2, 3 June 1853; JHA 1853, 4 June 1853; 16 Vic., cap. 2, An Act for the Encouragement of Education (15 June 1853).

577 *DCB*, s.v. "Prendergast, James Luke"; Assembly 14 June, *Express*, 19 June 1852.

Bennett boasted that the Council table "groans with petitions from the Episcopalians"), his clandestine backing of Prendergast's bow at a venture, and his several interventions in the legislature, exercised a significant influence on the outcome of debates. Patrick O'Flaherty has observed that Catholic bishops also influenced government policy, and Thomas Mullock was no exception. Apart from ordering the Council, in 1851, to change their legislation on pain of halting Catholic education, he was accused by the *Ledger* of constituting himself the Government of Newfoundland after a vituperative attack on the policy of the Liberal government. In 1860 he denounced the government's failure to institute a steamboat service, following it up by personally making a formal contract for a steamer without government authorization.[578] As shown earlier, Mullock justified his actions, at least with regard to education, by asserting he wielded an authority superior to that of the state in matters concerning schools and boards.

Although Newfoundland had some of the formal trappings of democracy—an elected Assembly, voted in by electors whose qualifications were the occupancy of a tenement of any description for one year—the governor had the power to dismiss the government (as LeMarchant did in 1861) and the Council frequently rejected bills sent up by the Assembly. More significantly, decisions of the Council, ostensibly an instrument of state, could be overturned by ecclesiastical interference. That political policy could be influenced in these ways can ultimately be traced to the weakness of the base on which the governmental structure rested, namely the fishery, the raison d'être for the imperial presence in the island. An economy grounded on a single industry subject to fluctuations, and operating on the virtually cashless truck-credit system (which inhibited the formation of a tax base) was a brake on the development of political-economic foundations for a strong, stable government which could resist outside interference. The fishery as constituted was, in

578 Council 14 Apr., *Express*, 17 Apr. 1852; O'Flaherty, *Lost Country: The Rise and Fall of Newfoundland 1843–1933* (St. John's, 2005), 41, 93; Gunn, *Political History*, 154; E.C. Moulton, "Constitutional Crisis and Civil Strife in Newfoundland, February to November 1861," *Canadian Historical Review* 48, no. 3 (September 1967), 252–53.

Cadgian's words, the root cause of "the slow development of settlements and colonial political institutions in Newfoundland."[579]

579 Parl. Deb. 3rd sers., 46, 26 Apr. 1839, 554, speech of Lord Aberdeen; Cadigan, *Hope and Deception*, 15.

CHAPTER 13

*Sir John Harvey's Cultural Revolution, 1841–1846**

> Culture: a particular form, stage, or type of intellectual development or civilization in a society; a society or group characterized by its distinctive customs, achievements, products, outlook, etc.
>
> *New Shorter Oxford English Dictionary*

The relationship of culture to the state or civil authority has recently begun to receive attention from historians, educationists, and anthropologists. The work of Edward Thompson on cultural forms in the pre-industrial state, of Corrigan and Sayer on culture and state formation in England, of Curtis and others on education and social structure in Upper Canada, of Hobsbawm and Ranger on the invention of tradition, and of Sider on culture and class in Newfoundland points the way to a widening of the concept of culture and to a dynamic treatment of the inter-relationship of culture and society. The focus has been on both the significance of popular culture and the role of the state in the creation and maintenance of cultural hegemony, but little of this research has been concerned with the culture of colonial states, or the attempts made by imperial powers to inculcate what might be termed a colonial consciousness. Newfoundland in the mid-19th century provides a particularly interesting example of a colonial state in the making, both materially and culturally. Attached to the British Crown since the 16th century, the island had long been used merely as a stage for the west of England fishing fleets until increasing population, the expense to Britain of direct administration, and a

* This chapter was first published in *Journal of Canadian Studies* 23, nos. 1 & 2 (1988), under the title of "Culture, State Formation and the Invention of Tradition: Newfoundland 1832–1855," and is reprinted with permission. It was written in the late 1980s and thus other chapters replicate some of the material; the text has been edited only for style consistency.

powerful reform movement in Newfoundland itself led to the granting of representative government on the Canadian maritime model in 1832.

The infant colony faced peculiar problems. Its economy was based on the infamous truck or credit system, in which the fishing population bartered the fish they caught for food and equipment with a small number of merchants. The latter were mainly Protestant; the fishing families were divided between Catholics from southeast Ireland and Protestants from southwest England. Newfoundland was regarded, together with New South Wales, as an "anomalous society," one which lacked a sufficient number of men of property, education, and loyalty to form a viable political entity.[580] Most general histories of Newfoundland have acknowledged its peculiarities, but failed to link them with either popular or state-regulated cultural activities. In these works culture has either been ignored, or interpreted merely as the arts and leisure activities, usually in an added chapter, or virtually equated with social history. The growth of political culture in the sense of the encouragement of popular cultural activities by the state, with the aim of fostering social harmony among the masses, has largely been ignored.

The work of Gerald Sider has opened a new dimension, both in the meaning of culture and in its relationship to the socio-economic structure of Newfoundland. Sider argues that the family fishery, dominated by merchant capital, was the breeding ground for the main popular cultural activity—Christmas mumming—which became a means of re-ordering social and work relationships. But Sider's thesis does not encompass political structures and, in common with nearly all historians of Newfoundland, he pays insufficient attention to the fact that from 1832 onwards Newfoundland was not only dominated by merchant capital but was also a Protestant colony in the making, a "state" which the Colonial Office and the local elite attempted to fashion on lines acceptable to the political, social, and cultural norms of the mother country. In this operation, Protestant ideology played an important role as a means of combatting the political militancy

580 J.M. Ward, *Colonial Self-Government: The British Experience* (Toronto, 1976), 124–26.

of the Catholic Irish, who formed half the population of the island.

The early attempts to construct a viable colonial community can best be examined between 1832, when representative government was granted, and 1855, when responsible government (with a prime minister and cabinet) was achieved. In the first years of representative government, the populace lacked a commitment to British colonial rule and the island was racked by political and sectarian antagonisms. It was when these tensions appeared to be making social and political integration impossible—particularly in the period 1837–1841—that the British government intervened, not only instituting constitutional reform but also "inventing tradition" by sponsoring and encouraging organizations and rituals which attempted to inculcate imperial sentiment on the basis of a "patriotic" and nativist outlook.

The authority of ruling groups is not only maintained by economic or physical power, but is also located in cultural hegemony, "the images of power and authority," the obverse of which are "the popular mentalities of subordination."[581] The ruling elite must establish or maintain the consent of the governed to the rulers' legitimacy, exact loyalty to the nation, establish conformity with "the norms of society," and so on. The social and cultural identities of the citizens of a nation must be constructed in such a manner that the beliefs and presuppositions of the ruling elite, the strategies of authority, even the forms of economic exploitation, are accepted as normal, natural, unquestionable, and transcendent. Symbols, rituals, and traditions, usually with vague or general connotations such as patriotism, loyalty, public duty, etc., are cherished, publicized, or invented, that is, continuously generated, rather than transmitted. Support for the status quo usually has a national and patriotic rallying point around which unity can be formed. Conversely, groups or classes with separate or alternative identities are marginalized, or represented as outside the pale of "normal" society.[582]

---

581 E.P. Thompson, "Patrician Society, Plebeian Culture," *Journal of Social History* 7, no. 4 (1974), 387.

582 P. Corrigan and D. Sayer, *The Great Arch* (London, 1985), 1–13, 182–208; E. Hobsbawm and T. Ranger, eds., *The Invention of Tradition* (London, 1984), 265–67.

Few societies found it more necessary to attempt to construct a unified "national" consciousness, or to denigrate those considered to be outside the mainstream, than Newfoundland after the grant of representative government. For centuries little more than a fishing station in which permanent settlement was discouraged, without constitutional traditions, an educational system, or established civil institutions, Newfoundland in 1832 had a written constitution, in the shape of instructions and commission to the governor, thrust upon it. These documents, blueprints for a settlement on the Canadian maritime model, instituted a colony with an appointed Council, an Assembly elected on virtually adult male suffrage (without which, as Lord Aberdeen pointed out later, there would have been no constituency at all), and gave wide powers to the governor. The Church of England was established as the lawful church under the aegis of the bishop of Nova Scotia, education was to be organized according to church principles, and the obedience of the people was enjoined.[583] The instructions took no account of the fact that exactly half the population was Irish, nearly all of whom were immigrants by choice (in the period 1812–1830) from Tipperary, Wexford, and Waterford, an economically dynamic region of farming and trade, centre of resurgent Catholicism, and one of Daniel O'Connell's nationalist strongholds.

The Roman Catholic bishop, Michael Anthony Fleming, an Irishman and follower of Daniel O'Connell, inspired by the new situation following the 1829 Catholic Emancipation Act, had broken with the policy of collaboration with the Protestant authorities pursued by his predecessors, the "gentlemen bishops" O'Donel, Lambert, and Scallan. Moreover, he encouraged the political activities of his flock, backed radical Liberal-Catholic candidates for the new Assembly, and supported the establishment of publicly funded non-denominational schools established under the Education Act of 1836.

During the period 1837–1841 there was, in the words of Gov-

583 Parl. Deb., 3rd ser., 47, 26 Apr. 1839, 554; Instructions to Our Trusty and Well-Beloved Sir Thomas Cochrane, Knight, Our Governor … (March 2, 1832).

ernor Prescott, "war to the knife" between the Liberal-Catholic Assembly and the Conservative-Protestant Council.[584] There were clashes over revenue bills, the supply vote, privileges, the election of officers, the administration of justice, education, and, above all, the Assembly's support for roads and agriculture, which directly threatened the merchant monopoly of the fishery in the outports.

Furthermore, the Assembly, after long and bitter struggles, secured the removal of Chief Justice Boulton for maladministration and briefly imprisoned Dr. Edward Kielly, the District Surgeon, and Assistant Judge Lilly for alleged breach of privilege, actions which infuriated the merchant class. It was the actions of the Catholics at elections, however, which most alarmed the Protestant elite. As was common in Ireland, priests preached politics from the pulpit (there being no other channel of communication, asserted Fleming), political posters and petition tables were placed in the vicinity of the Catholic chapel, and marches with drums and banners were organized at election times to boost Catholic candidates and intimidate those who might vote for the Conservatives.

The Catholic Irish, in the view of the ruling group, were outside the pale of "legitimate" political and cultural expression. Governor Cochrane was amazed at the extent to which Catholicism had penetrated the civic culture of the Irish and their "ordinary relations of life." The fact that Protestant and Catholic children were being educated side by side in the board schools created in 1836 on the model of the Irish National System, and that large numbers of Protestant fishers voted for Liberal-Catholic candidates, further undermined the hold of the Protestant rulers on the hearts and minds of the people. In the later 1830s and early 1840s something very like a class struggle was being waged in Newfoundland. Recent research has revealed several instances of collective action by fishers against the merchants in Conception Bay in the 1830s, and troops were called out on more than one occasion during this period. R.J. Parsons, editor of the radical-Liberal *Patriot* newspaper, declared

---

584 For the following paragraphs, see Chapters 3 and 4; CO 194/88, Cochrane to Stanley, 2 Aug. 1834; CO 194/99, Prescott to Glenelg, 14 Oct. 1837; CO 194/111, Prescott to Russell, 9 June 1841.

that the intervention of the priests in politics had cut the ties between merchant and fishers; the latter, Governor Cochrane noticed, voted against merchants despite the fact they were economically dependent on them. "The politics which developed in this nascent colony," observes historian S.J.R. Noel, "reflected not only the traditional cleavages of ethnicity and religion but also the underlying potential of the people to realign their loyalties on the basis of economic class." The cultural underpinning of the Catholic political offensive was provided by the Benevolent Irish Society, a charitable and educational body founded in 1806, but which had come under the influence of Fleming's supporters in 1834. The St. Patrick's Day festivals held under the auspices of the Society fused ethnicity and religion with a militant nationalism for all but a minority of the Newfoundland Irish.

The Protestant administration could not have maintained the ideological basis for a governable state if they had allowed this situation to continue unopposed. The counter-offensive began in 1834 with an attempt to persuade Rome to discipline or remove Bishop Fleming from Newfoundland. At the same time, the two Conservative newspapers, the *Times* and the *Public Ledger*, joining the "No Popery" crusade then being waged in Britain and the English-speaking world, attacked Catholicism, the Irish in general, and Bishop Fleming in particular with almost unbelievable ferocity, alleging that Catholics owed allegiance to Rome, which was directing "enfranchised papists" to sever political, cultural, and economic links with Britain and deliver Newfoundland into the hands of the papacy. The aim of isolating the Catholics and cutting the links between Catholic and Protestant fishers was also behind an attack on the non-denominational school system. A united front of Protestants—Orthodox Anglicans, Anglican Evangelicals, Methodists, and others—attacked the concept of non-denominationalism, using every device from backing school boards to keeping children from school, from attempting to force the Authorized Version of the Bible as a reading book into all board schools to persuading the Attorney General to reinterpret the Education Act. This campaign succeeded in making the act inoperable in many areas for seven years.

The protagonists of the Protestant crusade in Newfoundland

succeeded in presenting to the Colonial Office an image of the Catholic Irish as enemies of the state. The British government, seriously alarmed at what it took to be a condition bordering on anarchy, finally took action. The constitution was suspended in 1841, and a select committee on Newfoundland set up in the same year, which took evidence in a very partisan fashion. In 1842 the Newfoundland Act passed, which modified the franchise, joined the Council and Assembly in an amalgamated legislature, and effectively reduced the representation of Liberal-Catholics, thus satisfying the Conservative-Protestants who had maintained throughout the 1830s that all the ills of Newfoundland sprang from giving the franchise to "half-civilised ... hewers of wood and drawers of water."

In September 1841 General Sir John Harvey had been appointed governor, charged with the task of bringing harmony to the colony and of reconstructing its political and cultural life in a manner that would prevent recurrence of the conflicts of the 1830s.[585] Harvey was an eminently suitable choice. A professional soldier who had won his spurs in the American War of 1812, an experienced administrator who had spent the greater part of his life attempting to keep turbulent colonies in order, Harvey had the reputation of a conciliator and peacemaker. From 1828 to 1836 he had been inspector of police for the province of Leinster, before taking up his first major colonial appointment as governor of Prince Edward Island, where he played a mediating role in a conflict of tenantry against landlordism not unlike that which he had experienced in Ireland. In 1837 he was appointed governor of New Brunswick, where he achieved a measure of harmony by conciliatory measures and the judicious distribution of patronage among the warring factions of the colony.

As governor of Newfoundland, Harvey felt that he had been entrusted with "a mission ... to unite all in one common endeavour to advance the general good." He viewed the Amalgamated Assembly as "an experiment" designed to promote practical legislation, not

---

585 For the following paragraphs, see *DNB*, Vol. VIII; *Times*, 22 Sept. 1841; CO 194/112, Harvey to Stanley, 21 Dec. 1841; *Times*, 22 Sept. 1841; CO 194/112, Harvey to Stanley, 21 Dec. 1841; CO 194/116, Harvey to Stanley, 22 May 1843; *Gazette*, 27 Jan. 1843; *Ledger*, 14 Jan. 1842, 18 Oct. 1844, 18 Jan. 1850.

party interests, a forum in which "legislative harmony" could promote "public good." At the same time he took practical measures to consolidate his power, persuading the Assembly to grant him the right of initiating money bills, and securing a balance of parties and the support of the officially appointed members by judicious promotions to the Council. Abjuring force and fiat, he worked to change, supplement, or invent the outlooks and perceptions of his subjects. Shortly after his arrival he informed the Colonial Secretary that he had taken the first steps to unite men of all parties by inducing them to attend a meeting and send a joint Address to the Queen on the birth of the Prince of Wales. In addition, he had taken the initiative in forming an Agricultural Society, becoming its patron and presiding at its first meeting.

The establishment of an agricultural society was of great symbolic importance; Harvey persuaded both conservative merchants and Liberal-Catholics to serve on its committee, thus neutralizing one of the latter's chief grievances against the mercantocracy. Harvey saw the fostering of agriculture not only in economic terms (as strengthening the fishery and thus promoting the consumption of British goods), but also as a means to the creation of a yeoman class—"brave, hardy, loyal and permanent settlers" who would form the "Constitutional Defence" of the colony. To some extent Harvey's patronage of the society—he attended their ploughing matches and banquets—achieved its aim, insofar as the report of 1850 asserted that merchants were no longer hostile to agriculture, but recognized its growth to be in "the best interests of the trade, and the moral and social condition of the people." Despite the import of cattle and seed and an increase of the area under cultivation, farming did not prosper greatly beyond the St. John's area, possibly because of the reluctance of merchants to capitalize the project beyond a certain point, but more probably because of the lack of a viable road system. Harvey had plans for an extensive network of roads to link the capital with outlying areas and open up the country to farming and settlement, but despite increased allocation of revenue and some extension of roads around St. John's, the programme produced limited results.

The education question was settled two years after Harvey took office by dividing the grant between the Protestant and Catholic denominations, the guerrilla warfare of the Protestant forces against the non-denominational system having prepared the way for a settlement on these lines. The Education Act of 1843 was piloted through the Assembly by Richard Barnes, whose speech on the second reading was a masterpiece of both erudition and special pleading. A member of a long-established merchant family, a deacon of the Congregational Church, and a self-educated man, Barnes employed standard Protestant arguments against the concept of non-denominational education, and the bill passed easily in a House containing a minority of Liberal-Catholics. Harvey, who admired Barnes but disliked "class legislation," justified the "deviation" which his predecessor Prescott thought was the purchase of public instruction at too high a price on the grounds that a "peculiar state of society" existed in Newfoundland.[586]

The board schools were potential generators of support for the new colonial state; but the teachers were for the most part so under-educated and the buildings so poorly equipped as to make the provision of even basic education problematic. The function of "colonial" education was, in any case, being undertaken by the Newfoundland School Society, an Evangelical missionary body founded by Newfoundland merchant Samuel Codner in London in 1823, and supported by the British government.[587] The society's ideological position was based on the theory of Christian colonialism, which underwrote imperial expansion provided it was accompanied by the spread of the (Protestant) gospel. The Society's British teachers arrived in Newfoundland with the declared intention of giving Newfoundlanders "a participation in all the religious and intellectual privileges of this pre-eminently happy land, emphatically *their* Mother Country," and the society's Evangelical leaders in London and its teachers in Newfoundland unremittingly promoted the ideal of the British Empire and Newfoundland's place within it. In 1851 the secretary was declaring that the society was part of a colonizing effort, the objective of which was "to transplant England's laws, England's language, Eng-

---

586 CO 194/117, Harvey to Stanley, 25 May, 30 Nov. 1843; [H. Prescott], *A Sketch of the State of Affairs in Newfoundland. By a Late Resident of That Colony* (London, 1841), 61.
587 See Chapter 2.

land's children, England's Church from the mother country and give them room and opportunity to develop abroad."

Although the Newfoundland School Society's cultural imperialism did not conflict with Harvey's general aims, he had little to do with the Society, which was well-established before his arrival; he preferred to work with organizations over which he could exercise some influence. His major achievement in the campaign to modify the cultural outlook of Newfoundlanders was achieved through the support he gave to the Natives' Society. This was one of a number of ethnic societies which were founded in the late 1830s and early 1840s on the model of the Benevolent Irish Society. But whereas the British and Scottish societies, established in 1837, and the St. George's Society, founded four years later, were formed and run by expatriate merchants, partly as dining clubs fostering nostalgic memories of the homeland, partly as benefit societies for indigent compatriots, the Natives' Society was a quasi-political organization dedicated to the formation of a Newfoundland consciousness in opposition to the immigrants from Britain.

The Natives' Society had been conceived as early as 1836 by Dr. Edward Kielly, a "dissident" native Catholic, as an assertion of the rights of Newfoundlanders against the policies and practices of the Liberal-Catholic politicians, all Irish immigrants, and some political dinners were organized to that end.[588] Although opposition to Liberal-Catholicism was evident in its early years (and warmly reciprocated), the Natives' Society rapidly established itself as a "third force" in Newfoundland political and cultural life. Its significance was quickly recognized by Sir Richard Bonnycastle, an officer of the Royal Engineers stationed in Newfoundland and unofficial adviser to the Colonial Office, who pointed out that the natives held the balance between the "ultra Tory officials and merchants" and the "Liberal middle class and people," and yielded neither to "the absurd pre-eminence in thought, rank and puerile precedence claimed by the former, nor to the rash, ill-advised, undigested schemes of the most excited of the latter." Bonnycastle considered the Society "a most useful engine, if managed by skilful hands," and he hoped

588 See Chapter 8.

it would meet with every encouragement from the government.[589]

Harvey took the advice and gave the Society an unusual amount of support, attending its ball in honour of the birth of the Prince of Wales—symbolically opened by Dr. Kielly dancing the quadrille with Lady Bonnycastle—and laying the foundation stone of the Natives' Hall. A procession to Government House marked the ceremony, with speeches at the site and flowery patriotic language inscribed on the stone itself. But the support which Harvey gained by this action was somewhat undermined a few weeks later when appointments to the Board of Directors of St. John's Academy, the Road Board, the Board of Control, and the Street Building Board were announced; of 37 members, only one was a native.[590] Immediately, sections of the press and public opinion set up a clamour against Harvey, accusing him of prejudice against those born in Newfoundland. The *Patriot* and the *Newfoundlander* (both Liberal-Catholic papers edited by natives) led the fray, the former going as far as to declare that "the best system of Colonial Government is that which promotes the Native interest in lofty superiority to every other." A public meeting of protest was held and controversy continued in the press throughout the summer, Harvey's supporters ridiculing the accident of birth as fitness for office. Harvey defended himself by claiming that if the aggrieved parties had communicated with him they would have received a courteous explanation; the appointments had been made by him, not by the Council, and for the most part were re-appointments. He was in entire ignorance of whether or not the appointees had been born on the island, he added, but his feelings were, other things being equal, to give preference to natives.[591]

Whether or not Harvey's explanation satisfied the aggrieved natives, the incident did not appear seriously to damage his pres-

589 CO 194/113, Bonnycastle to Stephen, 14 Jan. 1841, encl. "Considerations upon the Political Position and Natural Advantages of Newfoundland, St. John's 1841."

590 *Ledger*, 7 Jan. 1842; 27, 30 May 1845.

591 Editorials and notices in *Newfoundlander*, *Patriot*, *Times*, *Gazette*, and *Courier*, June–Aug. 1945; The Rooms Provincial Archives Division, GN 2/2, "Memorandum of Sir John Harvey," 19 July 1845.

tige or his policy, and was not subsequently held against him. In fact, the episode stimulated the native cause. The Natives' Society, whose leaders were drawn from what Bonnycastle called the middle class—small merchants, agents, and clerks and "a growing, most important, and rapidly increasing number of the sons and daughters of those respectable men who have chosen Newfoundland as the country of their children"—fused nativism, patriotism, and a respect for social order into a political creed. They would co-operate, asserted Dr. Kielly at the first general meeting, with "the peaceable, orderly, respectable and well-disposed inhabitants of this Island in measures of general usefulness ... to be respectful and obedient to the laws of the land, and ... manifest on all occasions our loyalty and attachment to our most Gracious Sovereign and Constitution under which we live."

The cutting edge of nativist criticism was turned not against the mercantocracy or the administration, as was Liberal policy in the 1830s, but against "strangers" who had been "sucking the vitals of the country" and holding the natives in "vassalage"—rhetoric which penetrated the psyche of both Protestant and Catholic Newfoundlanders and was to be extraordinarily effective in creating a patriotic consciousness. This patriotism subjoined Newfoundland to Britain and expressed itself in adulation of Queen Victoria and the British constitution. As Richard Barnes, treasurer of the Society and an underrated architect of the emerging Newfoundland state, pointed out, the island had little in the way of stirring history, great men, or culture heroes. It was inevitable, therefore, that in seeking to forge an identity the natives should look to "the beloved Sovereign of the British Dominions ... [who] reigned not only over us but in our hearts," and conceive their role as educating the people in "a knowledge of the political gifts which they enjoy."[592]

An important role in the creation of nativist sentiment was played by ceremony and symbol; the annual dinner, with patriotic toasts, quickly became an institution. In 1842, 80 members of Carbonear Natives' Society walked in procession through the town, headed by the society's flag; committee members carried staffs dec-

592 *Newfoundlander*, 1 July 1841; *Courier*, 12 July 1851.

orated with a bow of red ribbon, officers wore a sash, and members a red rosette on the left breast. By the 1850s the other ethnic societies were adopting similar rituals, infusing their ceremonies with tributes to the queen and the British constitution and inviting guests from brother societies. The 1850 St. Andrew's banquet was held in a hall decorated with flags "emblematic of the union of England, Ireland and Scotland," and in 1852 the British Society marched through St. John's behind the band of the Royal Newfoundland Companies "with colours flying." It was becoming *de rigueur* for almost any group to show signs of patriotism; a Wesleyan Tea Meeting in November 1851 displayed the "Red Cross of England," thus showing, reported the *Courier*, "the undiminished and affectionate loyalty of the Wesleyans to the House of Brunswick." Annual treats for schoolchildren, inaugurated in this period, were infused with a strong patriotic and moralistic content—gratitude to benefactors, dutiful obedience, and veneration of the sovereign.[593]

These groups and societies were, in fact, inventing tradition, promoting cultural rituals which were moulding the consciousness of Newfoundlanders. Harvey, who knew the value of official ceremony and display in attaching people to the social order, enlarged upon the tradition inaugurated by the first civil governor, Sir Thomas Cochrane, who, believing like his contemporary Louis XVIII of France that "men are governed in large part by their eyes," made pageantry, love of show, and a display of official dignity his guiding principles.[594] Harvey attempted to impress the populace with the public display (publicly reported) of civil and military power and lavish expenditure on soirees, banquets, balls, and processions, a policy which reached its apogee on the occasion of the visit of Prince Henry of the Netherlands to Newfoundland in August 1845. "Every honor and demonstration of public respect," vowed Harvey, "as well as every degree of hospitable attention in my power shall be paid and offered."[595]

---

593 Editorials and notices in *Ledger*, *Courier*, *Express*, *Post*, and *Herald*, 1842, 1845, 1846, 1850, 1851, 1853.

594 A.H. McLintock, *The Establishment of Constitutional Government in Newfoundland, 1783–1832* (London, 1841), 164.

595 CO 194/122, Harvey to Stanley, 15 July 1845.

"Never ... have the deities of pleasure and festivity ruled for the time with a more undivided sway," enthused the *Newfoundlander*, "the entire population of both sexes, of all ages, grades and distinctions ... went forth to welcome and to greet him." Prince Henry was received under triumphal arches and proceeded to Government House through streets lined with green boughs, followed by the various societies marching in procession. During his stay he attended the races at Mount Pearl, made a cruise to Conception Bay (returning to a Royal salute and a display of fireworks), and attended a special regatta in the harbour and the Agricultural Society's annual plowing match and dinner. He was later entertained at a soiree at Government House, a dinner given by the military, and a ball at the house of Major Robe of the Royal Engineers. Only the *Patriot*, recalling the role of the House of Orange in Ireland's history, criticized the festivities.[596]

These "calculated occasions of popular patronage," in E.P. Thompson's phrase, simultaneously brought the different classes together and made manifest the distance between them;[597] or as the *Courier* expressed it, with more percipience than it realized, these gala-days allowed all classes of society, normally separated by "a visible line of distinction," to stand on "a species of equality." The annual Regatta held at Quidi Vidi Lake, and the frequent race meetings at Mount Pearl, both organized and controlled by merchant interests, had become, by the 1840s, a permanent feature of the cultural landscape.

The success of Harvey's programme was due in part to the lessening of the political pressure of the 1830s: Bishop Fleming concerned himself with the building of the Catholic cathedral; the Liberal-Catholics, under the new constitution, could no longer command the majority they enjoyed from 1837 to 1841; the Liberal movement was temporarily in disarray following the St. John's

---

596 Editorials and notices in *Newfoundlander*, *Ledger*, and *Patriot*, Aug. 1845.

597 For the following paragraphs, see *Courier*, *Newfoundlander*, *Ledger*, *Patriot*, *Times*, and *Express*, 1835, 1838, 1840, 1843, 1845, 1857; *St. John's Total Abstinence and Benefit Society: Jubilee Volume 1858–1908* (St. John's, 1908), 5–8; *Banner of Temperance* 1, no. 16 (Aug. 1851).

by-election of 1840; and many of the leaders had accepted positions of emolument from the government. But Harvey had helped to set in motion a desire for improvement which animated not only the middle-class—small merchants, schooner owners, shopkeepers, publicans, and the upper ranks of artisans—but also reached down to the common people, expressing itself not only in patriotic nativism but also in such movements as temperance and the provision of literary culture.

When the Natives' Society held its annual ball in 1844, it was organized on temperance principles. This was a significant acknowledgement of the growth of the temperance movement in the island, and a reaction against the staggering amount of alcohol consumed in Newfoundland; in 1838, 277,808 gallons of liquor of all kinds were imported for a population of 75,000. Several short-lived temperance organizations had been formed in the 1830s, but the movement did not begin to flourish until the 1840s. Bishop Fleming inspired the formation of a Total Abstinence Society in 1841, which grew rapidly, attracted some Protestant support, and began to hold large public processions, replete with flags, banners with improving and patriotic motifs, ribbons, rosettes, and regalia. In 1851 the Sons of Temperance, a Methodist-supported body largely patronized by "young commercial gentlemen," held what was by this time a "traditional" procession, with similar regalia and banners, which halted at Government House to give three cheers for the queen—"a burst of loyal feeling," it was reported, "emanating from hearts devoted and true to British rule."

Well aware that his support conferred "a public and official character" upon such proceedings, Harvey bestowed some attention on the temperance movement, recognizing its role in the promotion of "habits of industry and sobriety, strict integrity, and sound moral and religious principles" in the "patriotic individuals" of the colony. Temperance and nativism, he informed the Colonial Office, might seem "trivial and unimportant" in comparison with other colonies, but in view of the peculiar situation in Newfoundland and his desire to reconcile conflicting parties and creeds, reports on such subjects might have more than ordinary interest. Harvey became the Patron of the Church of England Total Abstinence Society, and addressed some of its meetings, linking temperance with Christian virtues, the maintenance of family life, and the greatness of the British Empire. He attempted to give "a less exclusive character" to the Roman Catholic Temperance procession of January 1844 by inviting Protestant congregations to join, but was too late to succeed; the procession, exhibiting "the utmost possible order and decorum," attracted nearly 8,000 people. As in Britain, the strategy of the Newfoundland temperance movement was "moral suasion"; social ills were explained in terms of individual moral failure, and little or no attention was paid to the environmental factors which created drunkenness; nor was any attack made on the merchants whose import of liquor created the problem.[598]

If the temperance movement, in addition to reducing the consumption of spirits, exerted a widespread influence in favour of respectable patriotism—the Catholic procession of 1843 was reported to have attracted 10,000 participants, including some Protestants—the establishment of libraries and reading rooms was indicative of a zeal for "improvement" among the middle classes consonant with the mood of the times. Significantly, there were connections between opposition to drink and desire for polite literature; in 1851 commercial clerks connected with the temperance movement planned to open a temperance hotel with a reading room attached. The clerks had established a reading room in St. John's as early as 1835, and provided much of the market for literary culture.[599] Their increasing numbers in the 1840s and 1850s reflected the growing centralization of commerce in St. John's, described in 1845 as "an almost entirely commercial town." The logic of merchant capital decreed that the outports be restricted to fishing operations and that the capital should be the locus of commercial transactions. Thus the clerks, educated young men sent out from England to join merchant firms, congregated in St. John's; they boarded in merchants' houses

---

598 *Times*, 2 Aug. 1843; *Ledger*, 7 Feb. 1844; *Express*, 13 Dec. 1851; CO 194/120, Harvey to Stanley, 9 Jan. 1844; *Banner of Temperance* 1, no. 16 (Aug. 1851).

599 *Courier*, 4 June, 26 July 1851; *Ledger*, 24 Feb. 1835; *Patriot*, 10 Mar. 1835, 11 Jan. 1843; CO 194/116, Harvey to Stanley, 7 Jan. 1843; CO 194/120, Harvey to Stanley, 9 Jan. 1844.

but were not treated as equals, and consequently found themselves in something of a social limbo. A reading room and library, the *Patriot* thought, would provide them with suitable conversation and social recreation. Under the leadership of the ubiquitous Richard Barnes, who became secretary of the institution in 1840, the library, despite some vicissitudes, grew fairly rapidly and in 1845 received a grant from the legislature. The following year the premises were consumed in the fire and the project had to be started afresh. By 1852, no fewer than 6,201 books were being borrowed annually, or 33 volumes to each shareholder and subscriber. Sir John Harvey, ever solicitous to stimulate cultural activities, persuaded some "leading characters" to give donations to the library, but by and large the elite did nothing to help the movement. It tended to foster literary culture of a "useful" or "improving" kind and to exclude publications having an "improper or immoral tendency." This policy, it was hoped, would form a "correct bias" in the minds of young people "destined to fill important positions in society." Similar considerations inspired the formation of a Mechanics' Institute in 1849, the sponsors of which hoped, by reducing fees, to attract members lower down the social scale; like similar institutions in Britain and the US, however, the institute was largely attended by the clerk and shopkeeper class. Two years later the library and institute joined forces to promote the formation of the St. John's Athenaeum, but the institution did not come into being until 1861.[600]

These institutions attempted to influence the minds of young adults in the direction of sentiments favourable to the status quo, to imbue them with the idea that knowledge was primarily useful as a means of personal advancement up the social-commercial ladder, and to avoid any genuine debate upon controversial topics. The rules of the proposed literary and scientific institution in 1840 excluded religion and politics as the subjects of lectures, essays, or discussion. Similar statements informed the outlook of the Debating and Elocution Society, founded in 1838 and again patronized by

600 Editorials and notices in *Gazette*, 1845, 1846; *Courier*, 1851; *Express*, 1852; *Times*, 1840, 1841; *Newfoundlander*, 1845; *Banner of Temperance* 1, no. 16 (Aug. 1851); *Patriot*, 1835; *Ledger*, 1837–1851.

merchants' clerks. This society remained in being until 1846, when it succumbed to the Great Fire of that summer which destroyed three-quarters of St. John's and seriously dislocated its commercial and cultural life. However, socio-cultural activities resumed when St. John's was rebuilt, and exerted an increasing influence on popular mentalities. If Newfoundland, by the time of the achievement of responsible government in 1855, had not become "the brightest gem in the British colonial diadem," as Sir John Harvey had hoped, it was certainly some way from the strife-torn colony which had alarmed the local administration and the British government in the later 1830s. Harvey wished to claim much of the credit for himself; many of his later addresses to the Assembly and despatches to the Colonial Office were filled with self-justifying accounts of the success of his policies of development and conciliation. The construction of roads, the increase of educational facilities, the extension of agriculture, and improved provision for the poor he ascribed to the beneficial working of the "experimental constitution," in whose formation he himself had played a part.[601] He viewed the Amalgamated Assembly as "a well-contrived political machine" for raising and appropriating revenue for general improvement. More importantly, he believed that his policy had contributed to the happiness, sobriety, and loyalty of the people and to the amicable relationship between the denominations, which he felt was exemplified in the laudatory address to which all members of the Assembly contributed on his departure in August 1846.[602]

Although Harvey undoubtedly had extended benevolent guidance and support, it is evident that large sections of the population were eager to participate in the ritual activities associated with the growth of patriotism, nativism, and various forms of self-improvement. As meetings, processions, celebrations, and festivities became regular or annual events, a sense of stability and continuity was added to the flux of everyday life, and the mystique with which these

---

601 *Gazette*, 23 Apr. 1845, 24 Jan. 1846; CO 194/122, Harvey to Stanley, 25 Oct. 1845; CO 194/125, "Papers Relating to the Proposed Changes in the Constitution of Newfoundland" (5 August 1842).

602 CO 194/122, Harvey to Stanley, 23 Apr. 1845; CO 194/125, Harvey to Gladstone, 17 Feb., 12 Mar., 22 May 1846; *Gazette*, 28 Apr., 6 Aug. 1846.

activities were imbued exerted a powerful attraction on a people seeking a "national" identity within the British imperial orbit. Patriotic Anglophile attitudes were perhaps most easily and securely established. The loyalty of Newfoundland to the crown was attested in the House of Commons in 1855,[603] and the Crimean War brought an outburst of patriotic fervour hardly matched in Britain. At the beginning of 1855 a Patriotic Fund was established to raise money for the relief of widows and orphans of soldiers who had died in battle. By June subscriptions had totalled £2,118 and collections had been made in at least 10 communities. It would appear that the campaign was spearheaded by a substantial number of citizens of the Protestant faith, for few Irish names appeared in the subscription lists and no purely Irish areas sponsored a collection. In St. John's a public meeting of citizens was held in January to express sympathy with "our brave troops in the Crimea"; the governor was in the chair and the band of the Royal Newfoundland Companies opened the proceedings with the national anthem. Again, the sponsors of the meeting were nearly all Protestant, and the resolutions identified Newfoundland with the queen and the English nation: the people of the colony had "the unanimous sentiments of British subjects" as to the justness of the war, felt proud that they were "fellow subjects of Queen Victoria," and like British subjects everywhere sympathized with the death of their countrymen in battle. Later in the year, when Sebastopol fell to the Allies, another public meeting was held; on this occasion the main speakers were Ambrose Shea, Lawrence O'Brien, and John Kent, all leading Liberal-Catholic politicians. They composed an address to Queen Victoria on behalf of "Her Majesty's loyal subjects resident in St. John's, Newfoundland, and deeply interested in the glory of their country."[604]

Newfoundland was about to enter upon responsible government as a state in which loyalty to the concept of Empire had been achieved. Paradoxically, this consciousness of being British subjects resident in a colony co-existed with a strong nativist feeling. This was dramatically demonstrated in 1857, when all parties and faiths,

603 Speech of F. Scully, Parl. Deb. 137, 20 Mar. 1855, 892.
604 *Times*, 3, 6 Jan., 6 Oct. 1855; *Ledger*, Jan.–Nov. 1855.

in a great outburst of national fervour, united in successful opposition to the British government's grant of additional fishing rights to the French on the west coast of the island. Though the British and the French—to whose leaders toasts had been drunk at public dinners at the height of the war fever two years earlier—were temporarily the objects of protest, little permanent damage was done to British-Newfoundland relations; but Newfoundland's sense of nationhood was greatly enhanced.[605]

Beneath the surface, however, antagonisms of class and denomination still smouldered. Harvey had perceived that though politicians might co-operate in the Assembly, the population was still divided into virtually two classes, the merchants and the fishers, whose interests conflicted and who were far from entertaining cordial feelings toward each other. The achievement of responsible government in 1855, which was largely the result of a 10-year campaign led by Liberal-Catholics, was excoriated by Conservative-Protestants as the triumph of the "Catholic minority" over "Protestant interests."[606] Religious and political divisions came to the surface in 1861, when a large and angry crowd of Liberal-Catholic supporters demonstrated outside the legislative building against the governor's dismissal of the Liberal ministry and the allegedly fraudulent Conservative election victory which followed. Troops were called out, the crowd was fired upon and a number of demonstrators were killed or wounded. This was a turning point in Newfoundland's political history, for it forced the Conservative forces to realize that they could either continue to govern by force—the "Irish solution"—or could choose a more conciliatory path, in effect a return to the mode of administration adumbrated by Harvey. The conservative-administrative elite felt that the latter course was in their best interests and began to extend the patronage system and to "share the spoils"—to allocate all offices of emolument and honour throughout society on a basis roughly equal to the strength of the main denominations. This strategy was formally introduced into political life in 1865 when two leading Liberal-Catholics, John Kent and Ambrose Shea, were

605 Gunn, *Political History*, 143–44; *Times*, 27 Oct., 1 Dec. 1855.
606 CO 194/125, Harvey to Gladstone, 12 Apr. 1846; *Ledger*, 13 Feb. 1855.

invited to take office in a Conservative administration. This marked the beginning of the end of the identification of Catholicism with Liberalism and Protestantism with Conservatism and the conflicts which flowed from it.

The years 1832–1855 were undoubtedly the crucial period in the formation of the state in Newfoundland. What emerged in the second half of the 19th century was basically a Protestant state, based largely on Protestant merchant capital and owing allegiance to a Protestant mother country. But it was also a state which was very different from that envisaged in the Instructions given to Governor Cochrane in 1832. The directing classes had not only successfully encouraged the growth of a patriotic nativism but, coming to terms with religious militancy (particularly that of the Catholic Irish) by the institutionalization of denominationalism, had also removed the underlying causes of religious conflict. The intertwining of the concepts of patriotic nativism and denominational allegiance in the consciousness of the vast majority of Newfoundlanders underlay the strength of the island's social fabric in the latter part of the 19th century, and after. The activities which supported this outlook soon became bathed in the rosy glow of tradition, but their roots lay in Harvey's "cultural revolution" of 1841–1846. Much of what today is regarded as immemorial Newfoundland tradition, enshrined in institutions, rituals, and attitudes, can be dated to the period under review.

Manuscript and Newspaper Sources

MANUSCRIPTS

These are listed at their locations when consulted.

London, England

National Archives (formerly Public Record Office)

Colonial Office Records:

CO 43/-	1824, 1828
CO 191/-	1824, 1828
CO 194/-	1801–1845
CO 195/-	1824, 1826, 1835, 1843, 1844
CO 197/-	1844
CO 199/-	1836

School of Oriental and African Studies

Missionary Society Records

Society for the Propagation of the Gospel Correspondence 1802–1852; Journal 1809, 1811; Annual Report 1817; Proceedings 1804, 1821, 1828, 1846

London Missionary Society Correspondence, 1800–1815

Methodist Missionary Society Correspondence, 1816–1838; Minutes of Mission Committee 1823

British and Foreign Bible Society, Home Correspondence 1820–1823; Annual Reports 1704–1850

Society for the Promotion of Christian Knowledge, Correspondence 1839–1841; Annual Reports 1840–1842

Guildhall Library

Colonial Church and School Society Reports 1851–1856

General Committee Minute Book 1850–1856

Rome, Italy
Archives of Propaganda Fide, S.C. Am. Sett., 3, 4, 5, Correspondence 1807, 1836, 1838, 1840

Dublin, Ireland
Archives of the Archdiocese of Dublin, Correspondence 1792, 1793, 1810

O'Donel, Remonstrance (?1788)

Killiney, Ireland
Archives of the Franciscan Order, Correspondence 1812, 1824

St. John's, Canada
Archives of the Archdiocese of St. John's, Correspondence, Statutes 1801, 1836

United Church Archives, Minutes of Meetings 1850

The Rooms Provincial Archives Division
- Colonial Secretary's Office
- GN 2/1, Replies to Correspondents 1821–1844
- Proclamations 1826, 1829, Memorandum 1845
- GN 2/2, Incoming Letters 1822–1845
- Duckworth Papers, 1810
- Benevolent Irish Society Minute Book, 1822–
- Conception Bay Board of Education, Minutes 1836–1841; Correspondence Book 1836
- Colony of Newfoundland, Blue Book 1844

Memorial University Queen Elizabeth II Library; Centre for Newfoundland Studies (Archives and Special Collections Division)
- Dr. Arthur Barnes Papers
- Letter of Phoenix Fire Company, 1845

NEWSPAPERS

London, England
Record
Standard
Times
Watchman
World

Newfoundland
Carbonear
Sentinel and Conception Bay Advertiser
Star and Conception Bay Journal

Harbour Grace
Conception Bay Mercury
Weekly Herald and Conception Bay Advertiser

St. John's
Banner of Temperance
Evening Telegram
Morning Chronicle
Morning Courier and General Advertiser
Morning Post and Shipping Gazette
Newfoundlander
Newfoundland Express
Newfoundland Indicator
Newfoundland Mercantile Journal
Newfoundland Vindicator
Patriot and Terra Nova Herald
Public Ledger
Royal Gazette and Newfoundland Advertiser
Telegraph and Political Review
Times and General Commercial Gazette

Index

About the Author

Chris Hammond/Memorial University

Phillip McCann is Professor Emeritus of Education in the faculty of Education at Memorial University of Newfoundland, and a Fellow of the Royal Historical Society. He is also a veteran of World War II, having served in Royal Air Force in Britain and India during World War II, from 1941 until 1946.

Born in Birkenhead, Cheshire, England, Dr. McCann received his doctorate from the University of Manchester. He taught in secondary schools in London for seven years prior to being appointed senior lecturer in Education in Goldsmiths, University of London. He came to Newfoundland in 1967 as Associate Professor in the Faculty of Education, Memorial University.

Throughout his career, Dr. McCann has written widely on the historical and social aspects of education in Britain and Newfoundland. His books include *The Educational Innovators*, Vol. 1, with W.A.C. Stewart (1967, reprinted in 2000); *Popular Education and Socialization in the Nineteenth Century* (1977, reprinted in Routledge Library Editions 2007); *Blackboards and Briefcases: Personal Stories by Newfoundland Teachers, Educators, and Administrators* (1982); and *Schooling in a Fishing Society 1836-1986* (1994). He has published numerous articles in academic journals and presented papers at education conferences in the US, Europe, Australia, and China.